THE SQUARE PEG

A TIGHT FIT IN A TIN CAN

By
Jesse E. Pond, Jr.

Published

By

The Pearl Harbor History Associates, Incorporated.

Sperryville, Virginia
1992

THE SQUARE PEG

A Tight Fit In A Tin Can

By Jesse E. Pond, Jr.

Edited by Lilja B. Powell

Published by The Pearl Harbor History Associates, Incorporated.
Post Office Box 205
Sperryville, Virginia 22740

Composed in Univers by the author on his P.C.

Cover and book design by Powell Printing

Printed in the United States of America by

POWELL PRINTING

Culpeper, Virginia

Library of Congress Catalog Card Number 92-85443
ISBN 0-9634347-0-5

TABLE OF CONTENTS

DEDICATION

This book is dedicated to the several million "good men and true" who wore those silly little round white hats and endured the whims, fancies, and peccadilloes of those fortunate enough to have worn the gold braid.

It is specially dedicated to my shipmates whose friendship and comradeship made things work: especially Jimmie; Red; Jack; Fredie; Bill; Earl; Elmer; George; Mazurk; Herbie; and "The Towhead". Some have finished life's journey and have gone on to better things. Most of these stalwarts were Reserves, in to do their bit in fighting a war and get it over with. Their desire was to return to civilian life and raise a family and leave the Navy to those who made it their career.

I have tried to present these enlisted men as fairly as possible. They were thinking, caring, hard working, capable people, and not parts of the scenery.

Time, the great healer, allows me to say "Hell, some of my best friends were officers."

ACKNOWLEDGEMENTS

This book could not have been written without the encouragement of my wife Edith, who is the heroine of this chronicle, and who had the task of editing for grammar, usage, and clarity.

My thanks to shipmates Virgil Gex and Glenn Thompson, who generously allowed the use of their memories of "The Date That Will Live in Infamy" to be a valued addition to the chapter when "All Hell Broke Loose."

My thanks to the Board of Directors of the Pearl Harbor History Associates, one and all, who had confidence in the viability of The Square Peg and decided to publish the book.

A separate thank you to Bill and Lilja Powell who added professionalism to my work, and made the task enjoyable.

SKETCHES OF MORAL PHILOSOPHY

"If you choose to represent the various parts in life by holes upon a table, of different shapes - some circular, some triangular, some square, some oblong - and the persons acting these parts by bits of wood of similar shapes, we shall generally find that the triangular person has got into the square hole, the oblong into the triangular, and a square person has squeezed himself into the round hole. The officer and the office, the doer and the thing done, seldom fit so exactly that we can say that they were made for each other."

Generally accepted as the origin of the phrase "A square peg in a round hole." Bartlett's Familiar Quotations, 14th Edition.

Sidney Smith (1771 - 1845)
English clergyman and essayist

"If one but tell a thing well, it moves on with undying voice, and over the fruitful earth and across the sea goes the bright gleam of noble deeds ever unquenchable."

Pindar, Greek poet, 518 - 438 BC.
Isthmian Odes, IV, i, 67.

FOREWORD

The first year after Adolph Hitler initiated the Second World War by ordering his troops to invade Poland in 1939, Americans were pretty much isolationist. They viewed the war in Europe as none of the U. S.'s business. President Roosevelt had begun revitalizing the Army and the Navy as part of the Great Depression recovery effort, but the two Armed Services were still very small and numbered about one hundred thousand active duty personnel each. The Air Corps was part of the U. S. Army. Most service equipment was obsolescent, of World War I vintage.

After the fall of France in the summer of 1940, attitudes began to change dramatically. Other changes were put in train which were to affect every American in the next five years. An early step was to call to active duty units of the National Guard and the Naval Reserve. THE SQUARE PEG is the story of a Naval Reservist whose unit was called up in the Fall of 1940.

It is an adventure story with a happy ending. It is autobiographical, and it is in large part, the story of a ship, the USS CHEW (DD 106), one of the oldest destroyers to be taken out of mothballs for return to active duty, and its crew, a cast of characters of every stripe. There is little about actual fighting against the enemy, with the exception of the attack on Pearl Harbor. The CHEW was in the thick of that and acquitted herself very well.

Jesse Pond left the CHEW the year before the war ended. It so happens that I can add a footnote to the CHEW history. I was a member of the ship's company of the USS PHOENIX (CL 46) which arrived in Pearl Harbor on Sunday morning, August 19, 1945, the day President Truman declared a day of thanksgiving for the Japanese having agreed to surrender. We were enroute from the Philippines to the Long Beach, California, Navy Yard for a badly needed overhaul. We stopped at Pearl for the day in order to refuel. Next morning we got underway in company with two destroyers, the CHEW and the ALLEN, also bound for Long Beach. We had to refuel them at sea about halfway there. The following Sunday as we were approaching Long Beach harbor, our orders were changed. All three ships were instructed to keep right on going. After one day in Long Beach all were ordered to go on through the Panama Canal to the East Coast, PHOENIX to go into mothballs, CHEW and ALLEN to scrap.

As the author says in the Preface he tells about things as they were. In my experience during that period, most of which I was serving on the cruiser PHOENIX, also in Pearl Harbor at the time of the Japanese attack. It went on to duty in the Southwest Pacific theater for most of the war. The book reflects accurately life aboard ship and ashore, the attitudes, and the moods of the times.

Francesco Costagliola,
Captain, United States Navy (Retired)

Frank Costagliola was born in Cranston, Rhode Island in 1917. He received a BSEE, United States Naval Academy, 1941; studied Nuclear Physics, M.I.T., 1947 - 1949; an MBA from American University, 1974. He served in USS PHOENIX at Pearl Harbor December 7, 1941, and subsequently in the Pacific. Among his commands was a destroyer during the Korean War. His decorations include the Legion of Merit and the Bronze Star. He retired in 1968 to become a member of the Atomic Energy Commission. He is a member of the American Nuclear Society; Military Order of the World Wars; Army and Navy Club; Naval Academy Alumni Club; MIT Alumni Association; Pearl Harbor Survivors Association; and the Pearl Harbor History Associates. He has contributed many articles to professional journals.

PREFACE

Many memoirs are written by many military people after retirement for many purposes and reasons. It is almost a requirement for retired flag rank gentlemen to take pen in hand and set down their career for posterity. This is not to be a memoir as such, but rather the story of one period of my life, written from a different point of view from most memoirs.

This is not a history of World War II. Many well-researched volumes have been printed on that broad subject. Many books have been written on the Japanese attack on Pearl Harbor of December 7, 1941. Most of the latter are the work of historians who are delving into previously written works with the hope of finding a new slant or something that has been overlooked, or to espouse the writers own pet theory. Then there are many more written that use oral histories as their theme. Oral histories tend to be overblown and extremely inaccurate and undependable. Most seem to be the recollections of a person endowed with X-ray and telescopic vision. An example is the oral history of a man who I have known for over a half century. None of what he relates as having witnessed is untrue, he is relating what he has read, not seen in person. He was at his battle station, by his own words, and that battle station was in the fire room of a destroyer. That destroyer was tied up between the one that I was on, USS CHEW, and the overhanging hulk of the ex Spanish-American War armored cruiser BALTIMORE. There was no way that he could have seen any of what he so vividly described.

There are also some articles written by eyewitnesses of all ages that bring alive some of the details of "The Date That Shall Live In Infamy" but my viewpoint, the viewpoint of an enlisted man, will cover that one day as a chapter and will shed some light on that sort of life and on the naval service in particular as it was at that period of time.

The United States Navy of 1940 was an antique organization patterned on the British service and just a bit more modern than that service. There was a great cleft between the officer class and the lowly enlisted man. A United States Naval Academy graduate with several years sea experience described the Navy as a "yacht club" for the officers and that the enlisted men were just part of the "scenery." An enlisted man with twenty years of exemplary service and a petty officers rating could be broken down in rating to second class seaman by getting on the wrong side of an officer. There was a definite line between the classes that was not to be ignored, and exists even today.

In the passage of time since 1940 many changes in procedure have made a great difference in life below decks. Military life still requires discipline and regulations but the atmosphere in 1940 was almost unbearable for an enlisted man with intelligence, ability, and pride.

The historians efforts seem to me to be dry as if the dust of the years on those old papers has infiltrated their writing. I hope that some of the following chapters may let a breath of fresh air in the readers idea of six years in the Forties.

All dates are accurate. Events portrayed are true. In cases where the comment is unfavorable to the subject I have omitted the name and used a nickname in its place. Several of my shipmates had sobriquets that were unprintable , and so they will be skipped over. My aim is to see that the facts are straight, to give a different slant on things as they were, and for posterity to know us in a favorable light.

Chapter I

Trying For a Fit

In the winter of 1939-40 it became obvious to most of the readers of the daily newspapers, as it did to me, that the United States was going to become involved in the war that had flared in Europe. Hitler was annexing his weaker neighbors and threatening the rest of the Continent. Our President, Franklin Delano Roosevelt, was an Anglophile and was open in his support for the British. My opinion held that it was only a matter of time before we would be in it.

At my age, just twenty-three and single without any dependents, I knew from the past history of the United States that if any draft procedure was ever put in effect, I would be in the first call up. My views on the non-romantic side of warfare had been distilled by listening to tall tales and war stories from the time that I was able to understand English.

I had two uncles, my mother's older brothers, who had served in the Army during World War I. Uncle Billy had been under fire in the American Expeditionary Force, and in his outfit "Over There", my mother's first beau, Joe Britten, had been killed. Mom's other brother, Uncle Charlie, spent the war in New Jersey training recruits. He had a boarder, Jack, who was living on a disability pension from his war wounds. Jack delighted in telling my cousins and me the most gruesome horror tales of the trenches in France. Art Bergeron, an orphan who had been taken in by my grandmother and was one of the family, had also been in Uncle Billy's outfit in the AEF. He was a frequent family visitor. "Uncle" Art lost half of his lower jaw as his contribution to his service in France. These men, despite their experiences, were patriots and active in the community. However, their reminisces on life in France had made up my mind for me that trench warfare, with all of its mud and rats and bayonet charges against dug-in machine gun nests, was not for me.

I was a fair woodsman and a good shot, after having tramped all over the Missouri Bottom Swamps for years - hunting. But, after Jack's vivid descriptions I resolved to find a better way to fulfill my responsibility to my country, if that need ever came. I was patriotic and anti-communist and anti-fascist enough to have inquired in 1939 at the Finnish affairs office in downtown St. Louis about joining in the effort against the Reds, but I was turned away by them and my name turned in to the FBI office for my troubles.

1

Hitler invaded Poland in September 1939 and the United States Congress was starting to discuss a draft law. Accordingly, I made a quick decision in April of 1940 and joined the Naval Reserve in St. Louis with two goals in mind: one to earn an officer's commission, and, two, to play on the Reserve's basketball team. I had another reason in the back of my mind - to avoid any possibility of that future draft and slugging it out in the trenches.

For a smart guy, joining that Reserve outfit was one dumb move. After about the second night of what passed for drills I discovered that this was a genuine first-class Mickey Mouse outfit. Right away I had a problem with my physical. My body was unscarred, and the Corpsman needed three identifying marks for his forms, until we finally counted a couple of moles. Then, (Oh, this was horrible!) my name was on file at the FBI office from that inquiry to the Finns. That took some pondering in the office before I was "officially" passed, even though I had been sworn in several weeks earlier. Before the passage of the draft law there were few recruits at the door, but, after the passage of the Draft Law in October those slots were in demand. It seemed that every eighteen-year old in town had suddenly realized his safest patriotic duty was to join the Naval Reserve.

The drills were a joke, presided over by a couple of semi-literate petty officers sporting hashmarks denoting years of service right there at the foot of Grand Avenue in St. Louis. Several of these worthies appeared saltier than Sinbad himself and passed the time trying to impress each other, and the recruits, with fancy manual of arms that involved a lot of rifle tossing and marching back and forth in the gym. Other than close order drill there were lectures on military subjects, which meant one of the petty officers reading from a manual. One of these snoozers was broken up when the reader got stuck on the word "vinegar" and his audience got up and left. When the orders came through for the Division to go to active duty these "salts" fell all over themselves arranging discharges for themselves for all sorts of reasons, real and imagined, to avoid leaving home.

By the time I had three months of this training under my belt, I was thoroughly disenchanted with the whole shebang. In addition to the weekly drills and lectures there was a two-week annual cruise on a real warship in which the Reserve Divisions would learn seamanship from using real machinery and real guns on a real ship. The cruise for 1940 was to take place in July on Lake Michigan aboard an old warship. The USS SACRAMENTO, a gunboat that had been retired from China duty to serve as a training ship. SACRAMENTO, first commissioned in 1914, had been converted from a coal-burner to an oil-burner after arriving in Lake Michigan.

The thought of wasting my valuable vacation time aboard an antique ship with a bunch of lint-headed teen-agers just wasn't in my plans. I told the Yeoman in the office that they could proceed without me. He promptly told me in no uncertain terms that I "had" to go on that cruise, that failure to attend would have a deleterious effect on my Naval career! That cracked me up. I was already a marked man, I was on file with the FBI, I wasn't very impressed by the petty officer-teachers, and now I was being insubordinate. He told me to be there on that date with my sea bag packed, "or else." At that time I was a civilian foreman in a large iron foundry bossing a big gang of laborers and I could get a lot more authority in my voice than the kid officer behind the desk could, so I just up and quit, walked out the door and went home. From that time on I did not attend their absurd drills and totally ignored the place.

The following is taken from the "Schedule of Activities" for the Second Quarter, 1940, shows the curriculum that was supposed to make sailors out of green civilians:

04 Apr	(1) Emergency Drills (2) Gun and Engine casualties.
11 Apr	(1) Emergency drills (2) Battle problem
18 Apr	Infantry Drill
25 Apr	(1) Inspection rehearsal (2) Emergency drills
02 May	(1) Inspection rehearsal (2) Battle problem
08 May	(Wednesday) FEDERAL INSPECTION
16 May	New Manual of Arms
23 May	New Infantry Drill
28 May	(Tuesday) Battalion Drill
06 Jun	(1) Bag and Locker inspection (2) Classes
13 Jun	(1) Gun Service (2) Safety precautions
20 Jun	(1) Gun Service (2) Classes
27 Jun	(1) Infantry Drill (2) Gun Service

From that Schedule it is apparent that it would take many years to make a sailor out of a raw recruit.

I sincerely believed that I knew more about operating various types of machinery than any of the instructors who had to instruct with a manual in one hand while trying to operate whatever dummy machine it was with the other.

There was a wooden-hulled sub-chaser left over from World War I tied up there on the Mississippi, but to my knowledge no one ever set foot on it. I did hear that they did get it underway after the war started and sent it downstream to the Gulf for duty. And to add insult to injury, the basketball program was scrubbed because of the emergency. What a complete bust my enlistment turned out to be - no commission, and now no basketball. I missed out on any chance of a commission, I was told, because I had enlisted first, instead of applying for the commission first. Commissions came through political influence from the inside, not from applicants from the outside.

However, things started to hum in October as letters were sent out to all hands asking for volunteers in certain ratings to serve on YP boats in New York Harbor. (YP meant Yard Patrol. Small vessels.) Then I received a letter dated November 25, 1940 setting a tentative date for orders to active duty, "about December 16th" and to get my affairs in order. Before receiving this letter I had been ordered by telephone to show up at several Thursday night drills before the end of October so the notice by letter was not a surprise. What *was* a surprise at the first meeting in December when we got orders to leave for San Diego on December 10th! I had received a personal notification at that meeting from Lt. (jg) Charles F. MacNish, who was to be the senior officer leaving with the Division, that I was on the roster and was going. If I missed that train, I would get an escort to the nearest Federal military base, which was Jefferson Barracks. I had knowledge of the stockade at that resort, which was left over from the War Between the States. Therefore, with that alternative in mind, I did get my affairs in order, sold my new car, and showed up on December 10, 1940, at the St. Louis Union Station. About 250 others from three of the four St. Louis Reserve Divisions caused a mob scene on the platform.

We all boarded the same special train. The petty officers were trying to create some sense of order by mustering the men in ranks. Adding to the confusion were parents (mine were there) and girl friends (mine was there, too). We all milled about amid shouts and tearful goodbyes, while railroad men tried to get the Special boarded and out of there on time. This gave me a good opportunity to get my first close look at the men assembled there in brand-new blue uniforms, and size up my new shipmates. Very few of the petty officers from the drills were there. It seemed that most of the "feather merchants" had been able to duck the call to duty. The greatest percentage seemed to be the youngsters who had enlisted in the Reserves in the last few months to avoid the two-month old draft law. The one or two, if that many, "drills" that they had attended, hardly qualified them as sailors. These were kids on an outing, and were acting the part. What an uproar!

Finally, the "bluejackets" were herded aboard the cars. The men wore the blue uniforms of the Navy and almost looked like sailors, but making them into sailors would take some time.

The train backed out and headed West on a four-day trip to our destination, San Diego. Our entire trip turned out to be a four-day reprise of the platform mob scene. We were, as far as I could see, unsupervised, and a festival atmosphere rollicked on, day and night. The only stops along the way were to change train crews and take on water. The Special rattled along over St. Louis-San Francisco Railway tracks to Fort Worth, Texas, then the Texas and Pacific to San Antonio, switching to the Southern Pacific to Los Angeles, where the last change of lines was to the Santa Fe in to San Diego. At most of the stops along the way, such as the one at Gallup, New Mexico, someone would dash across the tracks to a store, saloon, or whatever, and come racing back with a bottle held high. No one was left behind at any of these replenishment stops, although there were a couple of close calls.

To get away from the noise and hubbub I moved up to a car in the head end of the train and met a kindred soul, Earl Loeb, who became a buddy from that time on. Earl was also twenty-three, had two years of college, and he, too, had missed out on the commission bit. Earl persevered and finally did get a commission in 1944 by constantly applying, and hardest of all, keeping his "nose clean" and enduring all sorts of ragging and gibes from his shipmates about his good conduct. For example; one particular man aboard ship, kept up a barrage of insults on Earl that got under my skin. Earl was an athlete and kept in trim. I advised him to give that loud mouth one good smack in the mouth and he'd shut up, but Earl said that might endanger his quest for a commission. Earl had *real* guts, not a quick temper and stubborn streak like his shipmate to be.

During the four-day odyssey two of our Chief Petty Officers, Bill Hudson, the Bosn's Mate, who had been a Railway Express truck driver in his just departed civil life, and Jim Sullivan, the Machinist's Mate, who had been a locomotive engineer for the Wabash Railway, worked hard on the roster, making up assignments for the men for use when we caught the ship in San Diego. They were in for a rude awakening when we finally did get to the ship their efforts went for naught and the plans never saw the light of day. The Regular Navy took charge aboard ship, and the Reserve chiefs were shunted aside.

5

Late in the afternoon of the fourth day the train backed in to the Destroyer Base in San Diego. The mob poured off the cars to tear around as might be expected of a bunch of youngsters who had been cooped up on a train for four days, whooping and hollering, and carrying on in general. That celebration came to an abrupt halt when a voice of the type associated with Victor McLaglen, fog horns, and cheap whiskey, without need for electric amplification, roared "AWRIGHT, YOU DIRT FARMERS, LINE UP HERE LIKE TWO ROWS OF CORN." (Victor MacLaglen was a pugilist turned actor whose career spanned many years in the movies. He had actually fought Jack Johnson, the first Negro Heavyweight Champion for the title.) The powerful voice came from a mean-looking stockily built man in undress blues. This Neanderthal displayed a row of hash marks on his sleeve denoting many years of service, but with the one chevron of a coxswain (coxn) on his right arm, denoting that the wearer had not forged ahead in his rating, despite his years of service. He also wore a shiny badge on his chest, "Master At Arms." This was our first meeting with a Regular Navy "Jimmie Legs", and he impressed the lads at once. The ruckus ceased immediately.

"RIIIIIGHT FACE --FORRARD MAAARCH" the Master at Arms led us into a large old barn-like structure close by. When the column of men passed through that door it was out of the 37th Division, United States Naval Reserve into the United States Navy, never to return. Our transformation from a civilian rabble into fighting men was under way. Some of us would not live through the experience.

Chapter II

You're In The Navy Now

Inside that big barn a table had been set up, a Yeoman and a Pharmacist's Mate seated behind it. A portly middle-aged gentleman wearing an outlandish tweedy-looking jacket, topped off with a rumpled felt hat, perched on a chair just past the end of the table. Our names were called out one at a time, alphabetically, of course, then the man would step forward, be checked in, and then moved on in front of the portly gent in the racetrack tout costume. He was, it turned out, a Navy doctor (rank unknown) who had been called in at the last minute to check us in, medically. Goodbye to privacy, we were welcomed into the Navy. Each man, in turn, stood there in front of the entire group, lowered his pants, submitted to an intimate inspection, then on a word, turned around and bent over for further examination, until "Next." Needless to say, there were many nervous witticisms bandied about from the rear of the line.

Check in was far from being a rapid process. The necessity for standing in line started on our first real day in the Navy. Finally, Old Fog Horn Voice marched us right in to the mess hall without any intervening stops for hand-washing, or any other unnecessary or sanitary reason.

The influx of this unexpected train load caught the galley crew unprepared, but they rallied superbly. Food from the freezer was boiled and ready in minutes, and tasted like it. Then it was served on stainless steel trays: hot dogs, potatoes, and sauerkraut. Not like Mother used to make. We did have a choice -- take it or leave it. There was a large sign over the entrance to the mess hall "Take what you want, but eat what you take." The Destroyer Base had been notified that we were coming, but they didn't know *when* until we descended on them. Coordinated organization appeared lacking in this whole operation.

Four Reserve divisions were called up in this operation, to man four destroyers that were in the Reserve Fleet. The plan was for the men to take the ships out of mothballs and recommission them. In so doing we were to become familiar with the equipment as it was installed, and then sail the ships to Pearl Harbor, the assigned duty station. A good training idea, but the paper work took too long and the ships had to be made ready by Regular Navy crews to hold to the recommissioning schedule. The revised plan had the Reserves taking over the ships in San Diego, but, again, the calendar outran the paperwork, and the ships sailed on to Hawaii with the Regular Navy men.

We were fortunate in that we missed catching those rickety old ships in San Diego and sailing them to Hawaii. Instead of unloading from the train to the ships, we were put up in some nearly completed barracks and spent almost a month working in the Destroyer Base while we waited for transportation to catch the ships. That month was well spent in getting us used to the Navy regimen and customs. I shudder to think of what would have happened if that green bunch of boots had tried to sail those ships in our first taste of the sea.

The commandant of the Destroyer Base was the famous "Captain Mack," Byron McCandless, who was known throughout the Navy as a hard taskmaster who demanded a full days work from every man. He was also known for his insistence of feeding his boys three square meals a day. That was his sign over the mess hall door, spelling out to eat all that you took. I've often wondered about the reasoning behind the layout of the mess lines. The line started at the garbage cans, with screaming seagulls circling overhead, and then passed the steaming, smelly, scullery just before entering the mess hall to start the serving line. That layout might have had an effect on a not-hungry man's appetite.

Captain Mack was also known for his hatred of white socks when worn with a blue uniform, a fact that was brought home to me later. We were almost left on our own until the transportation came through, but Captain Mack was feeding several hundred extra mouths daily and he demanded, and got, something in return, which was our labor on all sorts of odd jobs about the Base. Mack was everywhere on his bike, and we all got to know his short, burly, figure and his voice right away.

Within a few days of landing on his base, I picked up a case of Athlete's Foot, probably from the gang shower. Accordingly I reported to the Sick Bay on the USS RIGEL, which was the Receiving Ship for the Base. Simple! The doctor took a look and gave me some powder to relieve the itching. He then signed a small, printed chit. When he handed it to me he said in a very serious tone of voice, "Keep this with you at all times." He had also told me to wear white socks instead of the black issue to prevent the possibility of infection from the dye. While hiking to the mess hall later that very same day, a voice from behind me roared out "HALT, ONE TWO." It was Captain Mack, on his bike, pointing at my feet. His face was not its usual cherubic pink, but was instead a flaming red. Without a word I pulled out that little chit and handed it to him. His face changed and he muttered something about using lye on the decks in the heads (toilets and washrooms) and pedaled off. I later learned that he had men tossed in the brig for wearing white socks. However, on the whole, that man was entitled to an idiosyncrasy or two.

One afternoon in January, 1941, right after evening chow, word came to pack our bags, and fall in out in front of the barracks. Without ado we were marched down to the dock and into an ordinary roofed-over freight barge of the type used for lightering goods out to an anchored ship. There was no way to see out of this contrivance as there was only the opening in the roof and no other means of access to the dark interior. Shortly we felt the slap of waves against the hull as were being pushed out in the Bay. It seemed like hours, until we bumped up against something solid and substantial. It was now fully dark and we could see a bright light above the opening that shone into our eyes and prevented us from seeing whatever it was that we had bumped. Our bags were tossed into cargo nets and hoisted up and out. Down came a rope ladder for us to clamber up and out of the barge, through a hatch into what seemed to be a machinery room of some kind. It was all steel with hoists and chain falls in the overhead and bright lights.

"Where are we?" "What is this?" we asked. "Mac, you are on the LEX." Sure enough, we were on the USS LEXINGTON. The next day would prove it, but not that night as we were not able to leave the compartment that we finally were stuffed in, until we were at sea the next morning. Our bags were dumped out of the cargo nets on the deck, from that pile we each retrieved our own bag and hammock, shouldered them, and climbed down a ladder into a large storeroom marked "Stores - Spare Parts." This was to be our stateroom for the next six days, no ports, no loudspeaker, just steel decks and bulkheads and a bright light in the overhead that never went off. We were on the LEXINGTON, the pride of the Navy, en route to Pearl Harbor, with the rest of the spare parts.

During those few weeks at the DESBASE we had liberty every week night until midnight to go into San Diego and have one of those ten cent beers. A ten cent beer was no big deal to someone from St. Louis where a 26-ounce schooner went for a dime, but the idea of getting away from the daily discipline was attractive. (More to some than to others, because there were houses there that were more than just a home.) Money was a limiting factor, as we did not receive any pay there, and we had to depend on what we had brought from home. However, I did get a week-end liberty, and with my buddy Earl

9

Loeb, took in Los Angeles. We splurged: the whole week-end cost us less than $5 each. We took the Pacific Electric train, stayed at the YMCA, and took in a show, Ken Murray's Review, with Marie Wilson. A good show, but the big thing to me was seeing a young movie actress of little renown at the time, up close and in detail, as the show was letting out and we filed out through the lobby. She was a knockout! WOW! Her hair was orange, she was over-lipsticked and all made up, but Lucille Ball just about knocked my vision out of kilter. Earl just sniffed at my rhapsodizing about her on the trip back to Base.

The trip on the LEX was supposed to be another one of those work-your-way Navy rides, but we were so unorganized that I was able to avoid getting shanghaied onto one of the working details. After my first breakfast on a ship, memorable only in that it was so bad, I went alone up to the flight deck to see the air groups come aboard. The ship having weighed anchor at dawn, was well out to sea, and it was preparing for flight quarters. The few planes aboard were warming up, roaring, and the excitement was thick enough to slice. I watched from on deck, out of the way, and stayed that way to avoid the work details and to see the action.

The planes got off and preparations for receiving planes aboard got underway. I went aft to get a better view of the planes coming in from the stern to land on the flight deck. LEXINGTON had four twin eight-inch gun mounts, two forward of the stack, and two aft, mounted one over the other, and I thought that up on top of the farthest one aft would be a fine spot from which to watch the action. From the flight deck side of the mount most of the rungs on a steel ladder were missing, so I went around to the outboard side where the rungs were all there, and clambered up to take a seat. I'd hardly gotten situated up there when one of the ship's company, a two-hash mark cox'n, yelled up at me, "Get offa dere, you dummy." When I got down he explained to me in very simple terms that the reason the rungs were missing on the inboard side was that planes kept bouncing off that gun mount. Anyone up there was in a very precarious position, indeed.

Wiser now I went back to my previous vantage point. In the very first wing of torpedo bombers landing, one got a wave off from the Landing Officer but it was too late. The plane hit the deck hard, the prop tearing a six-foot long splinter out of it, and the plane slammed into the safety barrier. The pilot got a bloody nose, and the plane looked pretty sad too, as the bent prop had damaged the cowling. This was no big deal to the deck crew, it just shoved the plane onto the elevator and lowered it to the hangar deck below to be dropped off at the next naval air station for repair. This particular plane was a Douglas TBD Torpedo bomber, the same type that would perform so poorly at Midway in 1942, earning the name "The Flying Coffin."

LEXINGTON did not proceed directly to Hawaii but instead went North and anchored just inside the breakwater at Long Beach. Passengers were allowed liberty ashore until midnight, and as I had a few dollars left I decided to see the place, for a change, and perhaps find something tasty to eat. LEXINGTON was not known for the quality of its food. As a matter of fact, it varied between poor and gosh-awful. Access to and from the Fleet Landing was restricted by the number of liberty launches available and the times of their operation. Most of the other recruits were too broke to go ashore for even a hot dog, so I went alone. Long Beach near the Fleet Landing was not an impressive place. If you wanted a beer, or a tattoo, or maybe something else if you had the funds, this was the place. It was a sailors hangout, cheap bars, entertainment arcades, a tawdry dance hall, all aimed at separating the sailor from his pay. I got back to the Fleet Landing after a stroll and a hamburger to find that I had missed a LEXINGTON launch, and that I had hours to wait, maybe even until the first one in the morning, right there in a drizzle without any protection from the weather.

The Shore Patrol on duty were in oilskins, and one of them took pity on the poor boot standing in the cold and told me that an admiral's barge from LEXINGTON was down at the Officers Landing and perhaps I could hitch a ride on it. No sooner said than done. I ran down there and asked the cox'n of this gleaming fifty-footer if I could ride out to the ship with him. This man had a whole armful of hash marks, and a Second Class Bosns Mate crow, and the spit and polish look of an "operator" who had the cushy job of being the admirals personal cox'n. He had clout, and he knew it. After giving me a long look, seeing the single cuff stripe of an Apprentice Seaman on my sleeve, he grunted his assent and turned away to continue his conversation with another of the boat crew.

I jumped into the little open air cabin at the stern to get out of that drizzle, and admired the furnishings. This was nice! Spotless white cushions, white mat on the deck, white MacNamara's Lace hangings as decorations. Not at all like the austere fifty-foot open motor launch that I had come ashore in just a few hours ago. I eased down on the seat to take it easy while I waited for the admiral to return to his command, let out a sigh of relief, when the cox'n's face appeared in the access hatch, roaring like the MGM lion, "OUT! UP FORRID, YOU STOOPID BOOT!" Up forward was just varnished wooden side seats

11

up in the very bow, but it was under a solid canopy, and it was dry. I had time to catch a few winks before His Nibs showed up, and the barge moved out smoothly and quietly to stop at the Officer's Gangway on the ship, where the admiral and his party debarked. I did not see the group, nor did it see me, and then the launch moved on to the boat boom to secure for the night. There were no other hitch riders like me aboard, just the three man crew, and there was no gangway, just a rope ladder hanging down from the boom, to scramble up and enter the ship. I thanked the cox'n for the lift and received a stern warning that if I had left one footprint or mark in the stern sheets of that barge I would now be swimming half way out from the Landing. I think he meant it.

Early the next morning the ship left the protection of the breakwater and set a course for Hawaii at a good speed. The carrier USS ENTERPRISE joined up with us on a parallel course and speed. Escorting the two carriers were four of the Navy's newest destroyers holding screening positions on the flanks. These were HUGHES (DD 410), ANDERSON (DD 411), HAMMAN (DD 412) and MUSTIN (DD 413). Several days out we ran into some heavy weather, which meant little to the heavy carriers, but, as some of us were watching the destroyers from the flight deck as they were taking seas up and over the bridges as they plunged ahead, we were commiserating with those poor slobs on those "itty bitty" ships until some wise guy observed that these particular destroyers were much heavier than the ones that we were trying to catch and board. A sobering thought.

As we broke from breakfast on January 19, 1941, someone said that one could see the islands from the flight deck which brought on a stampede to see our destination. The load of planes had flown off the previous day so the flight deck was bare and offered a high place to look but at that early hour the only thing I could see were some black mountains hidden by clouds. It was after lunch before the force made it to the South side of Oahu passing Diamond Head and Honolulu. That gave us time to get our bags and hammocks up to the hangar deck ready to debark. To say that we were eager to get off that ship and get to doing something, anything, is an understatement. We were champing at the bit, eager to see the ship that was to be our home. We had been cooped up for a month, doing make-work jobs, and I know that I was not alone in looking forward to duty on the USS CHEW (DD 106).

Chapter III

All Aboard

We were set in ranks on the flight deck as the ship entered Pearl Harbor, slowly and majestically moving through a narrow channel, a bright green sugar cane field on the West side running for miles back and up to steep and frowning mountains. The other side was bordered by a mixture of odd buildings, an Erector Set of what I learned later was the Coal Docks, then a point of land with high palm trees and green lawns around some white buildings - Hospital Point. The weather was putting on a show as we got deeper into the harbor. There were puffy white clouds, rainbows in the mountain valleys, varying colored fields, and over all was the intoxicating smell of flowers. This was a tropical paradise, no doubt about it. The water outside the harbor had been a beautiful deep blue, which turned to green as it washed up on white sandy beaches, then a different blue deeper into Pearl Harbor.

As the ship passed Hospital Point the view changed drastically to that of a busy harbor. Small boats, tugs chugging around, steam cranes chuffing along the docks, an imposing group of large shop buildings, various odd types of trucks and conveyances moving around - this was Pearl Harbor! Three large, brightly painted water towers stuck up in the middle, towering over the fascinating scene, the center one of which displayed colored signal flags. I recognized a foundry roof and a power plant stack among the shop buildings. Right in front of us was an air station with all sorts of seaplanes at the water's edge, a runway stretching off in the distance with a steady stream of planes landing and taking off from it. This busy place was the Naval Air Station and took up the entire Ford Island in the middle of Pearl Harbor. We turned left to take a mooring place on the West side of the air station.

The Island of Oahu was everything that had been promised. Beauty most spectacular, sea, sky, mountains, palm trees, Honolulu looked good, even the Navy Yard itself was a visual treat. It was bustling and humming, large gantry cranes, small steam cranes, all over the place, overlooked by those three water tanks and a tremendous "hammerhead" crane sticking up as the skyline of the Navy's "impregnable" Pacific base. We would find out just how impregnable it was in less than a year.

The two carriers tied up at quays with a minimum of effort and time. We passengers had been standing in ranks on the flight deck for hours without a break. At least we were standing "at ease" but it did seem that we had been forgotten. Finally, after the ship had secured from the mooring details we were marched down to that same port through which we had entered in San Diego, and the men assigned to CHEW were loaded into one fifty-foot open motor launch with our bags dumped in by a working party of the ship's company. Each man's gear was stuffed into his only sea bag, which was in turn lashed into his hammock and mattress wrapped around the bag in a sort of a horseshoe shape, all according to the Bluejacket's Manual. When one saw how his bag was handled he soon learned to pack anything fragile in the center of the bag and all hard items, like shoes, on the outside. Those bags were tossed from heights of twenty feet or so to land on top of the previous bags.

As soon as we were loaded, standing room only, the launch cox'n received orders to proceed to Berth Baker 6, unload his passengers, and return. The motor roared and we were off, around the apron of the Air Station, across the harbor to TenTen Dock, so named as it as 1,010 feet long, and on around and behind it until there in the rear of the pier two ships came into view. Someone said, "There it is, boys, your new home." There was a great collective in-taking of breaths at the sight, and the resulting letting out of sighs was almost enough to make the launch back down. There they sat, two rusty near-derelicts, the inboard one leaning out against the outboard one, and it in turn, leaning in on the other, much like two Skid Row drunks on a cold morning. These ships did not look a bit like destroyers. The word destroyer hardly appears in print without being preceded by "sleek," or "greyhounds of the sea." They were forlorn and seemingly abandoned, until several men appeared, to take our line and hold the launch alongside a sea ladder to allow us to toss our bags up on deck with the usual thuds, and scramble aboard. There was not much of a welcome ceremony. The men who had helped get our bags aboard were not smiling and looked at us about the same way that lifers at San Quentin look at a bus load of newcomers.

CHEW was the outboard ship, and we were standing in groups not knowing what to do until an officer appeared, together with a Yeoman with his clipboard and papers, and the officer posted us into ranks along the rail under the cold stares of the men in dungarees. These men were what was left of the crew that had sailed the hastily re-commissioned ship through a stormy passage from sunny San Diego to Pearl Harbor. They looked the part, as did the ship. Only the ship, if anything, looked more the worse for wear. The yeoman called off names, and some of the men, those who were to be in the Deck Force, were told to go forward. Those of us who were to be

14

part of the Engineer's Force were sent aft with our gear to find an empty bunk.

We stumbled down a steep ladder into a poorly lighted compartment full of empty bunks made from pipe stacked three high in the center and along the sides of the room. Playing cards at one of the mess tables bolted to the deck in the middle was a big swarthy man, cigarette dangling from a corner of his mouth, who was giving orders to a couple of sad sacks scraping paint off the bulkheads. He paused in his game to growl at us to take any bunk that did not have a mattress on it, and then cursed one of the other players in the game, who was grinning at the collection of sweating newcomers in winter blue uniforms who had jammed into the compartment. The big man was the Master at Arms for the Black Gang, Blackie Shimek, one of the Fleet Reserves that had been called back to active duty. We got to know Blackie well in the days ahead. He was just about the way he looked, mean, abusive to those he could bluff, and a smiling toady to any and all officers. The other man in the card game who had been grinning at us was Blackie's sidekick, Sam, another of the Fleet Reserves. Sam had done 16 years in the Navy, and then had gone into the Merchant Marine, where he had spent a dozen years below decks before being called back into the Navy. He was a perfect foil and henchman for Blackie. An absolutely venal person, filthy of mind, alcoholic, who delighted in telling the recruits of his perverted conquests in the dives of various waterfronts around the world. Sam left CHEW early in 1942 to be taken back to the Mainland on a hospital ship, where rumor had it that he died on the trip and was buried at sea. If that tale was true, Sam finally did one good thing in his life by feeding the fishes, unless the fish had discriminating tastes.

We had barely hefted our bags on the bunks when it was time for supper, never "dinner" in the Navy, and some unnamed stuff was brought down from the galley by one of the sad sacks who had been scraping for Blackie. This man was the "mess cook," whose duty was to fetch food from the galley to a mess of twenty men, set up plates and utensils, then wash the dishes and clean up after the meal was over. Mess cooks received an extra $5 a month for this duty and did not stand any watches underway. In their spare time they cleaned the compartment and helped the cooks by peeling spuds, cutting up onions, and similar little jobs. Mess cooking assignments were a requirement for recruits. It was a learning experience, to say the least.

CHEW was a WICKES Class destroyer [1] , built in San Francisco at the Union Iron Works, which later became a part of Bethlehem Shipbuilding Corporation, launched in 1917. That class was designed for World War I with a minimum of amenities for the crew but with a maximum of economy in every sense of the word. It was intended to carry its twelve torpedoes into battle and not much else. One of the other ships in DESDIV 80 was WARD (DD139), that had been built in just seventeen and a half days from keel laying to launch at Mare Island Naval Shipyard.[2]

Living conditions for the men in this vessel were Spartan. Crammed into the 310 foot by just under 31 feet wide by two decks deep hull of 7/16th inch steel plates riveted together (CHEW was built prior to the development of reliable welding - hence the rivets, which tended to rust and fall out.) were two firerooms; two engine rooms; storage rooms for food; tanks for fuel oil and water; magazines for gun ammunition, torpedo war heads, and depth charges. The wardroom, one deck below the main deck, was the living area for seven officers, with a small galley, and space to eat and sleep. Forward of officer's country was the Chief's Quarters, where thirteen men lived. Below that deck the sixty men of the Deck Force ate and slept. Just aft of the Seamen's Quarters started the engineering spaces, the two firerooms, the two enginerooms, oil tanks, and magazines, running aft to the Engineer's Quarters, where another sixty men lived. On the one main deck, aft, was a small building (called "shacks" in Navy lingo) that housed the Torpedo Shop, a washroom, with one small mirror, two spigots (that were only "on" in port when shore water was available), and a single stall shower for one hundred and fifteen men. It, too, was only "on" in port. Also in that shack was a four-seat open toilet - the Head. The last priority in the design of this class destroyer was living space for the men.

CHEW had lain in "Red Lead Row" in San Diego's back harbor for twenty years with no upkeep, then had a rudimentary recommissioning, and a rough, stormy passage to the berth where she now lay, and she looked the part. The memory of that ship, and the events that I had a part in, will never fade from my mind. From that point on my life would be different and changed completely.

The Engineer's Quarters, where I spent my first eleven months, were not designed to be anything but a place for sixty men to eat and sleep. There were no frills, not even a chair. To sit at the mess tables, one row of men sat on a folding wooden plank-top bench, the other side sat on the locker tops. Entrance was by an almost vertical ladder that landed amidships in the first compartment. The second, narrower compartment, aft, could only be entered through the first compartment. There were overhead escape hatches in each room, but the one aft had to be kept dogged tight to keep the sea out, and the one in the forward compartment could only be open when the seas were calm. The main difference between the two compartments was that due to the narrowing of the hull, there could only be one mess table aft while two fit forward. These three tables were secured to the deck. Each had a steel cage at the ends which was used as storage for the plates, cups, and bowls, and the mess cook's dish pans and gear. If one of these cages came open at sea, and one did, the plates, cups, and bowls would cascade across the deck and smash into bits with a resounding crash, with a loss of eating gear until the next time in port for replacements. There was no space aboard for spares.

Bunks were mounted three high outboard over built-in wooden topped lockers, the ones that doubled as mess seats. One of the first tasks for the Engineer's spare time was to clean up these locker tops, scrape off all the old paint, and bleach out the oily stains until they were white, plain wood, protected only by wax. The place was a pigsty at first, not fit as a living space for anyone who had any pride in himself. Light came from a few overhead bulbs, mounted in steel cages, and a single row of portholes outboard. Within a year the portholes were welded shut with steel plates as a protection from bomb splinters. The ports had to be kept closed at sea at any rate because of the water that would come through on every roll of the ship. Each man was assigned a bunk and a locker. There were no hangers for clothes, and as a matter of Navy rule, it was an offense punishable by extra duty for leaving one's clothing "adrift." Everything that you owned had to fit in the sea bag, and that removed the necessity for decent sized lockers. That one folding bench for each mess table had to be folded and fastened down securely as soon as the meal was over so that people could get to their lockers, and at sea that bench would be a missile if allowed to be loose.

Space was at a premium. Sixty men in those two small compartments without ventilation made it imperative that some sort of forced air was brought into that "hole" which a small group of us accomplished in short order. Blackie scrounged a blower from one of the shops in the Navy Yard and Red Grossman, Herb Schwind, and I got most of the ducting from the hulk of the Spanish-American War armed cruiser BALTIMORE that was tied up at X-ray 5 waiting to be sold for scrap. The close quarters made it a requirement for all hands to observe personal cleanliness, and once in a great while it became necessary to enforce that rule by using a scrub brush and salt water soap on the offending party. Just the threat of such a bath kept that from ever happening in the Black Gang.

There were more bunks stacked amidships in front of and behind the entrance ladder in the forward compartment. Off to one side of that ladder was a large hatch in the deck, padlocked heavily, leading down to "Jack O the Dusts" dry food storage. Jack O' the Dust, a title dating from the days of the sailing ship Navy, was the galley's fetcher and carrier, a man of all jobs, who was a cook striker learning the trade. In the forward compartment, all the way forward against the bulkhead between the compartment and the #2 Engine Room, and directly under the overhead hatch, was another hatch that led down to the Aft Handling Room and Shaft Alley. This passage led to the magazine for depth charges and torpedo war heads, and the two shafts passed through supported by bearings which had to be monitored hourly on each watch when the ship was underway.

We slept over the depth charges and torpedo war heads, but the main annoyance was the high-pitched whine of the shaft, and the Oiler's hourly trip to record the bearing temperatures. He usually was not too mindful of his sleeping shipmates' slumber and dropped the hatch with a loud clang. Often the Oiler left that hatch open, and that made the sound of the shafts even louder. The aft compartment was separated from the Steering Engine Room by a thin steel bulkhead that did nothing to keep the steady clunking of that mechanism out of our ears. It was a noisy place, and to live there one had to tune out the sounds. (Especially when one had turned in early in order to get some sleep before going on watch at midnight and some of the boys decided to have a poker game.)

No one was allowed in his bunk during working hours. The bunks had to be made up, blankets folded and strapped down in Regulation fashion. The lower two bunks were hooked up out of the way for meals - and the almost constant card games at the aft table, - until "lights out" at sea. Some of the games in port, and after pay day, went on all night, and it was worked out so that the card players had the bunks that had to be folded. Shortly after coming aboard I lay up in my bunk one night in port and watched three of the Fleet Reserves, who had spent the afternoon at the Tin Roof.(The "Tin Roof" was the enlisted men's official beer garden in a busy part of the Navy Yard. It was just a small shack with a dutch door, from which glasses of beer were dispensed. There were a few heavy wooden tables under a sheet tin canopy and some kiawi trees for shade. It was torn down shortly in the expansion of the harbor.) These three, after spending the afternoon there lapping up a few beers were playing a game that one of them thought was poker. The other two, Blackie and Sam, were cheating Eggie out of his pay. They double-dealt, slipped cards to one another, dealt off the bottom, until Eggie was cleaned out. Their slogan was: "Cheat your friends, your enemies never come around."

The reserves' introduction into our particular niche in the Navy's scheme of things started at once, with assignments to duty sections, steaming watches, repair and work gangs, battle stations, who was who, and what was what. Getting the crew lined up and familiar with what each man's duties were was an immediate requirement and no time was taken for any schooling or indoctrination.

I was assigned to duty in the Engine Rooms. On the next day we went to sea with me in the After Engine room for the very first look at what was one great big roaring steaming puzzle. There was a chief petty officer in charge of both Engine Rooms, with a First Class petty officer in charge of each room. No introductions, just climb down the ladder, and watch as several men were twisting valve wheels getting ready to go to sea. The chief was dashing about yelling orders (the noise made ordinary conversation useless) holding a watch list (a roster of men and ratings) and when he asked my name he just grunted and told me to "help Siegler." I carefully went forward in the room from the foot of the ladder that I had just descended until I found Siegler standing in front of two two-foot diameter spoked brass wheels that were mounted on the transverse bulkhead, and as calm as a cucumber as he watched some gauges on that bulkhead. I had clunked my head at least twice in making my way forward to him as headroom was limited. Large pipes ran in every direction without any semblance of order, but this man Siegler seemed to know them all by function.

He gave me a cheery greeting just as a bell clanged over our heads and he responded by slowly twisting one of those two wheels. A hiss came from a large machine behind us and the whole ship seemed to move. He had received orders to back down one third speed, as that order showed on a brass contraption overhead. He handed me a book and told me to record that "bell," and informed me that I was now standing a steaming watch as an Oiler. He was the Throttleman on the starboard set of turbines and I was his helper. Those two big spoked wheels controlled steam from the boilers to a set of turbines in that room. He was giving it "the gas." After a few minutes the ship took a lurch to one side, and then another one to the other side, which brought an observation from Siegler that we must have just passed the Entrance Buoys and we were now at sea. We had the "watch" to keep the ship running. My first steaming watch and I didn't know what I was doing and what was going on. Ed Siegler was one of the Fleet Reserves who had done 24 years and had retired to work as a machinist in a factory in San Diego only to be called back to

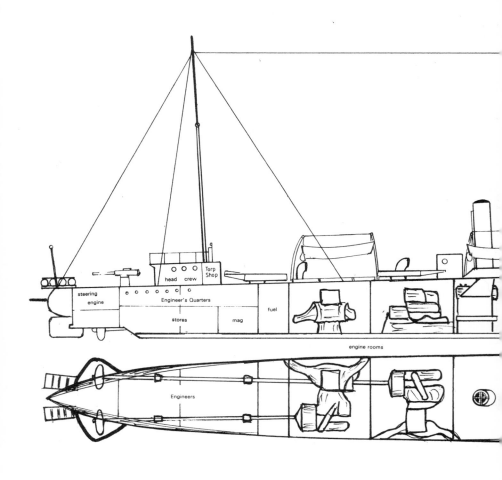

TYPICAL WICKES CLASS DESTROYER -

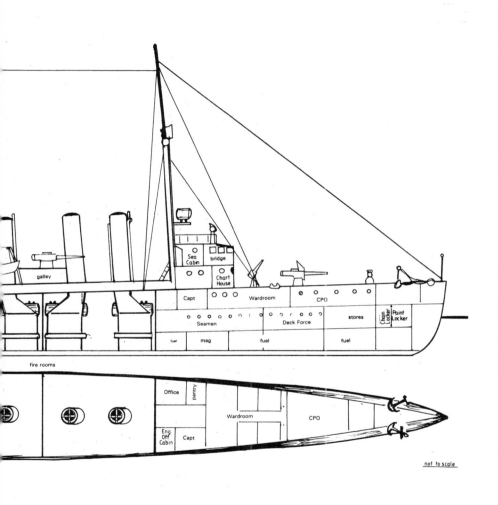

USS CHEW (DD 106) - 1940 Configuration.

21

active duty on the USS CHEW. I was fortunate in drawing him as a mentor, as he was patient and friendly.

That watch was soon over and we went topside to wash up and have lunch down below in the quarters. As soon as we had eaten the chief came along and told me and some others to get topside to work for Blackie in scraping the locker tops. That wasn't bad, the sea was beautiful with white caps and a fresh breeze, as we sailed along the South Coast of Oahu scraping the wooden locker tops. After about thirty minutes on that course the ship turned to head in the other direction. During that maneuver I suddenly felt the need to get to the toilet. I put down my scraper, and hustled aft to the Head. My lunch came up, almost everything, including my socks came up. Oh I was sick. The saying is about seasickness is that at first you fear that you are going to die, then you fear that you aren't. That is true. I went below and got in my bunk to await the Grim Reaper, but instead Chief Tracy appeared, grabbed me and pulled me out of the bunk and shoved me for the ladder with the admonition that I could be just as seasick scraping those locker tops as I was in that bunk.

Topside, I couldn't believe my eyes. The scenery was so beautiful, and I was so sick, and there was no sympathy anyplace. I was not the only sufferer and the ones who were not affected were having a ball with wise remarks and jokes. It took a while, but no one spent any time in his bunk trying to recover from mal de mer. You worked it out.

On the date of January 21, 1940 the crew was made up of thirty-three Regular Navy; twenty Fleet Reserves; and seventy-five Organized Reserves from St. Louis, for a total of one hundred twenty-eight. The thirteen chief petty officers were one Regular; eight Fleet Reserves; and four Organized Reserves. The rated petty officers, First Class, Second Class, and Third Class were nineteen Regulars; ten Fleet Reserves;and twenty-one Organized Reserves. Non-rated were split eleven Regulars versus fifty Organized Reserves. The four mess attendants serving the officers were two each Regular Navy and Fleet Reserves.

The Captain, Edward L. Beck, was Regular Navy, as were the Exec, Robert A. Theobald, Jr., and the Chief Engineer, Daniel M. Entler. The rest of the officers were Reserves: Charles MacNish, John Morrison, Virgil Gex, and John E. Tuttle.

The Reserve rated petty officers were the targets of jealousy and envy from the Regulars, especially the non-rated ones. A couple of the Reserve First Class Petty Officers, with little or no sea duty, drew the most resentment and had the hardest time.

Rates were hard to come by in the Navy at that time. A third class fireman, non-rated, like me, got $36 a month to spend any way that he wanted. Out of that amount one had to take all personal expenses: clothing replacements; toiletries; tobacco (although cigarettes were sold as "Sea Stores" for a nickel a pack!); stationery; and everything else not in the original "bag" of clothing issued. One of the Regular Navy Second Class Watertenders had two hitches in before he made Second Class Petty Officer, and then it was only after another man had retired. So it was no wonder that the Regulars resented a rating coming in over them with all of his experience in a shore-side Armory. Bill Hudson, as the sole Chief Bosn's Mate, had it easier with the kids in the Deck Force than Jim Sullivan had in the Black Gang. Sully had most of the Fleet Reserves and the Regulars to contend with and he was quickly shunted aside to be a maintenance man because of the resentment toward him. There were also two Fleet Reserve chiefs in the Black Gang that were down on him. Sully was a decent man, but he was not cut out to run a tough bunch like the Black Gang.

CHEW had been mothballed, and was the second to last ship to be recommissioned from San Diego. This meant that the ships finished ahead had their pick of the machinery and equipment, and the last ones got the leavings. It was understood that CHEW was to have been the third from last out, but when they worked down to the end there wasn't enough machinery for the last one, so it was made into a water barge. At least, there was a water barge in San Diego that had been made from a four-stacker to give credence to that story. Another story from that same file of tall ones was that CHEW was in such bad shape that the British refused it as part of the fifty "overage" destroyers that went to Britain in exchange for bases. [3]

I don't know how true that some of these stories may be, but it sure was interesting to those of us who had a part in getting her back in shape. She was in poor to terrible condition, hurriedly slapped back together, and then sent to Hawaii to work as an anti-submarine, anti-invasion, escort vessel, ship of all trades, with a crew of (mostly) Reserves. Many years later at a Pearl Harbor Survivors Association reunion in Hawaii, Captain Beck, who had commanded that first year, told my wife how proud he had been of that crew and the way it took hold of that old ship, whipped it into fighting trim, and made it into a home. Beck, who was to me the very epitome of a Naval officer, tall, ruggedly handsome, and every inch the gentleman, went on to a distinguished career after he left CHEW, and retired as a Rear Admiral. (We trained him well)

During the time I served in the engine rooms we of the Engineer's Force had to refurbish each and every piece of machinery in order for it to operate properly and dependably. In the meantime the entire crew went through drill after drill, exercise after exercise, maneuver after maneuver, individually as a ship, and as part of DESDIV 80. Destroyer Division Eighty, assigned to COM 14, Commander, Fourteenth Naval District, consisted at first of ALLEN (DD 66), the oldest destroyer in the Service, and a veteran of European duty in World War I, manned by the 36th Reserve Division from St. Louis; SCHLEY (DD 103), manned by the 35th Division, also from St. Louis; CHEW (DD 106), 37th Division; and WARD (DD 139), manned by the 47th Division Reserves from Minneapolis-St. Paul. The year passed, some of the Reserves were weeded out, most of the Fleet Reserves were transferred off for physical reasons, but from this group came a crew as good as any, man for man, as any ship in the Fleet.

FOOTNOTES

1. WICKES Class destroyers were 310 feet long; 30 feet, 11-1/2 inch beam; four boilers; two sets of geared turbines developing 26,400 horsepower with designed speed of 35 knots.

2. "USS WARD - THE FIRST SHOT" 1983.

3. To lay this rumor to rest see "Destroyers for Great Britain," Arnold Hague, Naval Institute Press. Revised 1990. The Brits did not turn down any ships and at least two of the fifty had been stricken from the Navy's list as unfit for service. From this book it appears that the Navy got rid of some of its junk.

Chapter IV

Life in the Pre-War Navy

The Navy was an organization of two worlds, far, far, apart. There were the enlisted men on one side and the officers on the other. Far away and removed from the world of the enlisted men was the cossetted world of the officer.

In the Spring of 1941 I had the midnight to 0400 watch in the engine room. The separation of officers from enlisted men was demonstrated to me. CHEW was in Pearl Harbor, alongside a dock, "cold iron." That is, no boilers were lit off, the ship was receiving water, steam, and electric power from the dock. There were two engineers on watch; one in the firerooms, and the other, me, in the engine rooms. The Deck Force had a gangway watch, a petty officer as JOD (Junior Officer of the Deck), a seaman as his messenger, and a roving sentry. On these late in-port watches the OD was in his bunk forward in the wardroom, subject to a call from the Gangway Watch PO, if necessary. This watch was usually boring and without incident, and this particular one began quietly enough, then from the silence above, a voice called down to me through the open hatch, "Do you have any coffee on?" and at my affirmative answer an officer in his dress whites clambered down the ladder into the forward engine room. It was the Chief Engineer, Lieutenant (jg) Daniel M. Entler, my direct superior officer.

Entler, who had been a varsity halfback at the Naval Academy, was a quiet, reserved, man, not given to a lot of talk. He was a lighter-than-air pilot who, rumor had it, had been sent to the CHEW as a punishment for some unknown infraction. I had recently been hauled before the Captain's Mast (The most minor "court" in which to judge an enlisted man.) on a charge of making a wise crack, and Entler had gone to bat for me at the trial. Because of his intervention I got off with a bit of extra duty. I had thanked him for his good words on my behalf, but he had kept his poker face, and I did not know how the thanks had been received.

Now here we were, a month or so later, and from the moment when he stepped off that ladder onto the deck plates it became obvious that he had been someplace where liquid refreshments had been served, and that he had taken on his share. He was not drunk, just to the point where some men become belligerent, and some become philosophical. He was, thankfully, in the latter frame of mind. After he had swallowed some of the java, he looked at me and said, "You know, Pond, this dash-dashed Navy is just a yacht club, and you men are just part of the scenery." No truer words were ever spoken on that subject.

Years later, in the Sixties, Dan Entler and I had a long visit in his office at a plant in Baltimore in which we talked over old times and a wide range of subjects. In that session he said that in the wardroom the general opinion of me had been that besides being a cheeky rascal, I was also a Communist! That ridiculous assessment of my character accents the wide chasm between the officers and the men.

The wardroom was populated at that time by two or three Regular Navy officers, three or four of the called-up Reserves, and the rest by Ninety Day Wonders (or, in several cases, Ninety Day Blunders), kids who had completed two years, or more, of college and then a three-month course to become a Naval Officer. As twenty-year olds, they made officers of varying quality. Some were all right and caught on, others were so - so, and some were absolute disasters. They came and went on the CHEW. Charles MacNish, a Reserve Lieutenant; Virgil Gex, also a Reserve but a Naval Academy graduate, and John Morrison, a Reserve ensign, came aboard at the same time as the rest of the Reserves. MacNish was a hard-driving straight arrow who went on to work his way up to admiral. Gex later skippered a Destroyer Escort that sank two Japanese subs. "Smokey" Morrison was downright bashful and had very little to say as Assistant Engineering Officer. Ensign Jim Rowe was one of the first young officers to come aboard after the war had started.Rowe was a decent man who got in hot water and was disciplined for going on liberty (fraternizing) with an enlisted man. Ensign Clair Callan was an excellent athlete who played on the ship's basketball team, and later went on to become a United States Congressman from Nebraska. But there were a few others who came along who the crew had a lot less regard for than for others, ones who seemed to think that the enlisted men were somehow or other a lesser breed of creatures.

Many years later Virgil Gex confided to me that, as an Ensign, he avoided any trips into the Engineers Quarters, as he would rather not risk life and limb in that inferno. The "Snipe's Quarters" bark was a lot worse than its bite, so to speak, although it did have quite a few noisy residents. That reputation was enhanced by a fight between Blackie Shimek and Tow-head Doeden that resulted in one man being taken to the Hospital for treatment and the other combatant to the hospital ship SOLACE for repairs. I was off the ship at the time and so missed all of the festivities, but it took pains and effort to get the two apart and cooled down enough for shipment to the hospitals. Blackie had used a dog wrench on the Tow-head, whose fists were enough. Incidents like this did not improve officer's perception of the men.

Some of the wily old Fleet Reserves could bring beer and whiskey aboard almost at will to help pass the time at the card games in the Engineers Quarters. The aft compartment, nicknamed "The Guinea Pullman," was a veritable casino. It was hard to get in there from topside easily, as one had to wend his way through the outer compartment past the rows of bunks, so the poker game was un-raided.

The after payday ritual crap game was held all the way around at the far side, unmolested in its remote spot, but for safety's sake that game also had a topside lookout who would rap on the deck as a warning. There were several unsuccessful attempts to raid that crap game, but in the main it was let alone. None of the Deck Force, for reasons of health, (their own) would even think of turning us in, although we did allow some of them to get in the games, but not too many. Sixto Tuangtuang, a First Class Officers Cook, was a welcome player in our games. A slim, quiet man, he was said to be a Moro, and the Filipinos in the officers' mess crew were extremely wary and respectful of him. All Catholic Filipinos knew the reputation of the Islamic Moros as fierce fighters and kept their distance. To this day the Moros and the Filipinos are fighting and the Moros have not lost their fierce reputation. In the pacification of the Philippine Islands after the Spanish-American War the United States Army developed the 45 caliber pistol in order to get enough power in a handgun to stop a Moro.

There were never any big games held up forward in the Seamen's Quarters as that place was too easy to raid, with entrances from both forward and aft. The kids up there did have penny ante games, one of which was raided by Ol' Mush Mouth, who at that time was now Commanding Officer. He was going to "make an example" out of those nasty gamblers. Three of the gamblers were Second Class Seamen, and had no rate to lose, but Leo Coe was a Third Class Sonarman, and lost his single stripe at the Captains Mast that followed.

Mail Call was an important event. Most of the crew had girl friends and/or families back "stateside" and the receipt of an envelope from home was something that we all looked forward to with enthusiasm. The Mail Clerk was a petty officer who had what was considered a

27

plum as he had all sorts of extra things to do, like go in from the ship by whaleboat with "guard Mail" and spend the day, and sometimes overnight, in port. It was interesting to watch the different reactions different men had upon receipt of a letter. Some would grab the letter and retreat to a remote spot to read his letter alone. Some exhibitionist types would read their letter aloud to entertain his shipmates, to their howls at some of the passages. Eddie Greco received several packages from home that contained some of the most delicious Italian sausage that must have made the entire mail ship reek of garlic. I received a box of cookies once that came in the form of crumbs after its passage.

In between Mail Calls were lonely times. One of the ships in the Mine Squadron had an antidote for loneliness in a dog named "George," a white, spotted mutt, of indiscriminate breed, with short legs and hound ears. He was the ship's dog, and how we envied that crew. George would go on liberty with the men, rode the bus to Honolulu with them and came back on the last bus with the drunks. We tried several times to shanghai a dog without luck.

Someone had picked up a mongrel pup off the sugar docks in Hilo on one of our trips to that port, and enticed it aboard. Several men were playing with the pup on the fantail when another man who had just returned with a skin-full of booze from town, stepped out of the head, and just to be mean, kicked the dog over the side into the water. The pup had hardly hit the water when Jack Grossman went over the side, grabbed the dog, and scrambled back aboard over the screw guards, put down the dog and flew into the mean SOB who had kicked the dog. Jack was a short, stocky, mild man, genial to a fault, definitely not a fighter nor a match for this man, who was a big, mean, brawler with a bad reputation. His reputation didn't mean a thing to Jack as he was ticked off. Jack charged the man, stuck his finger in his face, and chased him off the fantail. When we singled up the mooring lines and pulled out the pup was left behind as being better for his well-being.

When the ship was in Pearl, and one had liberty, in order to go into Honolulu there was a walk of about a mile to the Main Gate to catch a bus to the Army-Navy YMCA on Hotel Street, or a little longer walk to the Oahu Railway and Land Company railroad station for a ten cent ride into River Street. Or, if you were feeling flush, or in a hurry, there were the nine-passenger jitneys to take you to the Y. The train was too inconvenient and most men only rode it once. It was a rickety, narrow-gage, wooden seated, open-air relic of the past century and its clientele seemed to be mostly sweaty field hands.

The bus coming back to the Navy Yard was a hassle, especially in the late hours. One learned quickly not to sit in one of the rear seats as these buses always had all of the windows open for ventilation, and, it was not a rare happening, for some drunk up front to stick his head out of the window to throw up and the stuff would blow back in on the ones sitting in the back seats.

One balmy evening "Bones" Davis and I were in Honolulu walking off our dinner, strolling along aimlessly discussing world events until the conversation got around to the sad state of transportation between Honolulu and the Naval Station. About that time we were passing a used car lot, and we were struck simultaneously by the bright idea that *IF* we had a car, most of our problems would be over regarding transportation. We would have the means to go over to the Windward Side of Oahu and get away from the crowds of service men, and swim at the beautiful, uncrowded beaches, and really take advantage of being in Hawaii. No surly Shore Patrol, no noisy gin mills with watery drinks, and no gouging restaurants. We sauntered on the lot and started to kick tires, but most of the vehicles offered were far beyond our limited means. Until we saw Big Bertha 'way in the back of the lot. We haggled and negotiated and finally bought this beauty for the princely sum of $35 and took off for the Navy Yard. The car, a 1930 Chrysler Imperial 80 roadster, had seen better days, but it was running, and it was ours. Imagine huge washtub sized headlights, soaring fenders with two spare wheels in side mounts, rumble seat, and a trunk cantilevered out over the back bumpers. It was just about the biggest thing that Chrysler had ever built. Traces of the original white showed through the black that it had been re-painted. We theorized that it had been the property of some sugar baron's wastrel son who used it to help seduce dusky maidens with this ostentatious display of wealth.

In Hawaii at that time there were still many Fiat Topolinos put-putting around, and a Ford Model A was a big car. Next to a dog, young men love cars, and we had plenty of would-be suitors to help refurbish our vehicle. We could not take it in the Navy Yard, because they were fussy about insurance, and we didn't have the funds at the time to buy any. We parked it outside the Main Gate in a safe lot under the gaze of the Marine Detachment. In a matter of a few weeks it was tuned, shined, polished, and put in service every time we were in port up and over the Pali to the Windward Side of the Island and untrammeled idleness. I can only remember making one such trip when our idyll was interrupted by December 7, 1941 and we did not get back to see our car for more than a month.

When we finally returned the parking lot was empty! Where was Big Bertha? The first person to ask was the Corporal of the Guard. "Cars? Oh, yeah. A plane crashed on the lot and most of them got burned up, and then they were hauled away to the school yards so that the Japs couldn't land gliders on the flat places". We found the hulk of a burned out large roadster, no engine, no heavy running gear, in the middle of a football field. The heavy parts had gone to the Yard foundry for use as steel scrap, so that part wasn't wasted, and we talked about filing a claim "afterwards" against Hirohito. I've often wondered who thought the Japanese could tow gliders all the way to Hawaii to land on the playing fields.

I learned something that first few months that stuck with me for the rest of my time in the Navy. I had come from a background of a job in heavy industry during the late part of the Great Depression, where money was tight, and especially tight in industry, where a dollar spent for machinery or equipment had to be justified. No one ever bought a machine because it would be nice to have - it had to have a proven need before any real thought was given to the matter. Then I landed in the Navy, on a beat-up old second-rate ship, where creaky machinery either had to be repaired or tolerated. An officer had to get new equipment put on the ship's budget, then get the thing approved, and then ordered. The required procedure contained miles of Red Tape. If an item was not on the budget - forget it. It was make do, use it up, and wear it out. There was, however, another unofficial route to take, and it was one more lesson in my continuing education on how to get things done - without paperwork. That way was to scrounge something. There is a very fine line between scrounging and stealing, but the wise old Fleet Reserves were experts at skirting that line. The officers knew that some equipment got aboard without any paperwork, but they blithely ignored the facts.

CHEW was one of the last ships to come out of Red Lead Row and had more than her share of decrepit equipment. One of the worst examples was the boiler feed water pump in the Forward Engine Room. This pump furnished feed water to the boilers to make steam and at high speeds was called upon to produce great quantities of feed water. If the pump failed, no water went to the boilers and the ship could not move. This was the most important pump in the engine room. All the pumps were important, but this one had no back-up equipment, and it's failure would be noticed at once. This was a double-acting horizontal Worthington pump, a big one.

I had completed my three months as mess cook and was assigned to the Evaporator Gang, under the redoubtable Blackie Shimek, who was

30

a prime example to his gang, of how to get things done without a lot of paper-work being involved. He was far from being a role-model as a person, but as a scrounger, moocher, and general ear-banger with the officers, he was without peer. One afternoon Jim Graffigna and I were doing some minor job at the work bench in the After Engine Room when Blackie slid down the ladder in a hurry and called me over to one side. He handed me a metal tag, about two inches by four inches, with a name and some numbers stenciled into the metal, and a blank piece of similar sized galvanized metal. Taking our stencil set out of the tool box, he had me make a duplicate tag out of the blank piece of metal, only with USS CHEW DD106 stenciled in place of SS ESSO SOMETHINGOROTHER, but with the same numbers. Blackie had problems with spelling, and that was why I was drafted into making the new tag. As soon as I finished banging out the counterfeit tag he grabbed it and scrambled back up the ladder and out of the engine room. He crossed the gangway and growled something to the Gangway Watch to the effect that he had to get over to the "shop" to pick up something.

My curiosity was aroused so I followed him off the ship to see what he was up to and caught up with him as he hustled over to Tenten Dock. He didn't mind having a henchman in this operation, and told me to shake a leg to keep up with him. We finally came up to a large stack of miscellaneous crates and boxes, more than enough to fill a very large truck or trailer. Slipping around to the back of the stack, Blackie pulled a pair of pliers from his pocket and wired the "new" tag to one of the large crates that was almost hidden from view. Looking more closely at the crate, I saw that it contained a shiny new Worthington pump, fresh from the factory, that had been sent on to Pearl Harbor to catch an ESSO tanker that was limping in from the States.

Okay, so Blackie had found a pump that was the same model as our worn-out one, so what? My first lesson in creative acquisition followed. With a wink warning secrecy, he strolled over to the shade of one of the large cranes, where a group of yard workmen were, ahem, resting, and asked them if they had seen a crate with a big pump in it addressed to the CHEW? No, they had not, but one of them said he'd help Blackie look along the dock for it, as he would like to get rid of that pile of stuff that was in his way. "Eureka!" He found it right away. Within a matter of minutes Blackie had directed them to where the CHEW was berthed, and we left to return to the ship.

Blackie rounded up Eddie Siegler, who was the head-man of the

31

Engine Room, told him what he had done, and they assembled a half-dozen of the Black Gang. We pulled the old pump in a hurry, and had a Yard rigger to remove it to the dock. The crate from Tenten was soon dropped off. Carefully we opened the crate, removed the new pump, installed it, and while half of the men were installing it, Blackie and the rest of us put the old one (it looked good, as everything in the Navy had a fresh coat of paint) *into* the crate. Blackie put the original tag on the top. That night, after the Yard shift changed, he conned the night shift riggers into moving the crate back to Tenten Dock to await the ESSO WHATEVER. No muss, no fuss, no paperwork. Some one in the Wardroom should have noticed that the trouble with the main feed pump stopped mysteriously.

Another small thing that accented the gulf between the enlisted men and the officers were the newspaper reports after the fracas got underway. "Ensign Wilberforce Jonathan Tritters, son of Mr. and Mrs. Ashburn Q. Tritters, of 77 Wistful Way, Bug Tussle Acres, was killed in action while engaging the enemy on August 16th. Ensign Tritters was a graduate of Central High School, and attended Eastern State College, where he had been assistant manager of the Tiddledewinks Junior Varsity team. He had worked at Diederich's Drug Store soda fountain. Also lost were 57 enlisted men."

The valley between the men and the officers narrowed considerably when the bombs fell, but that gap widened again as the front moved farther away. Back came the "chicken" regulations, the squared hats, (the regulation way to wear that round hat, enforced by the Shore Patrol.) and all that came with them.

Chapter V

People in Uniform, or, Life in the Aviary

There are many names in this book, most are correct, some will be changed, especially if the comment is uncomplimentary, but nowhere will the name of the second Executive Officer be found, except as a nickname, "Old Mush Mouth," or "The Exec." Never is he referred to by his real name. There are many reasons for this procedure, and I hope that they will become evident as the story unrolls. The man had a negative effect on quite a few people, enlisted men and officers alike that forever colored their views of the Navy. The Exec who recommissioned CHEW was Lt. Robert A. Theobald, Jr., an admiral's son, destined to go on to bigger and better things. He served until April 1941, when he was relieved by Old Mush Mouth. Mush Mouth was the Exec until 2 February 1943 when he assumed command because of the illness of Captain Peter Horn. He was captain of CHEW until 10 January 1944, when he was relieved by Alan G. Grant.

Mush Mouth was held in such low repute by the crew that if anyone mentioned his name at the Deck Petty officer's mess table during a meal that man was fined a dime for each mention. The men from the bridge gang had the most trouble with this fine since they were in constant contact with him and they were baited by the others into more and more ten cent fines. Jack Wells and Jerry Pelletier were the prime targets of the baiters as these two, senior members of the bridge gang, would often show up for chow muttering and growling. This was a signal to the others to slyly inquire about the problem and another would keep track of the times that name was mentioned until the baited one would notice that all ears were turned to his conversation - "Oh Hell, how much?" and cough up, with a few choice words.

In 1983 I was "ordered" by Admiral Hummer to get up a ship's reunion. This "order" was given in a humorous vein (He had once "ordered" Dave Taylor to get a hit in a ball game, but the unhappy Taylor failed to deliver.). In the course of that effort I put notices into various veteran's magazines. One of the notices resulted in a letter from one of the petty officers chiding me for wanting to get up a reunion for that "Hell Ship, especially when Dash-dash was the skipper." As far as I know, this particular writer had never had any problems with Mush Mouth, but just from his observation of life under that command the writer said that his tour of duty in the CHEW was "Hell".

Harold "Red" Grossman had the ability to lay on a nickname that fit like a coat of paint. I cannot give credit to any one man for the names we used for the Exec. "Mush Mouth" was used by popular acclamation. Dave Taylor was a big, good-natured fireman, huge of foot, pigeon-toed, not at all light on his feet, but a good catcher on the ball team. Dave could trip over anything thicker than a sheet of paper, so Red called him "Twinkle-toes." It caught on immediately, and fifty years later Dave is still answering to a shortened "Twink." Skinny Henry Steele Davis was "Bones" right away. "Yap Yap" was perfect for a loud-mouthed Tennessean. Ozzie Grey was "Slop Chute" as Eddie Siegler said he ate with all the finesse of a slop chute. Most Navy nicknames show a lack of inventiveness, like "Big Polack" and "Little Polack," and anyone with a Slavic name like Yasulevich was "Murphy." Polish names were usually just plain "Ski," and there were lots of them. Other Navy names came from the man's rating: Jim Lennox, an Electrician's Mate, was "Sparky;" Radiomen were "Sparks;" Carpenter's Mate Johnnie Koester was "Chips" after his predecessor, Fleet Reserve Chief Anthony Bowers was transferred away and the name was "vacated." Frank Shimek had the old rate of Blacksmith, hence "Blackie," which fit him well as he was a dark, beetle-browed thug of Middle European extraction.

Another "Blackie" was good old Hank Emrich who had black hair and a constant five o'clock shadow. Art Clymer addressed his letters to his girl friend as "Dear Tootsie Boo" and so he became Tootsie Boo. Art was far from being a tootsie, boo or otherwise. He was a hard-working, willing, dependable, all around good guy. (He married his Tootsie Boo, by the way.) Almost all of the Bridge Gang and Radio Gang were called "girls" for their wearing of white shorts and clean white T-shirts on watch. Most of the Deck Apes (the Engineers term for the top-siders) called the Black Gang "Bilge Rats' or "Snipes" or "Greaseballs." All Gibsons were "Hoot" after the old silent movie cowboy star. What else to call Eggleston but "Eggie?" Gordon LeRoy Mountain had two interchangeable names; "Monk" or "Madame Foo Foo" the latter name from his use of gallons of after shave, hair tonics, and assorted emoluments. Monk was without a doubt the cleanest, neatest, most fastidious man in the Navy. He was a Watertender with a hot, dirty job, but he wore shined shoes on watch in a 140 degree fireroom. Most men were clean, and cleanliness was enforced, but Monk carried cleanliness to the extreme.

The Blacksmith had trouble pronouncing any name that was odd to him, so after he had stumbled over Graffigna a couple of times, Jimmie became "Graphite" as that was as close as Blackie ever came to "Graffeena." It was rare for the people from below decks to hang a name on an officer, but one of the first Ninety-day Wonders (or Ninety-day blunder?) to come aboard was reputed to have reported on the bridge during a drill wearing his slippers and he was "Bunnie Slippers" to us from that time on. At least that was the nicest name that he was called.

In one of the first drafts of volunteers that came aboard was a little 18-year old with big ears, so he was called at first, "The Little Pitcher With Big Ears." As this was too unwieldy he became just plain "Ears." A skinny torpedoman named Jacoby was "Snakey Jakey" but that boiled down to "Snake" which seemed to hit him right as he had a reptile tattoo put on to go with the nickname. Chief Machinist's Mate Al Mason took one look at a boot named Alsop and averred that this one wouldn't make shark bait, and so "Sharkey" was it. Mason also accused the Navy of recruiting monsters when he appraised another lad, who was no Arrow shirt advertisement, "Now they're bringing us monsters." The poor kid was "Monster" from that time on. Floyd Bacon, before he was carried off to the hospital for drinking some of his own torpedo juice, had the fitting name of "Plop Gut." Bill Brohammer had his head shaved for some goofy reason, along with a few other boot seamen, and he had an uncanny resemblance to one of Popeye's minor characters, Alice the Goon, so he became "Goon." As far as I know, he carried the name to his grave forty years later. With my surname, Pond, I was called every wet derivation that would come to mind; "Duck," "Lake" and so on. But no name here for Mr. Mush Mouth, the Exec.

There was a great deal of rivalry and chaffing between the Regulars and the Reserves. The Regulars resented any Reserve rating, as being a "feathermerchant rate" (a rate made by a stroke of a pen - not earned). A lot of the differences came, in my mind, from the majority of the Regulars having been innocent farm boys while the Reserves were wise guy city slickers. In our crew, mixed in with the innocent farmers and the wise guys, were the Fleet Reserves. Some had done long, hard, years in the Merchant Marine as bos'n's or as oilers in the Black Gangs. They were hardly the type one would want one around the innocents, but they did offer many years of experience in their specialties. Some of the Fleet Reserves were only interested in pay day and a bottle, but most of them, despite the physical problems that they had with the Spartan life on the old ship, tried to get things running properly and to teach the young men what they knew.

On the Deck Force Archie Moore and Newt Dupuy had many years of Maritime service as bosns after their Navy time and were constantly teaching the young seamen the ropes. "Pat" Sheedy was not a Fleet Reserve, having enlisted in 1914. Pat was a Chief Quartermaster, the most knowledgeable person, not excepting the Captain, on the bridge. In the Black Gang the outstanding mentors were Sam Callaway, John Ratliff, and Edward G. Siegler and Jim Cochran, who had been on one of the nine destroyers that ran aground off Point Arguello in 1923. There were others but these stand out in my memory. There were some rare birds in that covey, too.

Eddie Siegler had been called back to duty as a First Class Machinist's Mate and held forth in the two engine rooms. For some reason he took a liking to me, despite my seasickness at the start, and took me under his wing to learn that machinery. He was a good and patient teacher and in a short time I was standing the throttle watch in the after engine room, an important watch to stand. One night at sea, he and I were standing the watch in the forward engine room, he was the Throttle Man, I was his Oiler, we were enroute to Hilo from Pearl, and it was a stormy and rough trip. The Throttleman controls the steam to the turbines from orders from the Bridge. The Oiler was his helper, keeping records, tending to various pumps and machinery. On a platform deck in that engine room, up against the bulkhead to the firerooms, were the two generators that provided electricity for the ship. The generators were each driven by a small steam turbine, controlled by a governor. This equipment was old and worn, and the location up on the platform deck against the fireroom bulkhead was as hot as Hades. The open bladed knife switches on the panel board were a constant hazard to anyone going up on that platform.

We had just got into our four hour watch when one of the governors over-speed controls tripped out and the generator started to slow down, soon to stop. This overloaded the other generator, and it tripped too. The slowing down of the generators caused our lights to dim and the blowers to slow their high-pitched whine. Siegler grabbed a flashlight, climbed up behind the generators, and re-set the trips. The generators came back up to speed and all was normal again - for about fifteen minutes. The process started all over again. I again took Sieglers place at the throttle while he climbed up into that inferno and reset those damned trips. This problem continued. We had no other people to call on, so Siegler kept re-setting and re-setting the trips, time after time. During one of the dimming periods the phone rang from the bridge, "Keep those lights on!"

At last, after slowly coming back down to the floor plates, Siegler collapsed from exhaustion and crumpled at the foot of the ladder. I buzzed the bridge and yelled over the 'phone for them to wake the chief of the watch and get him down here as we had a problem. There was nothing else to do but carry Siegler up that ladder to the deck and dump him there to cool off, and I went back to the throttle position to maintain the ship's speed. After nearly an hour, when we had only about a half-hour left on the watch, finally Chief Tracy came down the ladder, "What is Siegler doing up there leaving you seasick Reserve alone down here?" I chased him back topside to take care of Siegler, which he did, returning down to see how badly I had screwed things up. We exchanged a few choice words, until Siegler came back down the ladder, and the two of us told Tracy what we thought of his ancestry. Shortly after that trip the ship went into overhaul and received a new, larger, AC generator to replace the two smaller DC ones. I was never seasick again, and Chief Tracy treated me with respect for the short period he remained aboard.

Siegler was put on the Report by Ol' Mush Mouth to go before the Captain at Mast one time for needing a haircut. This after we had been at sea steadily for about a month. The Chief Engineering Officer made the statement in his defense that he had never known Siegler to even need a shave. The charge was quickly thrown out by the Skipper. Eddie Siegler made Chief Machinist's Mate, a well-deserved promotion, to replace Tracy. Siegler was one rock of a man to stand watch with on a bad night.

In the Spring of 1941 I was assigned to my required quarter (three months duty) as one of the three mess cooks for the Black Gang. Red Grossman, Jimmie Graffigna, and I were on an assignment that was an un-buyable course in Human Behavior. Our duties were simple: bring food down from the topside midship galley to the quarters where you had set a table for twenty men. Then, after the meal was over, wash the dishes, stow them away quickly, and then clean the compartment under the watchful eye of the Master at Arms, the redoubtable Blackie. One of the three of us had the extra duty of helping the duty cook by peeling spuds, onions, or whatever little job he needed to prepare for the day's meals. The other two had to keep the living quarters clean. This duty was one that every enlisted man had at some time in his career, and the sooner he got it done and over with, the better it was for him. This was a miserable job, especially to one who was having his problems with mal de mer. Even the Navy recognized the difficulty of this job by adding Five Dollars each month to our pay, which was Thirty Six Dollars for Fireman, Third Class at that time. Plus, we picked up tips if we were speedy and wheedled extra servings from the duty cook for our table.

One of the rarest birds of the rare bunch of Fleet Reserves was

Edward J. Mumford. I vividly remember our meeting. One night while in port alongside a dock, I was just finishing up my chores putting away the dishwashing gear. I was thinking of the problem that I had in the previous week's inspection, when the captain's white glove had detected a smidgen of a smear on the underside of my galvanized dishpan. Said smidgen caused me to get a few hours of extra duty to remind me of my position in the scheme of things nautical. (The very bottom rung) On this particular night a sea bag came hurtling down the ladder from topside, followed closely by someone wearing a uniform bearing the crow and stripes of a Machinist's Mate Second Class. This person had to be an impostor! No sailor, no rated Machinists Mate, looked like this man. Short, rotund to the extreme, he was wearing a uniform made for a tall man, so the pants were rolled up at the bottom, but the jumper had crept up exposing a streak of light brown skin all around. The whites were dirty, wrinkled, and appeared to have never seen a wash bucket or a laundry. The Master at Arms, Blackie, looked up from his card game, evidentially knew this person, growled at me to "Git 'im a bunk" and continued with his game.

Back aft, in the guinea Pullman, (the common term for the aft compartment. "Guinea" refers to any swarthy Mediterranean type person, Greek, Italian, or Spaniard, who might consider this a luxury accommodation. This was Old Navy sarcasm.), there were two unused bunks hung on the bulkhead separating the living quarters from the steering engine room. These bunks ran athwartships, which made them almost impossible to sleep in at sea due to the roll of the ship, with the added disadvantage of being against that steering engine room with its heat and constant hammering and groaning noises. That's why these bunks were empty - no one could use them, but they were the only ones open at that time. I couldn't believe that this person belonged in the crew. He was obviously a Negro, and there were no black people in the segregated Navy other than those as Mess Attendants or officers' servants. How did he get that petty officers insignia? And he was built like a football, and could not be a sailor in that physical condition. He was of indeterminate age, but most likely was of the age of the older Fleet Reserves, in his forties.

He followed me, dragging his sea bag, back through the outer compartment to the guinea Pullman, threw the bag up on the bunk I had indicated, and when I opened the standing steel locker next to his bunk for him he reached up under his jumper and pulled out a roll of bills, held together by a rubber band, and tossed it into the empty locker where it bounced about like a baseball! He shucked his jumper to reveal a torso covered with faded tattoos of all kinds of scenes;

hearts, flowers, daggers, a veritable gallery of tattoo parlor art, emblazoned on a skin that wasn't dark or light, just a different shade of tan, cafe au lait. Taken as a whole, this man was a miniature tattooed Buddha! A wide smile came over his face when he saw my expression at seeing that roll of greenbacks. He seemed to be enjoying my puzzled expression. "Hi, shipmate. I wuz lucky," sticking out his hand, "I'm Mumford."

Eddie Mumford had been one of the original recommissioning crew of the CHEW at San Diego but had wangled his way into the Naval Hospital at San Diego and had been there for the intervening months, long enough to miss the hard passage in CHEW to Hawaii, and had just spent several weeks on a transport catching up to his ship, hence the filthy clothes. The man was one of two (as he told it) Negroes in the whole Navy to have a rate outside of the Steward's Branch. His story of how he got into the Engineers was that he was an Officers Cook aboard the old cruiser CINCINNATI when poison was found in the wardroom food. The entire bunch of officers' cooks, mess attendants, and stewards was broken down in rate to Apprentice Seaman and transferred away to other ships and stations. Then, the records of another man, and Mumford's, had been mixed up and they were assigned as if they were Third Class Firemen, and that is how they got into the Artificers' Branch. It also gave Mumford some basis for some of his tall tales about tough times heaving coal. Knowing him, I imagine that he was able to talk his way out of heaving very much coal. He did another fifteen or twenty years and retired into the Fleet Reserve as a Machinist's Mate Second Class. He was called up with the rest of the Fleet Reserves in 1940 and was assigned to CHEW. In between his retirement and call back he married and, as he put it, "made a few coins here and there" by running crap games in East Los Angeles.

Eddie Mumford was NOT a Machinists Mate despite that rate. He probably had been rewarded with that petty officer's rating for making some officer smile. He was, however, the absolute best morale builder that God has put on this earth. Never without a smile, and always with a tall tale about something that had happened on the "Ol' Cincy;" when they were coaling ship in Panama; or on the LEXINGTON when they were making that Clark Gable movie about Navy flyers. Of course, he and Clark had become fast friends - he said. He was an expert in getting someone else to put on the coffee, and he was far and away the best moocher of food stuffs from the hard-hearted cooks of any of the crew. He had a high, reedy, voice, and when he was accused (which was often) of having told a whopper, the voice would go higher in offended dignity; that someone would cast doubt on one of his stories, was just unbelievable. He referred to anything and everything as "that flicker" and so he was known as "Flicker" and "Flick" for short. Flick was of little use in the engine rooms, but he sure brought a breath of fresh air into what was a hard life on an old ship. A few months later, I was standing Throttle Watch in the Engine Room as a Fireman, Second Class, and Eddie Mumford was my Oiler, instead of it being the other way around as the rates would indicate.

On the morning of 7 December 1941 Flick was ashore in the Naval Housing area above the harbor and was left behind when we pulled out. Weeks passed before we got word that he had reported in to the Receiving Station and had been assigned as a guard up in the housing area. One of our men who had a wife up there, on his return from a visit to his bride, said that he had seen Flick on his patrol, at his very best, carrying a double-barreled shotgun upside down over his shoulder, muzzle down, greeting all the housewives as he passed, and followed by a group of admiring youngsters, like the Pied Piper of Hamlin Town, spreading good cheer right and left. A perfect job for him. But then things cooled off around Pearl and his guard job was abolished and he was assigned to run the galley's ice machines that were in the back room of the lower level of the Receiving Station building. He made that job into a little kingdom in short order. I often dropped by to see him when I was in the Yard for some reason or other, and he always had a pot of coffee on and a cheery greeting. "Come in, come in, Kid Pond, have seat and sit a spell."

I pulled a dirty trick on him. I had to go to the Receiving Station for something that required a belt and side arm, Tom Lewis, a kindred soul was with me, and as we passed Flick's place a bright idea struck me. We put on a couple of Shore Patrol brassards and walked in the door. "Mumford," in a stern voice and a frown, "we're here to take you back to the ship. Captain Hummer (the Skipper) has ordered us to bring you back and he's going to hold Captain's Mast on you for desertion right away." None of this was true, of course, we were putting him on. He grabbed me by the arm and looked up in to my face. "No, Kid Pond, tell him you couldn't find me. Oh woe is me" and more of the same , until he almost fell to the floor in his pleading. I don't know which of us broke first, me or Tom, but when Flick saw that this was a gag and a joke on him he jumped with joy and started to skip around like a kid. The three of us laughed until we hurt. We had kidded the kidder.

Some time passed before I got back up there to see him, and when I walked in the door I could see that things were different and that major changes had been made. Some dour Second Class was tending bar there and when I asked for Mumford it was "Who?" and after my description "Oh, that guy. He had a still over in the back and it blew up one day during an inspection and blew garbage all over the inspection party". Flick had started a project on his own to make "swipes," and it had double crossed him. Webster calls "swipes" a "thin, spoiled, beer," but Flick's Hawaiian version was made from whatever fruit that would ferment and turn alcoholic. It normally had vile and lasting after effects, ie: hangover. His replacement only knew that the man that he had replaced had been sent to some God-forsaken little island "Out there someplace," with a vague wave of his hand.

Wherever he went, whatever he did, Eddie Mumford brought his wide smile and good cheer along. Our paths never crossed again, an event that I rue, as an hour with Flick was always good for the digestion and general outlook.

Soon after December 7th we received a draft of recruits, mostly young men who had enlisted on December 8th. There were ten in the group who had names beginning with "F"; Flood, Freeborn, Fox, Frum, Fulk, and Forester were some of the names. They had been called from a list at the Receiving Station by a Yeoman reading from a roster. These young patriots varied in quality as the general population of the country varied: good, bad, and indifferent.

The Ordnance Gang was a close-knit group of about fifteen men, consisting of Gunner's Mates, Torpedomen, and Firecontrolmen. The petty officers of this group stood helmsman watches at the wheel, ready gun captain watches, and fire control watches. We usually had a Chief Gunner's Mate as the nominal head, under the Gunnery Officer, but we went for long periods of time without a chief, and the First Class Gunner's Mates were just not leaders, and the only Chief Torpedoman we had was hauled off in leg irons charged with a crime "against public morals," and as the ship did not rate a chief firecontrolman we just mucked along. At one time we had a First Class Gunner's Mate, "Ding Hao" Heckman, (ding how. Chinese for 'everything is OK') who was fresh back from the Asiatics, a happy-go-lucky type who made rapid trips along Hotel Street in Honolulu when on liberty and came back aboard ebullient and friend to the world. Sometimes he came back singing.

We needed a couple of strikers from the new men, and we lucked out with two exceptional recruits. Willie Cashel had been a bronco buster in Wyoming, and looked the part, short, wiry, bandy-legged, with a nose that had been broken by the kick from a horse, with a grip like a vise. Bill was serious, but a cheerful, non-complaining worker. Years later he became a minister of the Gospel.

The second gem of this pair was a lanky farm boy from the Ozarks, Fredie (The) Fox. Fred was a fine natural athlete who had gone to a little high school in Missouri that only had enough players for basketball and no other interscholastic sport, but he picked up everything quickly. Ensign Clair Callan and I tried to get Fred interested in going to college after the war (we were sure that it was going to end some day) but he was not at all interested. After high school he had ridden a bicycle from Missouri to California to find work. He needed work, he had no money, but he did have a bicycle, so off he went. He started working on a lettuce farm near Salinas, and because of his height was put to swamping - that is picking up the boxes that the braceros had filled and tossing them on a moving flat bed truck. "That got to be work," he said. Then came December 7, and he enlisted in the Navy at once.

Fred and I were in the same duty section so we stood watches at the same time and made liberties together. He was one fine sidekick. We corresponded after the war when I was married and living in California but he left Missouri for Oregon and I never heard from him again. Wherever he is, he is working. Bill Cashel is a minister in Wyoming. These two men were two of the best men to enlist in the Navy and we got them both on the CHEW.

There were other sides of the coin, as far as the recruits are concerned. One lad picked up the name "Stud" because he was anything but one. Liberty in Honolulu meant to him being brought back to the ship by either the Shore Patrol or his shipmates, passed out drunk and as limp as a dishrag. Others of his age, as soon as they got out of Momma's reach and put on that white hat, metamorphosed into the saltiest of the salty, could out-drink, out-fight, out-everything anyone else who came down the pike, until someone brought them back to earth with a thud. One kid had a good start as a pro boxer in California in the light divisions, about 120 pounds, but he did not use good common sense. He and a pair of his shipmates made a couple of bars on Hotel Street and on their way to another one, he decided to jay-walk on a busy corner with a traffic cop handling the traffic. The cop whistled him down to keep him from being run over, but the lad took umbrage and called the Hotel Street Red Light District 200-pound officer of the law several choice names, none of which amused the officer. He walked over to Jimmie and politely asked him to refrain from using such language. Our boy,

42

the lightweight fighter, quick with his fists, jabbed the officer a good, stiff jab on the nose, causing it to bleed. The officer drew his hand back from his nose, saw the blood, "You shouldn't have done that" and then our fighter said something like "Here's another one for you" and started another jab, but that was a mistake. The officer whacked him on the back of the elbow and took him to the station. After his arm had been set he was brought back to the ship briefly and he was transferred off to the hospital, and we never saw him again. Perhaps he was enrolled in a school to teach kids not to jab at big men who know and use Judo.

We acquired a thirty-year-old former mail-carrier from Chicago who enlisted in the Navy when his draft number was coming up. Never married, his entire working life up to that point consisted of carrying a pouch of mail on his back along a residential street, sticking letters in slots, after work stopping off at the local bar for a few beers, then home to bed. He did not play ball, or engage in any sport, just carry the mail, get paid, and drink beer, day come and day go, and God send Sunday. I tried to teach him how to paint, a necessary skill in the Navy, and I gave up. Another man also tried and failed. I don't know to this day if he ever learned how to do anything. He was unteachable, unless it was an act, and he wanted to be a permanent yard-bird. I don't know if he wanted to be one or not, but that is what he was.

CHEW had to go in dry dock for some repair or other, and we were in the new Dry Dock #2, a place where every minute counted. I had the Gangway Watch as Junior Officer of the Deck one afternoon, and this ex-mail carrier was assigned to patrol the edge of the dry dock, wearing a belt and carrying a rifle as a security watch. I received a report that there was a four-stripe captain crossing the caisson heading toward the gangway on an inspection tour. (Our captain was a Lieutenant Commander, two and a half stripes) I saw this man, and from afar recognized him as Captain John Shafroth, who was one of the driving forces in getting things done in the Navy Yard. This was a man who struck fear into the hearts of destroyer skippers like our Skipper, Harry Hummer. Shafroth did not walk, he strode. I wanted to make sure that we would make a good impression on this important person, and not embarrass Captain Hummer, so I called the sentry and gave him a set of quick instructions on how to treat Captain Shafroth and how to salute while carrying a rifle. Fine, he understood me perfectly, he said.

Shafroth left the caisson and headed for the gangway with a purposeful look, as if he wanted to chew on someone or something.

About halfway between the stern of our ship and the gangway he met our sentry, who stopped right in Shafroth's path, and started a hand salute, then changed in mid-wave as if to present arms, and then changed his mind again to just wave his hand. Shafroth came to a full stop, as the sentry shuffled off, and his jaw dropped, then he turned and came up the gangway, where he saluted the colors and returned my salute to him. "Is that your man," he asked, and when I nodded a slow assent he rolled his eyes Heavenward, and said to take him to see my captain. The man who signed up that mail carrier at the Recruiting Office should have been courtmartialed.

Along came an Apache kid from Arizona, Lorenzo Allison, who spoke broken English/Spanish, who had the eyes of an eagle. I had 20/10 eyesight, and I don't know if Allisons had ever been tested, but he had terrific distant vision, better than mine. Some of the recruits were careless with our binoculars, but not him, he cherished those 7-50 lookout glasses. Anything that helped his vision was something to take care of and protect.

Obsessions for unobtainable things were easy to come by, and there were plenty of men with hang-ups about many things: sex, women, girls, subjects that could be gone over and discussed hour after hour. My own obsession was for a cold drink. There was a scuttlebutt (Navyese for 'drinking fountain') mounted on the side of the refrigerator on the well deck, but it was never turned on at sea because of the chronic shortage of water for the boilers. There was always plenty of hot coffee, but something cold, no way. Barney Wolf became obsessed with a thirst for an alcoholic mixed drink. On his next liberty after payday he took off for lower Hotel Street in Honolulu, went in to the first bar, perched on a stool, slapped a big bill down on the bar, pointed up at the list of mixed drinks available that was painted on the wall, and told the bartender to start at the top and work his way through the list and to keep them coming. Phil Hanley and Hank Rogalski carried him back aboard ship, limp as a rag, and sound asleep. They said that he had almost made the entire list, but had passed out, fallen backwards off the stool and lain there until his shipmates had to leave to get to the ship on time, so they carried him back. They had been careful to stand over him so that no stranger would step on him lying there in front of the bar.

Water was always a problem aboard ship, not just for drinking, washing, and cooking, but for the all-important boilers. Their water priority came in first, second, third, and fourth, as there were four of them. There was an unofficial ration of one bucket of water per day per man. This ration resulted in a man shaving, then bathing in his bucket, then washing his clothes in the same water. The water valve to the single stall shower was kept locked. The Oil King, a rated Watertender, who was responsible for keeping the Engineering Officer aware of fuel and water supplies, held the key, but he would open the valve for about a half hour after the night watches came off duty from the fire rooms and engine rooms, because we really needed a shower after spending four hours below decks in temperatures up to 140° F. The Deck force did not get in on this luxury. It was a single-head shower and the Black Gang had to hustle in order for all to get in and out in that time period. Deck apes didn't need that many baths anyhow, as they never worked up a sweat.

Hollywood has always shown the Black Gang as being bare to the waist, covered with sweat. The sweat part is authentic, but we never stood a watch without wearing a shirt, denim jumper, or a sweatshirt, and *always* a hat. A "hot drop" from one of the overhead steam line flanges was enough to knock you down. No bare arms either, brushing against a line or a pump meant a burn. One of our new Ninety-Day Wonder ensigns will never know how close he came to being thrown overboard after he told a group of off-duty engineers how he had to take two showers in one afternoon to cool off, this while we were living under a ration of one bucket a day!

For being good little boys Jim Graffigna and I were granted a special overnight pass to the Royal Hawaiian Hotel, after the Navy had taken it over as a "Rest Station." Water was so important to us, we ignored the bottled beer (after a quick one), and the big-name band holding forth in the ball room, (Artie Shaw was the resident band leader there for a while) to spend time in our room. It was a nice room, with a garden view of the lovely grounds, but what was beautiful to us was the wondrous green sunken bathtub. We flipped a coin to see who would be first, and then we took turns soaking in that tub. We limited the turns to thirty minutes at a time, and added to our luxury by smoking a good cigar while in the tub. Late that afternoon shouting broke out down stairs - Doolittle had bombed Tokyo. Made our day complete. A luxurious bath, no watch to stand, a good cigar to enjoy, and Tokyo received a few greetings from our bombers.

Navy Yard workmen sometimes were a problem to some of our shipmates. Many of the Yardbirds were Oriental and our Midwestern boys were suspicious of anyone with "slant eyes," unfortunately. Some of the Haole workmen were just draft dodgers. Others were loafers, and looked it, hence some of the problems. However, as CHEW was attached to COM 14 Pearl Harbor was our home port. We spent a lot of time in port and we made many acquaintances with the

45

yard workers. We made some friends, too.

Having an "in" with the Yardbirds meant that we were able to scrounge a few extras for the ship. One exceptional man who did a lot for us "cumshaw" (on the cuff - free) was a Rigger named Lum. Lum was Chinese, about 5'6" tall by 200 pounds wide, built like the proverbial fireplug. Most of the yardbirds wore the required hard hats, but Lum usually wore a greasy fedora. It might have had something to do being Chinese, but other Chinese, like well-known photographer Tai Sing Loo, with his pith helmet, wore other than the prescribed hard hat. The Chinese yard workmen that I had contact with were aggressively hard workers. They had esprit. Lum would come aboard actually looking for work. Lum Da Riggah was welcome aboard at any time. He had many meals after the mess tables had been vacated and there was never a cross-wise look at him. We got many odd jobs done through Lum's efforts with the other "trades," welders, shipfitters, that never had a scrap of paperwork involved. He was a sort of "resident agent" for CHEW to the Navy Yard, and we appreciated his assistance.

The crew of the old CHEW was a motley one made up of all sorts of individual characters. Some of the recruits were greener than grass, some of the Fleet Reserves were weary and tired, but in each "gang" there were at least one or two men who took the lead and got things done. The ship itself changed as the crew changed. More items were added: radar; sonar; better radio equipment; K-guns to toss depth charges out in a wide pattern; until it was a better warship. Then it changed again, slowly, to become a school ship for training sound men and submarine crews as the war moved westward to its conclusion.

Chapter VI

Hula Girls, Coconuts, and Other Tropical Things

In my first year of service, before the war started, CHEW did a lot of running around the island of Oahu training, drilling, and maneuvering. Our schedule was hectic, but we did get in to other ports in the Islands. After the war started our training was mostly over and done with, but we made many stops at the other ports in our capacity as ship of all work;   convoys; submarine scares, and patrol. The outer island ports were a welcome change from liberty in Honolulu, which did not offer a great deal of variety. None of these ports of call were intended as rest and recreation stops, but the crew took all the advantage that it could at every stop to get in a little R & R. My favorite was Hilo, the main port on the Big Island of Hawaii.

Hilo was not used to being a liberty port for sailors. It had no permanent Shore Patrol, few restaurants, and really no facilities to handle an influx of sailors. A source of amusement to me was the appointment on one stop-over of easy-going, quiet, Earl Loeb as one of our two patrolmen. It was obvious that the Exec, Ol' Mush Mouth, did not read the character of his crew very well, for Earl was quite possibly the poorest choice as a shore patrol out of the entire crew. Not that he was a drinker or would shirk his duty, but he was a mild, religious man and hardly cut out to be a cop.

I did find a place on our first stop there that made the port a good one. I had walked in and out of the few downtown restaurants looking for a good meal, and had almost given up, when one of Hilo's taxicabs went by. These were not regular cabs but were called "sampans" by the locals. They were Dodge or Plymouth panel trucks converted into open air passenger vehicles and each one reflected the tastes of the owner/driver by the various decorative motifs. (Note: In 1991 there was a big public discussion going on whether or not these 'historic' vehicles were taking business away from regular metered taxicabs.) This particular cabbie had just taken a load to a local brothel and was returning to the waterfront for another fare when I hopped in his vehicle and greeted him with "Mabuhay" (showing off my command of the Tagalog language to impress the man) and asked for his recommendation for a place that served steaks. He suggested one of the several greasy spoons that I had just rejected. When I shook my head negatively he said he knew a place up above town that might be what I was looking for, and drove up out of the business area to an old mansion that had seen better days. He let me out and assured me that he'd be back at 1500 as I had to be aboard CHEW by 1600.

There was a sign over the entrance "Athens Club" to give some legitimacy to its business, so I opened the door and went in cautiously. When my eyes got used to the dark interior I was in a large barroom with a heavy-set, swarthy man eying me suspiciously from behind a bar that he was wiping down. "What'll you have?" Obviously he thought I was in search of a short romance, and when I responded that I was looking for something to eat he bellowed out something in a tongue that I didn't catch. Out from a door in the back of the room came a short woman with an astoundingly buxom figure, hair pulled back severely into a bun. She was so ugly that she could have sold surplus ugly to the Army. At that time of the day, it was about 1000, it seemed that the Athens Club did not have much lunch business. All that I could have on such short notice was a steak. As the Big Island raised a lot of beef, she had a wide selection, from which I picked a $4 T-bone. When the host heard me order that expensive steak he brought over a tall rum drink that he put in front of me with a flourish, as part of the meal. I had almost finished my tall drink when she was back with a platter mostly covered with a steak and a bowl of salad. That woman would never get a prize for her looks, but for her cooks, that would be a different story. This was my introduction to George and his cook/girl friend at the Athens Club. The next time CHEW pulled into Hilo I brought a few select shipmates along to share in this hide-out, and we made it a home away from home. We left the drunks, fighters, and roisterers out of it, they could do their roistering in the places along the waterfront where the Shore Patrol could keep an eye on them. We would have our steaks and drinks up there on George's veranda and be far away from steel decks and petty discipline. Someone had a camera along for a series of snapshots, one of which is in the photo section of this book.

On a subsequent visit to Hilo we tied up about 0600, liberty started at 0800, to be up at 1600, as we were leaving again that same day. Our group piled into a sampan and scurried up to the Athens Club in a matter of minutes to find the door locked and the place dark. We banged on the front door, and someone went to the back door to bang on it too. Finally George came down and opened the door and let us in. He was in bad shape, obviously the club had been busy until the wee hours, and George had been the master of ceremonies. He had a World Class Number One case of the shakes. From the magnitude of his shake, he must also have been a major participant in the celebration. But he was a business man and loved our custom, and was glad to serve us. But first, he had to do something about those shakes. He put a shot glass on the edge of the bar, and with two hands poured a stiff drink. Then, grasping the edge of the bar with both hands, he bent over and took the full shot glass in his mouth, stood up and bent over backwards so that the liquor went down his throat. He shook, shuddered, and took the glass out of his mouth. "OK, Gents, call your drinks". He was back to battery.

I returned to Hilo many years after the war had ended but the Athens Club was gone. The neighborhood had changed into a subdivision of nice homes with a view of the harbor. The Athens Club brought fond memories of comradeship and good times. It would have been nice to find George and Amapola (or whatever her name was) and thank them for what they did for some hungry and thirsty sailors.

On November 11, 1941, CHEW and WARD were sent to the island of Molokai to make a parade in Kaunakakai, the main city, as part of an Armistice Day ceremony. The pier at Kaunakakai stuck out unprotected into the sea, and the two skippers, Captain Beck on CHEW and Captain Wood on WARD had trouble bringing the ships in alongside the pier with the tide running away from it. The landing took some time, but we finally made it and tied up. While this was going on an InterIsland freighter was standing off waiting for the two destroyers to tie up. As soon as we were out of his way the freighter skipper brought his small, stubby, ship in with a remarkable bit of seamanship. He put the bow of his ship against the pier on the opposite side from our two tin cans, and a man jumped over to the dock with a mooring line, which he looped over a bollard and secured. Then the ship was swung around hard from it's own momentum as it still had way on. That same lone deck hand ran back to where he caught a line from the stern of the ship and tied it up, with the bow facing out to sea, ready to load and leave. It didn't take that skipper any more time to bring his ship in and tie it up than a truck driver would take to back his truck up against a loading dock. We watched that maneuver with admiration. I, for one, felt like giving that skipper a hand. That Hawaiian skipper gave a virtuoso performance.

After the docking was over the two Navy ships furnished two columns of men in leggings and belts, carrying our 1903 Springfield rifles, following our color guard, from one end of town to the other, before what I estimated to be the entire population of Molokai cheering on both sides of the street. It was a warm feeling to march down that street and see those faces, most of which were Oriental, many Hawaiians, and a few Haoles, smiling and waving. After the parade was over there was a barefoot football game in our honor at a field on the outskirts of town between two National Guard teams. The field had a very definite slope to it, but the team going uphill had the wind at its back to even things up. After the game was over several of us were treated to a home-cooked dinner at the home of the manager of the local power utility, who we had met at the football game. That was a most interesting slice of small town America. A cheering crowd, the big turnout for the parade, the game, and the warm reception that the sailors got at every place.

Many years later my wife and I sailed into Kaunakakai on a big catamaran to find the only visible change in the town to be black-top paving on Main Street and air conditioners sticking out of windows. It was still Small Town America and had escaped the Miamization of Hawaii.

Late in 1941 Harold "Red" Grossman and I had been invited to a luau by a Chinese woman who operated a jewelry store on Kalakaua Avenue in Waikiki. We had bought some Jade from her shop. This was not a novelty store selling trinkets for tourists, but a real jewelry store. Red had bought from her before and it is my opinion that his flaming red hair brought on the invitation to the party. Not too many Chinese have a big bush of hair of that hue. It was a good party, with a professional hula troupe entertaining, and plenty of food and drink. A real treat for two young sailors. I was smitten by one of the minor hula dancers. She was a tall, lissome, eighteen-year old girl with hair down to her waist. She was a striking beauty. After the hula show there was dancing by the guests to the music of the ukes and steel guitars. Not being one to let grass grow under his feet, I asked her to dance with me. We took a turn around the floor, which was a grass lawn, and as she was barefoot and I was no Fred Astaire, I had to be very careful with my regulation Navy shoes and her bare toes. We had hardly made one turn when some klutz cut in on me and whirled her away. I found out that one of the musicians was her father, the big one who had been watching me like a hawk, but I got her back for an encore anyway and got her 'phone number. The war started in a couple of weeks and I lost the slip of paper but I'll never forget that beautiful wahine, Nora Johnson.

Some time later I had a bright idea to write a book about a sailor and his Hawaiian girl friend. I had a sad ending all planned for the man to have been assigned to the USS LISCOMBE BAY, a light carrier that went down with most of the crew. But like a lot of bright ideas, it died before pen got to paper. All this was based on my brief encounter with Nora Johnson.

Most of the port calls were too brief for any liberty for the crew, which made it tough for us. On that ship with short water rations, to be so near to, and yet so far from, a welcome shore was real torture. Many times when CHEW came to a port to pick up a another ship to escort to another port, we would find that the ship wasn't ready yet. We would then have to stand off and keep circling and moving in case a submarine had been lurking around. We could not just lie off shore and wait, or even go in to tie up for an hour, we had to stay out and keep moving all the time. So near and yet so far to a source of a tall, cold, drink.

"A life on the ocean wave

A home on the rolling deep

Where the scattered waters rave

And the winds their revels keep!"

Epes Sargent, 1813 - 1880.
"A Life on the Ocean Wave" 1843

Chapter VII

Chow Down

Food was the subject of much discussion aboard ship and usually came up whenever sailors got together. Napoleon is supposed to have said that an army travels on it's stomach, probably true, it is also said that Robert E. Lee would not embark on a long march without onions to make the dried meat and hard tack palatable to his men. The surprising thing is that there is not a similar statement credited to either Mahan or Nelson, as food is an important morale factor in life at sea. Could it be that generals are more concerned with morale than admirals?

When I received my call up orders in 1940 I made my family goodbyes, one of which was to Uncle George Pfennig. Uncle George had been an Oberlieutnant in Bismarck's army before the turn of the century. His framed commission, along with a photograph of a dashing young officer sporting a fierce mustache, hung on a wall in his den. Now bedridden in his final illness, he called me to his side, rumbling from under that now white mustache, he imparted a truth of military life; "Always tip the cook, Kindt," he said. As I left I thought how droll that advice from one of Otto von Bismarck's men was. It wouldn't mean a thing in the modern navy that I was about to enter. Horsefeathers! It didn't take long aboard ship to learn to tip the mess cook every pay day. Those ignorant dummies or cheapskates who didn't tip always had problems getting seconds. Ashore, the watch cooks couldn't buy a drink. I am sure that Caesar's Legions tipped the cooks in Gaul, and the savvy crew men will tip whoever microwaves their chow on the way to Mars.

When CHEW was recommissioned in 1940 the first Chief Commissary Steward was a laconic, cadaverous, man who had served many years in the Asiatic Fleet, and had retired only to be called back to active duty as a Fleet Reserve. Other than his complete inability to get his cooks to serve edible food, he sticks in my memory best for his tattoos. Tisinger, for that was his name, was covered from head to toe, and I do mean 'toe', with works of "art." When he stood for inspection each Saturday morning wearing his whites, the only tattoos that showed were his tattooed rings and the words "True Love" on his fingers. There is an old sailors superstition that pigs and roosters tattooed on ones feet would prevent the wearer from drowning. He had them, plus many others to cover almost every square inch of his epidermis. I regret that there are no photographs of him available. He had to be seen to be appreciated. He was the supervisor of the galley cooks, and whatever control or guidance he gave them was not readily evident.

At the mess table we could tell which cook had the watch and had prepared the meal from the consistency of the mashed potatoes. If the spuds were watery, Pappy had the watch; if they were lumpy, Stormy was the culprit; but if they were decent, Ben Wimer had taken the trouble and made the effort to make them edible. It took some time for the Reserve cooks to get on top of their jobs, but the main improvement came after the ex-Asiatic Fleet gent made his unlamented departure. Tisinger was shipped ashore in mid-1942 and was replaced by Sanders G. Bondurant, a Louisianian who had been raised in an environment of tasty food. Bonny's hands-on supervision made all the difference in the world in the quality of our chow.

From the time the ship was recommissioned, long before Bondurant came aboard, the men had mess kittys into which each man kicked in a dollar each payday to a fund to buy additions to our diet. Such items as Worcestershire sauce (bug juice), tabasco sauce, and real Heinz ketchup made all the difference between unimaginative bland food and something edible. Later, when I was eating in the Deck Petty Officers Mess we also bought the little tin cans of syrup that were shaped like log cabins in which to wash down the stacks of collision mats that the cooks termed "pancakes." The Navy's home-made syrup, a watery concoction of sugar and coloring, never made it to that table. It had a well-earned vulgar nickname.

The Reserve First Class Cook, Pappy, had been a steamfitter in civil life. Despite an armful of hash marks denoting his many years of service, and his First Class crow on his left sleeve, he was still a steamfitter. He had to have been a better steamfitter than he was a cook, as he was not a cook by any measure. He did not like cooking in the cramped, crowded, hot galley, and constantly voiced a complaint "Twenty years in this dash-dashed outfit and I can't get shore duty." He seemed on these occasions to have forgotten that his twenty years had consisted only of a weekly drill and an annual two-week cruise.

One extremely hot day in port Pappy had the watch and was preparing the noon meal. Because of the intense heat in the cramped galley the overhead hatch was open wide to allow some heat out to help the sweating cooks a bit. Up on the stack above the galley deck house Barney Wolf was painting away. Barney was perched on a bosn's chair hoisted up in the air, slopping yellow zinc chromate primer on the stack with a four-inch brush, when "Ooops," the brush slipped from his hand and fell down through the open hatch into the galley, just as Pappy opened the lid on the copper holding the soup, ladling the stuff out into tureens for the mess cooks to carry down to the messes. "Kerplunk," perfect timing. The big, wet, brush went right in the open pot of soup. No problem. Pappy, without a moments hesitation, scooped out the brush and tossed it back up and out through the hatch and continued to serve his soup without comment, a' la zinc chromate.

Under Bondurant's direction CHEW soon got a reputation as a "feeder." During an "investment seminar" (nickel and dime poker game) he asked the rest of the players something about what they missed most in the Navy's food. Several of us mentioned barbecued spare ribs as something that we would probably kill for. The ship had a beer party scheduled for several months hence and that man somehow or other, by hook, crook, or connivance, got us a big box of pork spare ribs in time for the party. At this time very little meat was shipped overseas "bone in" in order to save shipping space. But Bonny finagled that box all the way from Iowa.

Many years later, in the 1970s, at a meeting of Pearl Harbor survivors in Ohio, I was telling of this reputation and using as an example the story of four flyers we had picked up after they had been shot down during the Battle of Midway. One of these men had been so taken by our food that he ate one meal with the watch going on, and a second meal with the watch that came off duty. We were transporting these men back to their outfits and I couldn't recall this chow hounds name, other than it had been a long, German one. Abruptly a man at the other end of the table pronounced the name. He had been one of the other four! Then a third man spoke up. He had been a crew member of the submarine USS DOLPHIN, that had plucked the four out of the water and had turned them over to us as a faster means of getting the men back to Pearl. Bondurant's comment on the approval of his food was that he was glad to get rid of those four airmen as one more day of feeding those vultures would have exhausted our food supply.

The famous skipper of the Destroyer Base at San Diego, Captain Byron McCandless, had a well-earned Navy reputation for his many quirks, but his greatest reputation came from his mess hall and his food. Captain Mack had a small table reserved for him set up in the center front of the mess hall, facing the serving line, where he took at least one unscheduled meal each day. The cooks in the serving line never knew when one of those steel mess trays would appear in front of them, held by a pair of arms with four gold stripes on the sleeves.

The appearance of that man, unannounced, for a meal had a marvelous effect on the quality of the food served in his mess hall. He could have had his meals served to him aboard RIGEL by his own staff of cooks and mess attendants, but he ate one meal each day of the regular fare with his men.

Throughout my business career I have copied as best as I could his system as a guide and it has been extremely successful in dealing with labor unions at factories that I have had a part in managing. In fact I have never eaten more than one meal in an executive dining room, and preferred to eat in the company cafeteria.

Captain Mack insisted on a full days work from the men, from morning until the noon whistle, and then again from 1300 to the quitting whistle. The men worked long and hard for him in getting those ships out of mothballs with the knowledge that the food they got in his mess hall was going to be plentiful and well worth the sweat they put out to earn it.

As should be evident by now, whenever we could we went to a restaurant to eat a meal that was not Navy food. Anything, almost anything, would do. Some of us, with higher tastes, would go to a seafood place on Kewalo Basin in Honolulu, Felix' Florentine Gardens. It was decorated in South Seas style, with nets, glass floats, harpoons, shark's jaws, all sorts of things associated with the old South Sea life. Felix had a six or seven course meal that laid a ton of food on the table. After about two hours of steady stuffing, the tab, with drinks, would add up to an outrageous six dollars, and sometimes all the way up to Ten Bucks! The meals at Felix's always ended the same way, with the satiated diners relaxing on a park bench, slowly inhaling, exhaling, and sighing.

It was easy to become obsessed with getting something to eat that had not been prepared in great quantities by a disinterested steamfitter for a gang of roustabouts who were not very discerning in their tastes. Accordingly, many of us headed for a restaurant every time we hit port in order to satisfy our craving for decent food served in a quiet place. There were exceptions to my choice of shore-side restaurants. The infamous Black Cat Cafe on Hotel Street, right across from the Army - Navy YMCA in Honolulu, was an exceptional place in which to partake of a sumptuous repast. It was a greasy spoon of the first order. The patrons certainly added to the ambience with their atrocious manners, yelling, swearing, fighting, and even one or two passed out sleeping in a corner. The Black Cat was not swept out in the morning to get ready for the days' business - it was hosed down right out the open front in to the gutter. After one meal there I never went back again. That decision was fortified by the revelation by Eggie Eggleston, a Fleet Reserve First Class Machinist's Mate. According to his wife, who was a cook there, any morsels of food left on a plate by a drunk was thrown into the grinder to use in the hamburgers. That was carrying thrift and economy a bit far.

Nowadays, in an attempt to keep enlisted men, the Navy has scrapped the entire method under which we existed and now is even offering menus and choices at meals. We had a choice too. Take it or leave it. But remember, *always tip the cook.*

"That packet of assorted miseries which we call a ship."

Rudyard Kipling.
"The First Sailor." 1918

Chapter VIII

Medical Care, On Or Near The Golf Course.

DESDIV 80 had a doctor assigned to it, but we saw him so rarely that he has faded from my memory. He did spend a week aboard once well before the hostilities started, but that is all that I recall about him. He probably made a berth on the beach some place with the Paymaster's group. Each of the four ships had a pharmacists mate aboard to tend to the well-being of the crew. His duties seemed to be mainly the regularly scheduled inspections for venereal disease, which gave rise to the vulgar nickname for all pharmacists mates.

Our man was James G. O'Dell, a short, wiry man, a Chief Pharmacist's Mate with many years experience in the Asiatic Service. Whenever a man came to him for treatment, O'Dell always recalled how he, himself, had whatever it was previously, only in a more virulent form.

During our first full day aboard CHEW the newcomers were assembled on the foc's'l for a lecture by the chief on the pitfalls of Honolulu, mainly the whorehouses, and the awful diseases that they gave to unsuspecting young sailors. O'Dell's main theme was that if one came down with a venereal disease he would have his pay docked for "misconduct". Misconduct was his threat, played for everything imaginable. How well this lecture on venereal diseases was received was shown by the alacrity with which many of his audience sped off to check out his advice! If Sex Education in our schools today should lead to a similar reaction by the pupils the poor parents are in for tough times.

It is probably a good thing that there wasn't a doctor aboard regularly. Living conditions for the enlisted men could have driven a thoughtful medical man to drink, they were so primitive. Both the forward living compartments had steam lines running through them to the anchor windlass that were covered with asbestos insulation., The Engineers Quarters aft had an active set of lines to the steering engine room insulated with that same fragile old asbestos that kept a continual film of white dust on the mess tables. The mess cooks would use a dust pan and brush to clean up before serving a meal, but when a meal had been served and men were seated at the tables eating that dust continued to fall. During the war when a depth charge was dropped the asbestos dust fell like a snow storm. The engineers also worked with powdered asbestos, especially the evaporator gang. I was a member of that bunch for a while. The "vaps" had to be re-insulated on a regular basis and that involved mixing the powder with water and then smearing the glop several inches thick on the evaporator casing . Asbestos did "get" Jimmie Graffigna and Jack Grossman thirty years later. Jimmie died from Asbestosis and Jack from Mesothelioma, a more virulent and deadly form, if that is possible, of the disease.

The Black Gang got dirty and greasy as a common occurrence and the use of kerosene, lube oil, and even carbon tet, to remove whatever it was that was clinging to our epidermis was the usual cleanup practice. I was part of a "gang" of four assigned to wipe down, scrape, and then paint the bilges with Red Lead. That was one of the filthiest, dirtiest jobs imaginable, and anyone with a slight bit of claustrophobia could not have done it. In preparation for this job the bilges had to be pumped as dry as possible. Then the "bilge diver" went head first under the turbines and between the ribs of the ship, pushing rags ahead and wiping the bottom with kerosene to remove the grease that had accumulated in the past twenty years. Another "diver" followed behind the first one, only the second man went feet first and used a steel scraper on the bottom to get the surface ready for the third "diver", who slid along feet first with a paint pot and a brush coating everything with Red Lead. We alternated in this task to spread the work evenly. The ship's ribs were about eighteen inches apart, which meant that we made many trips through the bilge. Under the turbines and the reduction gear cases it was a tight fit for me to squeeze through. That is where the claustrophobia part came in. I know that I thought that I was stuck several times, but Jim Graffigna pulled me through, as I did the same for him. After that job all of our clothes went over the side, uncleanable. We wiped each other off with kerosene before scrubbing off. When a crew had cleaned and scraped their bilges no one, *no one*, threw a cigarette butt or spat in those bilges. The perpetrator of such a deed would have had serious health problems in short order. We earned the title "Black Gang."

I went to Chief O'Dell for help in combating my problem with keeping food down at sea, and his advice worked out very well - "you'll get over it," and that is the way it went. In the meantime I kept feeding the fishes, along with most of my shipmates. O'Dell had a good job on CHEW as most of the crew were young and healthy. The Fleet Reserves were a problem to him, as some of those Ancient Mariners were up in their Forties. They used various and sundry ailments, real and imagined, to try to get off the ship and assigned to shore duty. Their successes varied, but I felt deep sympathy for those with dental problems. "Bathless" Morris and "Pappy" Callaway came back from a visit to the Yard Dispensary dentist minus ALL of their teeth and were fitted with ill-fitting false choppers. I felt particular compassion for Callaway, as he had a hard time of it right after his extractions. Morris was much younger than Callaway and it seemed to me that the dentist was premature in yanking his teeth, but yank he did. Both men did get transferred away fairly soon, but at that terrible price. Those dentists did not take the time to fill teeth - they yanked them instead.

The ship's company did get regular inoculations against Typhoid, Malaria, and several other diseases. Schedules were kept by the Pharmacist's Mate in cooperation with the Navy Yard Dispensary where the shots were given. The first series was given aboard ship in the forward passageway up by the sick bay. That first series of shots was a simple affair that got screwed up in the administration of it. The crew was to pass in line past the Sick Bay, where a Yeoman was making the record entries, as the Pharmacist's Mate did the needle work. The passageway was narrow, hot, and dimly lit, making for a slow process, but the line did move. Even that slow process came to a halt when big Eddie Ketchum fainted right in the hatch and stopped traffic. It took a lot of men struggling to get him up the ladder and out on deck in to the fresh air. The next series of shots was given at the Yard Dispensary and it was an efficient production. We were bused from the ship, unloaded, marched in a column through the office and then though a double line of Pharmacist's Mates, the first pair of which on each side swabbed the shoulder on his side with alcohol, then the next pair stabbed a needle into the clean spot, then another pair hit the arm with another injection, and out the back door back into the bus. Eddie Ketchum fell just before the alcohol swabbing station, which meant he got his shots from one senior petty officer, who hit Eddie on one arm and then rolled him over to get the other one. Then he was carried to the bus.

In a softball game, playing first base, I took a low throw on my right thumb, and obviously broke the digit. O'Dell gave me a break, he said, that as long as this accident occurred in a "ship sponsored" game, he would not charge me with misconduct! What a Grinch! He proceeded to tape the thumb to a tongue depressor as a splint, and that was the treatment. At this time we in the Engineers Force were busy working on all sorts of jobs to make the ship livable, and this thumb in a splint did not keep me from doing my bit daily. I was in a gang removing sheet metal ducting from the hulk of the ex-BALTIMORE and installing it in the aft living quarters so that there would be forced ventilation in that "Black Hole." In the installation process we fabricated hangers and straps to fasten the ducts to the hull by means of hand riveting.

The hammering made my thumb throb and it bothered me badly at night, so I "pestered" (his word) O'Dell to do something about the pain in my thumb, but I was wasting my breath. He finally removed the splint after it had become black and bedraggled and then I found that the joint would not bend.I had a stiff end joint on my right thumb. This gave me a problem as whenever I had to wrap my thumb around anything, such as a hammer handle, the thumb would stick straight out and interfere with everything. It also made it very difficult to peek at your hole card when playing stud.

A couple of months later when we tied up to a repair ship to get some work done to our ship, I discovered that it had, in addition to a first class gedunk joint, a real doctor, so I dropped in on him. He took a quick look, then an X-ray, and the following day told me that I had a growth around the joint on that thumb that prevented it from bending. The problem had been caused by me not having had proper attention paid to the break. He assumed that he was the first medical person to have seen the thumb. He didn't know how close to the truth he was. It was, he said, a simple operation to remove the growth. I had split the large bone, and it had knitted back properly. He gave me a note to O'Dell instructing him to get me to the Naval Hospital where they could take care of that simple little operation.

O'Dell was very unhappy with me for "going over his head" and making him look bad, but he wasn't one to hold a grudge, he said. To keep from making a fuss he would arrange things for me on the QT to hold down our accident rate and none of the Gold Braid would be the wiser. I went along with him, as my primary concern was getting that job done on my thumb. In a few weeks we were back in port, and sure enough, O'Dell seemed to be as good as his word. He had arranged it for me to go to the hospital and had a large envelope for me to take along. I was off for the hospital almost as soon as we tied up. I was happy, I was going to have my thumb fixed, and, that hospital had the reputation of feeding Nectar and Ambrosia compared to the grub we were getting aboard ship.

The hospital was a beautiful place, two-story white buildings, tall palm trees, set on a point sticking out into the harbor, with benches along the waterside for the patients to relax on while recovering. I was looking forward to spending some time in this Elysium, eating good food, no mid-watches in a steaming hot, noisy, engine room in a ship that was doing corkscrews in and out of the water, and relaxing on one of those benches watching the ships glide by. I reported in to the Main Building to a reception desk where a bored corpsman on duty opened the envelope, looked at the contents, grunted, handed it back after stuffing it in a larger envelope, and directed me with a vague wave of his hand to go back outside, and inland to Ward 5. I found Ward 5 with no trouble. It was a one-story tin shack of OD green, one of about four in a row, facing the hospital from across the road. The sign over the door was puzzling, "Eye, Ear, and Throat Clinic", but, so what, I was there to get my thumb fixed, and maybe they were short of beds in the big building. I entered into a room with a couple of desks, another bored corpsman behind one of them, reading a pulp magazine. He barely glanced at my envelope, then directed me through the next room. This appeared to be a working clinic office, big chairs, cabinets, but it was unoccupied as it was "after hours." He then took me through into a large ward with two rows of beds in it. He threw some freshly laundered sheets down on the first bunk, stuck the envelope in a holder at the foot of the bed, told me that was my bunk, and advised me that chow was now being served and I'd better get going if I wanted to eat. It seemed that this ward did not have any heavy eaters in it, but that didn't mean anything to me. I took off for the mess hall, and waded into a big meal of good, but bland food. It was a good start, even though the date was the 13th of October.

The next morning I was up, shaved, showered and off to breakfast and back before the 0800 muster. By this time the office and clinic were full of people, corpsmen all over, and a nurse who was, no doubt about it, in charge. Her name, behind her back, was "Fish Face," and it was close. She could have played the Wicked Witch in the Wizard of Oz without makeup. No chin, a prominent nose, and a mean mouth, sort of like a Gar. She was a Lieutenant (jg) and this was *her* ward. A corpsman, with three chevrons on his skivvie shirt denoting First Class Petty Officer, from the door into the ward, called out my name, and herded me into one of the big examining chairs. I was the first name called, I guess, because I was in the first bed, but he was calling out some other names too.

As I sat down I noticed a chubby gentleman, wearing a white smock and one of those Cyclops mirrors on his head, reading the contents of what turned out to be my envelope. Miss Fish-Face addressed him as "Doctor," so it was logical to assume that he was a doctor, and as he approached me I could see the double bars of a full lieutenant on his shirt collar under the smock. "Open up", he said, and proceeded to shine a light in my mouth and peer inside. "Hmmmmmmm" the usual doctoral conversation starter, "Have you had any pain lately?" I sat up straight, "I'm here to get my thumb fixed" and raised it up for him to see. In response he picked up my Medical Record, for that was part of what had been in that envelope, and showed me entries

63

wherein someone had written times and dates when I had been treated for Tonsillitis! A full page of small entries. It was evident to me that all of these entries had been written at the same time, and not at intervals, as all were of the same hue and tint from the pen and ink handwriting. (Ball point pens had not yet made their way into Navy supply.) They were all in the same handwriting too. I showed all this to the doctor, and told him that I had never had a problem with my tonsils, and this was all some kind of a mistake. By this time Miss Fish Face was in on the conversation, standing there frowning at me, she had heard sailors attempts at getting out of something unpleasant many times before, and she wasn't going to be taken in by this one's blarney, and she was muttering into the doctors off ear something that I could pickup a word now and then, words like "malingering" and "afraid" and "dodger".

The good doctor, in the voice that medics use when approaching a patient who may become violent, "let's take another look, Son" and poked around deep down in my throat. "Your tonsils are badly enlarged, and although there are no signs of infection, I think we'd better get them out and have it over with. Next" and I was pushed out the door and back in the ward where I sat on my bed and watched while one sailor after another was examined. I sat there and considered my course of action, and my options. I could walk out that door and go back to the ship, and never get my thumb worked on, and probably be in some kind of hot water for ducking out on that operation, or, I could submit to the operation, which probably was needed anyway, if that doctor could be trusted, and take a chance on getting the thumb worked on while I was right there convalescing from the tonsillectomy. About that time the man in the next bed broke into my thoughts with the suggestion that we go down to the waterfront and park on one of those benches until chow call at noon, which was not too far off. I made a decision. I'd stay put, lose my tonsils, take a couple of weeks to recuperate right here, and live high off the hog. That afternoon reality set in. The First Class came by my bed, where I was taking five, letting my lunch settle ,with the word that I was going to be operated on the next morning, first thing, and that I could not eat dinner that night, nor breakfast the next morning, as I had to have an empty stomach. Thank God for that Navy lunch! No matter that we were in the tropics, the Navy served hot soup, beef or pork, mashed potatoes, and canned peas or green beans for lunch, plus dessert. Real rib-sticking heavy food for hard working men, suitable for lumberjacks working in the cold North woods.

I was up early the next morning, shaved, bummed a cup of coffee from the office, and went back to my bed to wait for developments, which were not long in coming. There were all sorts of comings and goings in the office, and from my ringside seat in that first bed I had it all before me. Miss Fish Face was everywhere, pointing, ordering, keeping the half-dozen corpsmen hopping, getting the place organized. She knew what she was doing, and was apparently good at it. Into this bedlam strode a dapper Lieutenant (jg), resplendent in his white uniform, humming, taking imaginary putts at a golf ball, having fun, there to take a look at the night's new crop of patients. "Good morning, Miss", and kept up his humming. "Good morning, doctor, you have six tonsillectomies scheduled for this morning." "WHAAAAT? I have to tee off with the admiral in two hours. Get 'em in here." and he started to peel off that uniform jacket and slid into a smock, putting on one of those mirrors. "Get 'em in here." No longer humming, but with his jaw set in determination not to keep that admiral waiting. I saw all of this and jumped out of bed and in that door. I was going to be first. This turned out to be a wise move. A corpsman put a stool behind me at a sink, another handed me a curved steel half-pan with orders to hold it under my chin, another was shifting a light around. I had hardly gotten my bottom on the stool when that doctor-golfer had a hand with a needle in it in my mouth. A few snips and I was back in my bunk within minutes with a corpsman giving me a shot in the rump. I laid there watching the fun, bemused, in a half-stupor. I am sure that the golfer-doctor made his tee off time as he fairly flew through that schedule. But the last man through the line got my sympathy. He was a little black man and in the course of his operation he coughed, and blood flew all over the doctor, to that worthy's dismay, and the patient's regret. The doctor was rough on him for the rest of the operation.

After the tonsillectomy I couldn't eat solid food for several days. The very thought of food made my sore throat sorer, but the hospital had plenty of ice cream for sustenance. My next few days were spent between one of those water-side benches and the Mess Hall slowly eating ice cream and then "dental soft" food, mush, and more ice cream. I was starting to feel the need for real food and the smell from the Mess Hall was torture. Soon I was able to handle a pancake soaked in syrup, and I was looking forward to two more weeks digging deeply into the good stuff three times a day. On my tenth day at the hospital I was back on my favorite bench admiring the view, when suddenly O'Dell appeared, my papers in his hand. "Come on, we've got to hustle, I've checked you out and the ship is about to leave and you are needed." "What about eating? I have to have dental soft food." "It's all taken care of, I have a note from the doctor for our cooks right here." I picked up my ditty bag and followed O'Dell back through the Navy Yard to the ship. He set a fast pace as he didn't want to hear what I was trying to tell him and kept well ahead of me. When we got to the ship all special sea details had been set, the lines were singled up, and it shoved off almost at once. The noon meal was about to be served and on his way to the chief's quarters O'Dell stopped by the galley and yelled in "Pond gets dental soft food for the next week" and disappeared into the ship's office to check me in. From the galley came raucous laughter. That was one tough week at sea, dunking bread in coffee to soften it.

I had more experience with the Medical/Dental/Golfing Corp in 1945. After the Japanese surrender, while I was still at Mare Island waiting to be sent to Camp Shoemaker for discharge. I thought it would be a good idea to see a Navy dentist at Mare Island and have my teeth checked at no cost. I had not had a dental examination in over five years. There was a well-appointed Dental Clinic there so I dropped in to set up an appointment. No bored corpsman on duty here, instead there was a comely Wave at the desk. She was happy to set up an appointment for me the very next day. I gathered from her that this clinic was not very busy. The next morning when I walked in, the dentist, a Lieutenant Commander, was actually putting a golf ball around his inner office at one of those little gadgets on the floor for indoor practice. He put down his club and strolled into the office where that Wave had already seated me and was putting a bib around my neck. This examination did not take long. He picked around, poked and peeked, and put his mirror and tools down on the tray with a clatter. He said that my teeth were in fine shape and that I did not need any work, and went back to his putting practice. I had fully expected him to find some cavities at least, but I was satisfied with his diagnosis. Regular brushing with Colgates had paid off.

Within three months of my discharge after I was home in St. Louis I underwent oral surgery on an emergency basis to remove an impacted wisdom tooth. The surgeon said the "I should have had that work done before I got out."

I did get my thumb fixed within a year of my tonsillectomy. I caught a line drive on it and broke the calcified growth around the joint. Enough movement came back so that I could once again wiggle the end of my right thumb.

Chapter IX

The Crossroads of the Pacific

It has been said that the port of Honolulu is the Crossroads of the Pacific. If the number of foreign warships and major vessels that passed through are any criterion, the assessment is true.

I had kept a daily diary of events and ships I saw that would have been a great help to me in recalling events and ship sightings. Alas, during the big flail right after the war started we were ordered to destroy all personal diaries. Not throw them over the side, as they might fall in enemy hands, but completely destroy them. My little red book was burned.

One of the first notable ships to make a call in Honolulu was the Free French destroyer LE TRIOMPHANT. She had escaped from the German takeover of the French Mediterranean ports and was enroute to New Caledonia, and so she stopped off in Honolulu to refuel. She was in port for just a short time. Some of our crew went aboard her and came back with horror stories about how dirty she was in comparison with our ship. One of our radiomen said that the French radio gang kept some chickens in the radio shack! (With a deleterious effect on the atmosphere.) I did pick up a snapshot of this ship taken by one of our men, showing a modern ship with almost three times the displacement of the CHEW at 3,230 tons and 434 feet in length. An impressive ship. LE TRIOMPHANT was the source of some good tales from the South Pacific about how the crew shifted political allegiance from time to time, from Free French to Vichy French and back again several times, to the discomfiture of the local U. S. Navy commandant. This vacillation ceased when Admiral Halsey took over that part of the Pacific as an area command. Halsey severely limited the supply of oil to the ship so that it didn't have enough to go to sea for any distance, thus keeping LE TRIOMPHANT under U. S. Control.

HMS WARSPITE, the famous British battleship that had taken thirteen hits in the World War One Battle of Jutland, had been hard hit by a Stuka (German dive bomber) near Crete and limped into Pearl in early 1941 for repairs. The story that circulated was that she was originally to be repaired at Pearl, but that her crew and the Americans fought almost every time they had contact. To avoid confrontation WARSPITE was sent on to Bremerton for repairs in a more peaceful environment. Another very good story was that one particularly nasty British tar had been bad-mouthing the "Yanks" about not being in the war. He irritated a few bright American sailors enough that they got him plastered at one of the bars. They then hauled him to a tattoo parlor and had "God Bless America" inked in on his chest.

Jim Graffigna and I met one of the Britishers in the Navy Yard and were invited to go aboard for a tour, which we did gladly. Several things about the ship were outstanding. Our guide showed us the bomb damage where timber shoring was in place to support the deck. Trying to impress us and to explain away the stench, he said that bodies were still in the wreckage. We didn't buy that, as we could not believe that a ship would sail from the Mediterranean, through the Suez Canal, cross the Indian Ocean, and most of the Pacific, all in hot, tropical seas, without giving her fallen men a decent burial at sea.

In our tour we passed by an entrance to "officer's country" where we could see the difference between the crew's quarters, and that red mahogany paneled area. The crew lived in rather austere circumstances including hammocks just like in Nelson's days. The officers country was plush and reminded me of a deluxe Pullman car, except that it had stubby little British Marines standing sentry at the entrance instead of white-aproned dining car stewards bustling about.

Our host invited us to share a spot of tea in the crew's eating space. We sat with a group of the WARSPITE crew and listened to some of their stories about the fighting in the Mediterranean against the Germans and the "Eyeties." There were no nice names for the Germans. It was obvious that these men feared and respected the Germans. Our guide reached up into the overhead to bring down a box of "biscuits" (crackers) to offer his guests to go with the good, strong, tea, but when he brushed a few large, active, six-legged critters off the box we declined the honor. Jim and I found these men to be friendly and eager to talk to "Yanks" and to try to sway us to their point of view on the ongoing war. We felt compassion for these men, who seemed to be generally undernourished and with poor teeth.

As we left the ship we paused topside to watch a man, described as the ship's heavyweight boxer, working out. This man had obviously taken more than a few blows to his face, as it was a flat mess, and as he skipped rope his breath whistled through what had been his nose. Red Skelton must have seen him and got his idea for his comic character "Cauliflower McPug." Tied down on the catapult was a Fairey biplane that was an anachronism of naval aviation. It had fabric wings and guy wires for supports. That old crate looked like one that had fought the Red Baron. We left the WARSPITE with a feeling of sympathy for the Brits who had to use this relic against the

Germans. The ship did get repaired by the United States and aided in the bombardment of Sicily in 1943 and France in 1944.

In October of 1941 there was a series of well-publicized passages of Japanese NYK (the biggest Japanese shipping company) liners in and out of Honolulu. We did not exactly escort them but we did trail them and watch that no spies were dropped off. How they were supposed to drop anyone off at the speed at which they traveled was beyond my comprehension. Following one of those big, good looking, fast ships with CHEW was hard work for the Black Gang.

Many of the great liners from the age of ocean travel came into our view in those years. "Ile de France", of the French Line and "Aquitania" of the English Cunard Line stand out in my memory. "Aquitania" was a sister ship of "Lusitania" that got the United States into World War One. The Cunard ship took Captain Hummer's wife and two young daughters, Yvonne and Rene', back to the States when dependents were evacuated from Hawaii after 7 December 1941. CHEW escorted "Aquitania" around Diamond Head to the open sea, where her speed was her protection against submarines in the open sea. CHEW really scoured the narrow channel ahead of the ship bearing the Skipper's family. We ran alongside the big liner as it opened up and turned East but it drew away rapidly as we turned back to our patrol station. The top of CHEW's main mast came just about up to the same level as "Aquitania's" main deck.

In Honolulu, at the busy intersection of Kalakaua Avenue and Kapiolani Boulevard, called "Kaukau Corner", there was a multiple sign post with arrows pointing and mileages to cities all over the world. This intersection could rightfully be called "The Crossroads of The Pacific."

The clouds of war that had been over Europe since 1939 and over Asia a decade earlier were not in evidence in Hawaii. The sun was bright, the atmosphere was calm and unhurried, people went about their business as usual. Despite a large military presence on Oahu, there was little thought of war. There were thousands of miles of open Pacific all around Hawaii and the mighty United States Fleet controlled it. The winds were changing.

"Wars may be fought with weapons, but they are won by men. It is the spirit of the men who follow and of the man who leads that gains the victory."

George S. Patton, 1933

Chapter X

- And Then All Hell Broke Loose

Saturday, December 6, 1941, was a good day. On that day, after a week on the Offshore Patrol, CHEW was relieved by WARD, and we entered Pearl Harbor well before noon and were ordered to tie up at Berth X-ray 5, out in the harbor. X-ray 5 was the first mooring just past "Battleship Row," around the corner just off the Northeast corner of Ford Island. There were two small islets, Mokunui and Mokuiki, sticking up out of the shallow water between the mooring and Ford Island. The swept channel made a complete circle around Ford Island back to its starting point off Hospital Point. X-ray 5 was a far better spot than those out farther along the channel where the repair ships "mothered" their nests of Fleet destroyers. Our liberty boat ride in to the Fleet Landing was much shorter, and drier, in the liquid Hawaiian sunshine.

That particular mooring location had another advantage over the ones farther out. When the battleships were in port, as they were this day, we were able to hear and enjoy the excellent music from their bands, starting with the Star Spangled Banner at Morning Colors, through the noon hour concerts, to Tattoo at sundown. We in the "dungaree Navy" could sit on our little ships and hear and watch the spit-and-polish uniform-of-the-day battleship sailors answer the constant squeal of the bosns pipe calls, the bugle calls, and the squawk box's - "Now hear this ---" and count our blessings as not being part of that scene. Battleship sailors used the term "dungaree Navy" derisively in describing destroyer sailors, but most of them when transferred to our duty preferred the lack of spit and polish. The sound of the band music coming over the water was a pleasant and stirring sound.

We passed the line of moored battleships, the most formidable force in the world, to our port side. Past the last one, NEVADA, we made a hard turn to port to find that ALLEN was already tied up at our berth. We prepared to tie up outboard of ALLEN on the side nearer the row of battleships, with our bow headed South toward them and Ford Island. On the other side of ALLEN, also tied up to X-ray 5, was the hulk of an old relic of the Spanish-American War, Ex-BALTIMORE, an armed cruiser. Her pair of tall, rusted, stacks were a landmark in that part of the harbor. On the other side of BALTIMORE were some barges and white submarine rescue caissons that were kept there in ready storage. Those white caissons would soon be needed.

The old hulk was not one of our favorite mooring places as it was far away from any of the amenities, such as they were, in the Navy Yard. There was the Tin Roof, an open-air 3.2% beer dispensary, where off-duty lads could sit in the shade of the corrugated tin roof and quaff ten-cent glasses of poor beer. Several coffee wagons catered to the civilian yard workers. There were several flat places where one could have a catch or toss a football. All that BALTIMORE was good for was a source of scrounged material, and a place to try to hide out from the working parties. The only time that members of the Black Gang could hide out was when they had liberty and were too broke to go ashore. If they stayed aboard ship, they were subject to being pressed into a working party detail.

ALLEN being there first made it easier to tie up as her crew could catch our lines, instead of our having to put a boat over with a line-handling party. We tied up, secured from sea details, and set in-port watches. No power or water was available at this berth. The Engineers kept one boiler fired up and on line to furnish steam to run the pumps and generators, to provide light and power and water to the fire main. The Deck Force manned the motor whaleboat and the Captain's Gig, the Gangway Watches, and the Security Watches. The boats required a qualified boat engineer from the Engineer's duty section.

The crew was divided into three sections: Liberty; Stand-By; and Duty. The Liberty section was free to go ashore during specified hours granted by the captain, and, when moored to a buoy, subject to the availability of boats. As DESDIV 80 was a part of COM 14, our liberty was usually up at 0800, allowing the married men to spend the night at home with their wives, if the women were in Hawaii. The stand-by section was used for working parties and working details. They were able to get off the ship for many reasons but could not get their liberty cards, and had to stay on the Base. The duty section, engineers and deck force alike, pulled all of the watch details. I was in the duty section this day. I had drawn the first dog watch, which meant that I also had the watch from 0400 to 0800 the next morning, in the engine room, running the evaporators to keep the ship supplied with fresh water. The rest of that Saturday afternoon and night were the usual duty section routine, work at your station until knock-off for evening chow, and then you were free until time to go on watch.

Just after lunch on this Saturday, December 6, 1941, there was a brief ceremony on the foc's'l with all hands present. Our captain, Edward L. Beck, LtCdr, USN, was relieved by Harry R. Hummer, LtCdr, USN as our new commander. Beck left the ship after having been the skipper through the period of re-commissioning the old ship and then training the crew. He had done a good job.

We did not get to see much of the new skipper. Hummer was quite a contrast in physical appearance with our just departed Captain Beck, who was tall, handsome, and was a reserved and aloof man. One of the Reserves had gone directly to Beck with a chit for a transfer and had been put on Report for not going to the Executive Officer first. Hummer was huskier, with dark curly hair, and an athletic appearance. After we did get to know him we found him to be a real go-getter and a good skipper. But that Saturday he went ashore in the evening to be with his wife and daughters for the night and left the Exec in charge.

Of CHEW's two boats, only the motor whaleboat kept anything resembling a schedule. The Captain's Gig could be used as a water taxi, but it served the skipper first, and often, under orders from the Officer of the Deck, it and its crew of three, would spend hours sitting at the Officer's Landing just waiting for the Captain to appear. The whaleboat had made several trips that Sunday morning before the scheduled 0800 departure. In one of those early trips it had taken quite a few men ashore to go to a Catholic service that was to be held aboard PENNSYLVANIA over in the Navy Yard in Dry Dock #1. Included in that group were the Saffa brothers, Chouteau and Joe, Jimmie Graffigna, and Matt Agola. All were devout Catholics, and glad to get off the ship early. A mystery is how Clarence Wise, who was a "prisoner at large" waiting a Deck Court Martial, was able to wangle his way ashore in that group. He was hardly to be expected to attend any church service, but he had talked his way ashore that morning.

I had turned in early that Saturday night to get some sleep before being roused at 0330 to be able to relieve my man in the Engine Room at 0345, fifteen minutes before the official time. The fifteen minutes was called "watch standers courtesy." This was necessary for the oncoming watch to get all the standing orders, what the settings were for the various pieces of machinery in operation, and what was going on in general. The four hours on that particular watch would be spent making tank after tank of water, testing each tank for salinity, and recording the readings. I would drink black coffee from the pot made by my predecessor, and then make a fresh pot just before going off watch so that my relief would have a hot pot. This was a boring watch with little to do other than watch those tanks fill. I would spend the time reading, keeping one eye on the clock for 0745 and the appearance of my relief man. Then breakfast, wash and shave. It being Sunday and my having the duty, I would try to figure a way to get off the ship somehow. Even a working party detail would have been welcome, anything to get on solid ground. The deck of a four-stacker at sea is a live and moving thing, never still, and it was good to get off it. My relief, Slop Chute Gray, a dependable man, was on time as usual.

It was with great relief that I climbed the ladder up and out of that Engine Room, to stand there on deck and breathe in that warm, fresh, scented, air, in the sunshine of what was starting out to be a beautiful day in a place noted for its beautiful days. Clouds were scattered in profusion, great puffs of bright, white, cotton against a brilliant blue sky. It was good to get out of that hot, steamy, Engine Room and breathe this air. I stood there and slowly took off my damp denim jumper and inhaled more of that air. My reverie was rudely broken by the mess cook, Lefty Paul Fernau, in his white shorts with a white apron flapping around his bandy shanks. He yelled at me as he scurried by headed for the Galley amidships: "Come on, Pond, get below, I'm getting your chow now and I want to catch the eight o'clock liberty boat." He waved an empty steel platter and a coffee pot to emphasize his need for my cooperation, and kept going. I turned toward the after deck house to go below to the Engineer's Quarters, but as I stepped in the hatch I saw an airplane, with red markings, diving down toward the last battleship in line.

I paid no attention to the plane at first, because our crazy fly boys always skimmed the mast heads and buzzed the harbor as they came in, showing off. This was nothing unusual. The fly-boys kept up this stupid practice even after the war had been joined until one of them crashed in the Navy Yard and killed a few valuable Yard workmen. Admiral Nimitz then put a stop to it. I swung into the hatch with my jacket over my shoulder, grabbed the brass handrails and slid down to the deck below, intending to crash loudly on the deck plates in order to disturb any of my shipmates who might be trying to sleep in on a Sunday morning. I hit the deck hard, but whatever noise I might have made, was drowned out by a simultaneous explosion from above and outside. My first thought was "That stupid zoomie has accidentally dropped his bomb." There was a second explosion, seconds after the first, and then another! Fernau stuck his head in the hatch above and yelled "The Japs are bombing us, and that's no s--t!"

The General Alarm klaxon sounded and the bells began to clang. Gene Lindsey was on watch on the bridge getting ready to signal Colors and saw what was happening, and without orders, hit the alarm and sent us to General Quarters.

GENERAL QUARTERS! BATTLE STATIONS! KLANG AH-OOO-GAH KLANG AH-OOO-GAH, over and over again. A sound to wake the dead.

Everyone (except Monk) took off for his battle station. I headed for the foc's'l and my station as Pointer on the three-inch anti-aircraft gun, wearing no shirt, no hat, nothing but my sweaty dungarees and squishy shoes that I had been wearing on watch for the previous four hours. I went forward on the starboard side at a sprint. When I jumped through the hatch in the bridge house onto the foc's'l it was as if Hell's door had opened and I had just fallen in!

CHEW was several hundred feet off the starboard quarter of the last battleship in the row, NEVADA, with ARIZONA just ahead of her; next ahead of ARIZONA were WEST VIRGINIA and TENNESSEE, moored in pairs, and OKLAHOMA and MARYLAND an another pair ahead of that pair. That was as far as I could see along the row of huge ships. Two other battleships were in port that day, CALIFORNIA and PENNSYLVANIA, but they were out of my line of vision. The ships that I could see were under heavy bombardment, with great clouds of smoke starting to billow up.

As I burst out on the foc's'l bombs were exploding in an ear-shattering rhythm, one right after another. Planes were snarling by close enough to almost touch, some pulling out of a dive, others at wave height after loosing a torpedo. Explosions rocked the air, dense smoke, and an overpowering smell of cordite and burning oil choked the air. Machine guns from the planes added their deadly staccato to the din. The noise was like a heavy, suffocating blanket.

The bright sun was suddenly gone, obscured by a low, black cloud of suffocating smoke, lit by brilliant red flashes in it as more bombs burst. It seemed that the entire world had exploded.

I was the only assigned member of that gun crew aboard, all the others were ashore! That feeling of being desperately alone lasted less than a second, for men popped through the hatch behind me. "What can I do?" Need a hand?" Volunteers were ready, willing, and able. Without an officer or senior petty officer in sight, just the six of us acting as a team restored order out of what could have been chaos.

We yanked the heavy canvas cover off the gun. Because of our tropical duty the entire foc's'l was covered with a heavy canvas awning, held up by steel stanchions set in sockets in the deck, supporting heavy, varnished wooden strongbacks as overhead ribs. The canvas was lashed at one foot intervals along its edge to steel cables running along over the gunwales. The assembly had to be strong to withstand the wind and the sea. Knives appeared from the Galley. The awning was down and over the side in a trice.

The key to the ammunition ready locker was locked in the Captain's cabin, and he was ashore overnight with his wife and two young daughters. Elmer Anderson brought a bolt cutter up from the Engine Room and solved the key problem. We now had a few rounds to fire. The fuze setting wrench was locked in the Armory, and that key was also locked in the Captain's cabin. The bolt cutter was in action again. Jack Grossman had a pair of slip-joint pliers in his pocket and was able to turn the fuze setting on the nose of the projectiles. All that I had to do was to show Jack how far to turn the indicator so that the shell would explode in one-and-one-half seconds after firing. (That was my quick calculation to make the shell explode at 3,000 feet.) Jack had taken and passed the ten-second course in fuze setting.

As the only "experienced" member of the gun crew on hand it fell to me to show the volunteers how and what to do in the operation of the piece. We worked quickly under conditions of great stress, noise, and confusion. Art Clymer learned how to shove the shell into the breech; Jules Schoeneberg how to train and fire the weapon; "Red" Grossman put on the asbestos gloves to catch and remove the hot shells; Dave Taylor put on the headphones and plugged them in to became our contact with spotter Eddie Greco up on the Flying Bridge.

As soon as we were ready and had a shell in the breech, we fired. No orders to "Commence Firing" were given, or necessary. No officers in evidence, we just loaded that first round and fired at a target of opportunity, of which we had plenty. The time of firing that first shot was logged at 0803, just eight minutes after the sounding of the General Alarm. All of the preparations took just eight minutes. A trained and practiced gun crew could hardly have done better. Motivation and purpose made for quick learning and response. One of the stanchions that supported the awning was directly in front of the muzzle of the gun and would have interfered with firing dead ahead. I tried to pull it out of its socket to no avail. It had too many coats of paint securing it in place, so I merely bent it over out of the way. It was a three-inch steel pipe. Motivation again. There were twelve rounds of ammunition in the ready box, but we never had a pause in firing for a lack of ammunition. That bolt cutter took care of the lock on the hatch to the magazine and we were kept supplied.

Within minutes of our getting the gun in action a torpedo plane crash landed softly off our port bow, about halfway between us and NEVADA. I could see two men trying to get the canopy open to escape the fiercely burning plane. Someone yelled down from the bridge to turn the gun on it but I turned away as we had many more live targets, and this plane was no longer a threat. The next time I looked in that direction the plane was gone, sunk, and there was a ring of burning oil or gasoline where it had been. Word came down from Flying Bridge Control that another plane was diving in at a low angle to cross our starboard bow. We trained around in that direction as it came in our view, fired, and caught it with a lucky direct hit that cut it in half. It tumbled down to the earth. No other ship was firing at this plane. After it went down we stopped, to the cheers of our crew and from ALLEN, shook hands all around, and then got back to the business at hand, just as if we had scored a touchdown.

In our position, behind and upwind out of the smoke, we had a close up view of the burning and sinking ships that were the main targets of the attackers. A Repair Ship, USS VESTAL (AR 4), had been tied up alongside ARIZONA. It was cut loose during the early part of the attack and went by us slowly, sinking and on fire, on its way to be run aground on Aiea Shoal. (VESTAL's stack is visible behind NEVADA in one of the photographs taken from CHEW during the attack).

We were able to fire at the dive bombers on the way down, but not at the torpedo planes, as they came in low and behind their targets. We could not see them until after they had dropped their fish and were zooming away. Many of the planes we fired at were also under fire from other ships. We were pretty sure that we had hit one over WEST VIRGINIA, in addition to the one we had cut in half previously, and possibly one more. ALLEN's log has us shooting down a torpedo plane headed for ARIZONA, but I disagree with that assessment. Captain Hummer, in his official report, claimed two-and-a-half planes shot down and in the final tally we were awarded but one, out of the twenty-nine that the Nips lost to all causes that day. Given our position, if we had better and more modern anti-aircraft weapons we could have hit many more planes. A giant fly swatter would have worked wonders, especially for the ones that had just dropped their loads and were jinking away over the harbor to get out of there. Many of these low-flying planes fired off a few machine gun rounds at us as they passed, just to say "Hello."

Our two fifty-caliber machine guns mounted on the Galley Deck House were ineffective. The starboard gun was in too close to ALLEN and had a very limited field of fire. Phil Hanley on that gun did manage to put a round through ALLEN's whistle that gave her a unique toot until it was replaced some months later. Leo Theodore on the port gun had a clear field but his problem was that the planes whizzed by too closely and too fast to be able to get a bead on. Perhaps one of his rounds is the spent one that hit Admiral Kimmel over in CINPAC as Leo was firing in that direction.[1] In "At Dawn We Slept" Gordon W. Prange relates that Kimmel was struck by a spent fifty-caliber round. Such a round *could* have come from Leo's piece as he fired in that general direction.

NEVADA backed out of her berth to a point opposite our port side, then took off through the smoke past the row of burning battleships and the capsized OKLAHOMA, heading for the harbor entrance and the open sea. As she made her sortie, to the cheers of all who saw her moving, the attackers saw a golden opportunity to sink a large ship in the channel and bottle up the harbor, so they gave her a working over from all sides. She passed from our view into the smoke and we did not see her again until we sortied at 1000. When we passed her, NEVADA was aground on Hospital Point. Later in the afternoon she was shoved across the channel to Waipio Point stern first so that her forward turrets of five 14" guns would greet anything trying to come in that harbor.

From 0803 until the last Japanese plane left at 0945 we had fired 74 rounds. Early on we had a hang-fire, the shell did not go off in the gun. Safety regulations on hang-fires and mis-fires are thorough and time-consuming. In this case, with everything blowing up and on fire around us, I re-cocked the piece, and we tried again. Still it didn't fire, we had a dud. Procedures be damned! I had the breech opened, caught the bad shell, took two or three quick steps, and threw it over the side between us and ALLEN. This happened three or four times, and each time we went through the same routine, open the breech, catch the shell, and give it the Deep Six. Later, one of the crew said that as I threw one of the duds over the side it exploded, but I didn't see or hear such a happening. If one had gone off, I doubt if I would have heard it as I was not holding on to one of those babies any longer than I had to, and I was deaf, as we all were for about a week afterwards. None of us had cotton in our ears and it is hard to tell which was the most damaging noise to our ears, the bombs and explosions on the battleships, or the bark of that short-barreled gun right in our midst. In that short period of intense action, our makeshift gun crew performed excellently and entirely on its own without supervision or control.

While the gun crew was doing its best to defend the big ships the rest of the crew aboard were getting ready to take the ship to sea. At about 0815 the fireroom crew lifted safety valves as part of the procedure for getting underway. When those safeties roared as they lifted, we up forward on the gun, jumped about a foot straight up, thinking that we had been hit amidships someplace.

After dark that same day, when CHEW was standing offshore on guard, Art, Red, Jack, Twink, and I were huddled on top of the magazine hatch out of the weather reflecting and talking things over. We had all expected that the ship would get underway as soon as it was ready that morning, and lay a smoke screen down along battleship row to hide the ships and make it harder for the attacking pilots to take aim through the smoke. We were ready, one of the drills we had gone through was the laying of a smoke screen, and a heavy layer of black smoke that early in the attack might have caused some of the torpedoes to miss the mark. There is also the distinct possibility that we would have been sunk in the attempt, but that duty, and that result, is right out of the destroyer book. During the lull in the bombing we had wondered why we weren't getting out of there, and in that lull the Executive Officer, the senior officer aboard, came up on the foc's'l carrying a bottle of Coke. He stayed a minute and left with his drink. In the gun crew's discussion that night, it was our consensus that if he had taken that ship out and laid down a smoke screen he could have had the Navy Cross in his hand instead of that shaking bottle of Coke. That morning was his chance, and he blew it.

There was nothing but open water between our berth and the last ship in the row of battleships, but I did not see ARIZONA blow up, I was either in action facing the other way, or otherwise occupied. It was impossible, given our gun crews exposed position, not to have been aware of that tremendous explosion, but Ensign Virgil Gex, up at his battle station, did see it, and has recounted what he saw succinctly and well.

Here is his account as taken from the Archives of the Naval Academy, Class of 1940:

> "0800 7 December 1941 aboard USS CHEW, a destroyer, Ensign Gex, Class of 1940, tells his story.
> The CHEW was moored to another destroyer about 400 yards astern of the battleship ARIZONA. My battle station was with the two fifty-caliber machine guns on the boat deck. I remember watching two or three dive bombers pulling out of

their dives, crossing from over battleship row to Ford Island and jinking away over the northeast harbor, saying to myself, 'These guys are good,' and being surprised that Japs could be that good! I remember watching a dive bomber diving over the ARIZONA. The plane seemed to leap from its trajectory as the bomb was released. I followed the bomb down, as it hit the ARIZONA, apparently on the far side of her stacks. There was a small explosion as the bomb hit, followed one or two seconds later by a much larger explosion, and a split second later by a tremendous explosion in which a ball of flame seemed not to rise from the ARIZONA, but to materialize instantaneously to a height of two hundred feet above the ship (twice the height of her foremast). Her foremast lurched forward sickeningly, and it was obvious that no one could live in the forward part of the ship. I have read that the ARIZONA was sunk by an armor-piercing shell bomb dropped from a horizontal bomber. It may have been an armor-piercing shell bomb, but I am sure a dive bomber dropped it."

Virgil Gex's description brings the scene to my mind as clear as a photograph.

Our boat brought Captain Hummer aboard at 1000 and as he scrambled up the sea ladder he ordered the lines cast off. We backed out of the mooring into the channel, not waiting to take the boat aboard and swung around the North side of Ford Island. We passed DETROIT and RALEIGH, down by the stern, the upside down UTAH, CURTISS with a fire on deck along the West side of Ford Island and NEVADA now aground at Hospital Point. We steamed out through the entrance buoys at 1020 doing about twenty-five knots. We had barely cleared the entrance buoys when Sonar picked up a contact and we dropped depth charges at 1030.

CHEW searched for submarines off the South coast of Oahu, picking up more contacts and dropping more depth charges, with unknown results. On one swing close to shore after dark we could see flames rising up from fires in the harbor. The flames would momentarily subside, only to flare up again and again. Up on the gun crew, isolated at our battle stations, we were now wearing WWI flat British style tin hats that had been brought up to us from the armory, and we were shivering in the wind. The realization then set in that our battle fleet had been seriously damaged, maybe beyond repair and salvage. When we cleared the entrance buoys at 1020 we had expected to see the Imperial Fleet lined up waiting for us to come out, but the Nips had gone back home with their purpose accomplished - the destruction of the United States Pacific Fleet.

Our church party had landed at 0715 at the Fleet Landing and had joined a large group of men walking toward PENNSYLVANIA for the Catholic service. They had reached 1010 Dock when the bombs started to fall. The group broke up immediately into smaller groups and joined fire fighting and rescue parties near the Dry Dock helping out in any way that they could. PENNSYLVANIA had a donkey boiler on the dock lit off to furnish steam, as none of the battleship's boilers could be lit off in dry dock. Bombs fell on and near PENNSYLVANIA, wiping out the donkey boiler and its operator and many of the volunteer fire fighters. Eighteen-year old Matt Agola had been seen in that area earlier but none of the CHEW men actually saw what happened to him. His body was later identified. The story is different on Clarence Wise. No one recalled seeing him after leaving the boat at the Fleet Landing and no identifiable body was found so he was listed as "missing in action." It is possible that his body was one of the mangled remains that were hurriedly buried at Red Hill and then reinterred at the Punchbowl when that extinct crater overlooking Honolulu was made into a National Cemetery. He could lie under one of the "Unknown" markers there. He just vanished.

There were other men ashore who had overnight liberty; most were married petty officers. No log records were kept on who was ashore, just the duty lists that would show who was on duty and those records have long since vanished as being too unimportant to retain. The ship's Log for December 7, 1941 does not even list the names of the volunteers on the gun crew, men who did more than just their duty.

Some of this group of overnighters hitched a ride on USS CONYNGHAM'S (DD 371) boat intending to have the cox'n drop them off at X-ray 5 to board CHEW on their way out to CONYNGHAM, which was berthed alongside the destroyer tender USS WHITNEY (AD-4) at X-ray 8 farther out in the harbor. When that boat got near they saw CHEW hightailing out to sea, so they went on to CONYNGHAM and boarded it. CONYNGHAM did not sortie until 1712 and did not leave the harbor. Instead it moved from its WHITNEY berth and tied up with USS TUCKER (DD 374) at the Coal Docks for the night. The group from CHEW included First Class Bosn's Mate Hugh Scullin; Signalman Jerry Pelletier; Chief Machinist's Mate Morris Cox; Fireman Jimmie Graffigna; and cook-striker Chouteau Saffa, who had become separated from his younger brother Joe in the confusion on Tenten Dock. These men did not catch

CHEW until the next day when CHEW's whaleboat picked them up. Those of us on CHEW were happy to see this group of shipmates come back aboard with big, square-jawed "Pat" Scullin standing in the bow of the whaleboat. Scullin had several hitches in the Asiatic Fleet and was a veteran of the Yangtse and the PANAY Affair. He was a rock in the Deck Force and a steadying influence on the young men with his strength, experience, and an active Hibernian sense of humor.

At 0800 on Sunday morning our two boats had been in the water; the Captain's Gig had been sent to the Officer's Landing with orders to wait there for him. The Gig and its three-man crew sat right there until he finally got through the traffic. The whaleboat had taken the church party ashore and was scheduled to make another trip to the Fleet Landing at 0800, but it was side-tracked into doing some ferrying around the harbor before returning to the ship. CHEW's log, a sparsely worded document, does not record the names of the boat crews, which had Larry Meier, Joe Meadows, and John "Red" McKenna as cox'ns. The log does record the names of the men who were NOT aboard, and the names of some men from other ships who came aboard with our whaleboat, including LtCdr R. H. Rodgers, commanding officer of USS AYLWIN (DD 355). His ship had gone to sea without him, conned by four new ensigns. Rodgers came up to our gun position and asked if we'd mind if he acted as our spotter. We appreciated the honor, a Fleet destroyer skipper spotting for a makeshift gun crew of bilge rats.

There was an exception to the mass exodus from the aft crew's compartment and the mad dash to our battle stations. Fastidious Monk Mountain had the watch in the Fireroom from midnight to 0400, and had come off watch, washed, and turned in in his bunk with the intention of sleeping until noon. Monk loved his sack time, and with the ship in port, he would have kept sawing wood until time to get up, eat, and go back on watch at 1200. When the alarms sounded Monk growled at one of the mess cooks who had given him a shake, that they could take their damned drills and shove 'em. He was going to sleep in, and covered his head with his pillow and went back to sleep. The shaker took off and left Monk alone. At 1000 the screws started to turn over when the ship backed out of the mooring. The rumbling and shaking roused Monk and he came topside as the ship was speeding out past the burning ships, "What in the Hell is going on?"

While the men of the CHEW hustled to get the ship underway and took our best shots at the Japanese planes, future shipmate Glenn Thompson was having problems of his own over on WEST VIRGINIA.

He had turned in on Saturday night, but instead of sleeping below in his bunk in the crew's quarters, he decided to miss the heat, and bed down topside under the aft cage mast. On Sunday morning he was rudely awakened by the terrifying blast of bombs landing on his ship someplace forward of where he was sacked out. General Quarters sounded as he ran to his battle station, Fireroom Number Five, dressed only in the shorts he slept in. The noise was compounded by more explosions and planes zooming by firing machine guns. With four or five men assigned to the fireroom, they were attempting to light off the boiler preparatory to getting underway. Fireroom Number Five was on the port side of the ship, and WEST VIRGINIA was hit on that side by six torpedoes one right after the other, blowing that side of the ship open and doing tremendous damage. Glenn was left alone in the dark until someone opened the hatch from the outside. He was able to crawl out and up to the relative safety of the second deck. He was the only man to get out of that fireroom.

In the melee on Second Deck Glenn and some other crewmen formed a human chain to get up to the Main Deck and in to the Crew's Library, where the situation was hardly any better. The Library was flooded and fire ranged all about making that place untenable. In that desperate situation it became every man for himself. They bailed out, over the side, which was at water level now, into the oily, flaming, water slick with oil, to swim to safety on Ford Island. Glenn crawled up on shore dazed and "fairly well shaken up" only to find that his situation had not improved with the change of location. Bombs were still falling, and the smoke made it impossible to see what to do and where to go.

Wet, oily, and beat up, he stumbled into a bomb shelter, full of women and children, dependents of the officers living on Ford Island. He went in and crouched down to see just how badly he was injured. He was covered with oil and red lead and was stark naked - he had lost his shorts in that swim to safety. In his battered condition he was just glad to get away from the danger and the noise on the ship. One of the women in the shelter saw his condition and came over to help and covered him with her bathrobe, saying that he needed it more than she did, and as she turned away he saw that she too was in the buff. In the Winter 1991 issue of "Naval History," a woman who had been a teen ager in that bomb shelter describes a nude blonde sailor.

Sometime later in the day, in scrounged Marine Corp sun tans, he made his way to the Receiving Station where he was cleaned up and patched up and received an outfit of dungarees. Those remained his only clothes when until a few days he was assigned on December 16 for further duty to USS CHEW as Fireman, Third Class. **2**

Thompson is a blue-eyed blonde.

One of the many questions asked of me many times is "Were you scared?" The answer is "No," as I was too busy in getting things started and then after we did get started I was too busy to think. I was aware, at all times, how close we were to those burning battleships, and what little margin for error there was, but there wasn't any time to dwell on that fact. (Note: see illustration "TARGETS") But that night, after dark, when the CHEW was back off shore, we, the impromptu gun crew, all started to shake and shiver from release of tension that we had been under for about twelve hours. It may be that we were scared then, but that feeling was soon replaced by one of cold anger. The anger was directed mainly at the Japanese for hitting us the way that they did while highly publicized negotiations were going on in Washington, DC. The passage of time has lessened that anger toward the Japanese and directed some of it toward our leaders who had so mis-read the situation and had just failed to prepare for something out of the ordinary.

In the year, 1941, that had just passed we had gone through drill after drill, day and night: collision; man overboard; fire on the ship; fire and rescue; smoke screen; submarine action; daily exercises at the loading machine for the four-inch surface battery (4" fifty-caliber naval guns). They were guns that were excellent against surface targets but unable to elevate for aircraft; we had several runs firing these guns at towed targets, and those gun crews had become skillful and accurate. We had but one drill in which we fired the three-inch anti-aircraft gun. I fired one (1) round at a balloon that had been released from the bow of the ship. I had come close, but we had no range finder that would give us the elevation of the balloon, so the fuze setting was a guess. We had no other drills for that gun, just that one shot that was really a proof test of the piece to see if it would burst when fired, rather than a target shot. Come to think about it - that's the way it was when we fired for real - by guess. The drill schedules were set by the commodore, who must have received his instructions from COM 14, so the accent on surface warfare reflects the thinking of the Naval hierarchy of command. Old battleship men.

Another question is about medals. "Did you get a medal?" "Do you think you deserved a medal?" The answer to these is "No." My battle station was that gun, and my duty was to shoot it at the enemy. I did my duty. However, the rest of that gun crew were volunteers, and should have received a commendation, or even a mention in the ship's log, but the Executive Officer that day was far from being an efficient second-in-command.

It is a testimonial to the accuracy of Fuchida's men that we were not hit by an errant bomb. (Commander Mitsuo Fuchida was the leader of all the Japanese planes) The little group of ships at X-ray 5 were not targets, and although we were strafed, no bombs even fell near us. It was a memorable moment when the horizontal bombers went over, well above our range, and all that we could do was to watch them fly over, and listen to the bombs landing on the battleships in front of us.

Much has been written about the state of readiness, or unreadiness, of the ships and stations on Oahu. Without any attempt on my part to rehash the many books, articles, and reports, I will address one facet of the readiness situation as rumored and then amplified by some writers. It has been said that many of the crew members were drunk or incapacitated by drink, or sleeping one off, and were unable to perform their duties. This is completely untrue. CHEW, as part of DESDIV 80, was under the command of Admiral Claude C. Bloch, COM 14, whose people were allowed overnight liberty if they had a legitimate shoreside address. Many of the petty officers were married and had quarters at the Naval Housing area, just outside the base. An unmarried sailor had to have permission to get an overnight pass. A pass was not given as a matter of right, but as a reward for excellent service and behavior. Drunkenness among the married petty officers was, in my opinion, less than that of the general population. There were no people on CHEW incapacitated by drink on that night. None. The Fleet was under the rule that all liberty was up at midnight, and that rule was enforced. Other than the very few who had special overnight liberty from the Fleet units, all the enlisted men were back aboard by midnight. This would have applied only to the liberty section, or one-third of the ships crew, so two-thirds had been aboard all night. The Honolulu Police Department and the Shore Patrol reported a quieter night than usual. I reject out of hand the inference that alcohol had any part in the Pearl Harbor affair. It is a base canard laid upon thousands of good men by irresponsible sensation mongers. Or, in the case of the Temperance League of Hawaii, something started in a blatant attempt to advance their cause.

Footnotes.

1 Prange, Gordon W. "At Dawn We Slept" Page 516)

2 From transcript of interview. February 1, 1992. Glenn A. Thompson, 342-38-69 Fireman, Third Class, USN.)

See also: Naval History, Winter 1991 issue. Vol. 5 #4 "Only Yesteryear" by Mary Ann Ramsey.

USS CHEW at sea, 1943.

Hull 106. October 8, 1918. Bethlehem Shipyard, San Francisco.

#N 3497.

USS CHEW and USS WARD. Sugar Docks, Hilo, T.H., July 22, 1941.

Pond photo.

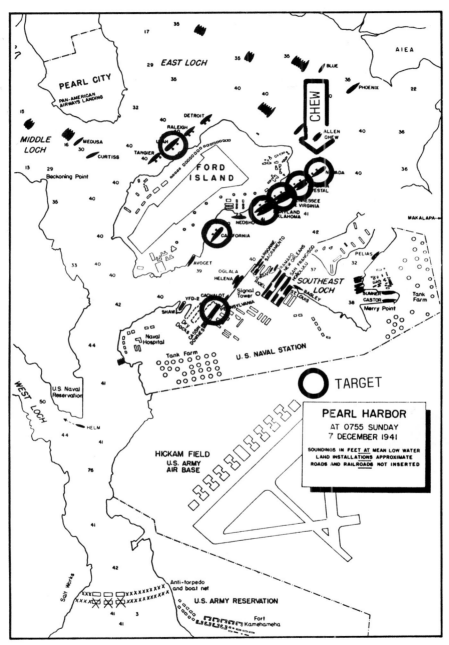

Targets at Pearl Harbor.
Chart by the Pearl Harbor History Associates, Inc.

Pearl Harbor, 0800 December 7, 1941. Japanese photo taken from over Beckoning Point.

NH 50930.

Pearl Harbor, 0800 December 7, 1941. Japanese photo taken from directly over CHEW.

NH 50931.

USS NEVADA on left. USS ARIZONA, burning, on right. December 7, 1941. Taken from CHEW's bridge.

Sheedy photo.

ARIZONA burning, NEVADA on left, with VESTAL stack visible. Taken from CHEW's bridge.

Sheedy photo.

USS NEVADA on left. USS ARIZONA, burning, on right. December 7, 1941. Taken from CHEW's bridge.

USS ARIZONA burning. 0830 December 7, 1941. Taken from CHEW's bridge.

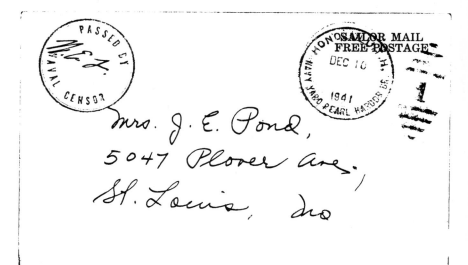

SAILOR MAIL
FREE POSTAGE

DEC 10
1941

Mrs. J. E. Pond,
5047 Plover Ave.,
St. Louis, Mo

NOTHING is to be written on this side except to fill in the data
specified. Sentences not required should be crossed out. IF ANYTHING
ELSE IS ADDED THE POSTCARD WILL BE DESTROYED.

I am well   ~~(sick,~~   - ~~(serious~~

~~I have been admitted to hospital as~~   ~~(wounded~~   - ~~(not serious~~

~~Am getting on well. Hope to return to duty soon~~

~~I have received your~~   ~~(Letter dated~~ ....
          ~~(Telegram dated~~ ....
          ~~(Parcel dated~~ ....

Letter follows at first opportunity.

I have ~~received no letter~~ from you   ~~(for a long time~~
                                         ~~(lately~~

Signature ...Jesse Pond.........................

Date .....IX/13/41.........................

Censored post card, December 10, 1941.

CHEW at Philadelphia Navy Yard, November 5, 1945. The end of the line.

NH 36331.

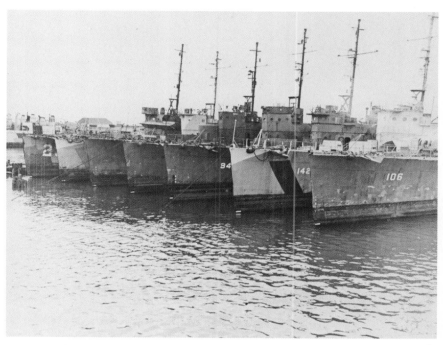

CHEW and others, Cape May, N. J., NAS, awaiting disposal orders.

NH 3497A.

Firecontrol Repair group, USS NEREUS (AS-17), August 24, 1945 at Mare Island, California. Rear, left to right: Bob Pastor, FC3/C; "Red" Strom, FCI/C; John Johnson, FC3/C; Cliff Miller, FC2/C. Middle row: Pond, FC1/C; Lou Clement, CFC; Bill Kapfer, FC3/C. Front: Hiram Seppi, FC3/C; Charles Boyle, FC2/C.   US Navy photo.

Reunion of CHEW crew at Pearl Harbor Survivors Convention in St. Louis, December 7, 1963. Front, left to right: Wayland Roberts, George H. Barrow, Jesse Pond, Robert Hartman. Rear: Elmer K. Luckett; William Hudson; Larry Meier; William Locklar; Mark Ferris, president; M. Gene Lindsey, president-elect.

Pond speaking at dedication of the USS ARIZONA Memorial at Pearl Harbor, October 10, 1980.

Miss Edith Anne Mary Lazar
Brooklyn, New York, March, 1945.

Jesse Pond

Lorstan photos.

Newlyweds. Daly City, California, January 15, 1948.

Pond photo.

Chapter XI

Rumors and Fantasies

The Japanese attack on Pearl Harbor gave rise to many rumors, some based on but a sliver of fact, others pure fantasy.

One common rumor was that an arrow had been cut in a cane field pointing at Pearl Harbor for the attacking fliers to follow. This was based on an unrelated fact. One of the intelligence agencies did check on one of the plantations, only to find that the large bare piece of ground visible from the air was made by the workers with a bulldozer shoving cane stalks together for burning. The need for an arrow to point out Pearl Harbor is unnecessary. The story did make some newspapers. It was repeated many years later on a radio talk show that I participated in with another man who "knew" it was a true story, as he had read it in the paper.

Another rumor grew from an advertisement that ran in the Honolulu Star-Bulletin a few days prior to the attack. Someone tried to make a big deal out of the "Silk Ad". The text in this large advertisement supposedly told all the local Hawaiian Japanese when the Japanese were going to hit the United States Fleet, and what ships were targeted. That rumor had a pretty long run but it did die out after a few years. This was a concoction of someone's great stretch of imagination.

Bits and pieces of many news items have made some people voice a theory that FDR knew all about the pending attack. This is simply another fantasy fueled by his political opposition. Some revisionist historians have mined this empty lode for years. One writer put out a book that the whole affair was a conspiracy of the admirals and politicians in order to get the United States in the war on Britain's side. This theory is ridiculous on the face of it. The idea of getting that egotistical collection of men to conspire is hilarious. They were too busy fighting among themselves and in protecting their own bits of turf to cooperate with a potential rival in any such scheme.

The stories about German pilots flying the Japanese planes, blue-jumpered paratroopers landing, and men with machine guns jumping out of a Dairyman's Limited milk wagon to gun down sailors returning to the Base are all fantasies. Even the Navy contributed to the tales by actually sending out a warning about the blue-jumpered paratroopers. The Oahu military took the paratrooper bit seriously. They actually put old automobiles on the playing fields to keep the gliders from landing! They awarded the Japanese the impossible ability to tow gliders for thousands of miles over open sea from the Mandated Islands. Stories ran in newspapers and news magazines about the Japanese "Fifth Column" in Hawaii and how spies and saboteurs were everywhere. To put it mildly, there was quite a bit of hysteria in the air at that time, but no gliders.

In order to protect Pearl Harbor from Fifth Columnists sneaking in from Honolulu a system of night patrols in the harbor was instituted. The craft for this patrol were taken from the pool of motor launches and admiral's barges that were available from the sunken battleships. These resplendently gleaming white and polished brass launches were spray painted a dull black and machine gun mounts were screwed into the mahogany foredecks. I was especially distressed by the treatment given a launch from the WEST VIRGINIA that had a hand-hammered brass wind screen with a spread eagle embossed on it. That elegant eagle was sprayed black too. These patrol craft would slowly circle the harbor after dark with an eye out for someone swimming or rafting over to the Navy Yard to spy or commit sabotage.

CHEW may have contributed to some of the rumors about saboteurs and snipers in a small way. In the first group of December 8th volunteers to become crew members were ten men with names beginning with the letter "F." One of these men was a young Iowa farm boy, strong as an ox, and just about as smart. One of his first days aboard he was assigned a watch from midnight to 0400 on the foc's'l to look out for - whatever. I don't know what his instructions were from the Petty Officer of the watch, but he could not have received much direction. But on this January 1942 night, young Mr. F. was alone on watch in the blacked-out ship in the blacked-out harbor, carrying a Springfield rifle with a clip in the magazine.

Suddenly out of the shadows along the bank slipped a dark shadow going to pass our bow. "Halt, who goes there?" challenged Mr. F. No answer. Possibly the cox'n of the launch that was making that shadow, couldn't hear the challenge over the sound of his powerful engine throbbing at his feet. "Halt, who goes there?" again. Again no answer. Our young man had enlisted just a month before and had some rudimentary training. Whether or not that training included rifle work, I don't know, but this farm boy did know how to fire a rifle, and that he did. As luck would have it, the range and the darkness made him miss, but the shot did ricochet off the launch. The cox'n rocketed out of there, calling the while on his radio for help that he was under fire from a sniper. Help soon arrived in the form of a PT boat and another launch, but the sniper had eluded them. Things cooled down by dawn. Young F was immediately transferred to the Black Gang where he would be below decks and out of reach of any rifles.

The military command of Hawaii had many things to worry about and foremost was the constant fear of helping the enemy's intelligence in some way. "Loose lips sink ships" was a well-known slogan, but our military intelligence people went overboard on one event to keep the Japanese in the dark. In 1942 there was a major eruption of Kilauea volcano up on the slopes of Mauna Loa on the Big Island of Hawaii. Some bureaucrat on one of the staffs came up with the brilliant idea that the glow from the volcano would help the Japanese home in on Hawaii. Therefore the news of the eruption was ordered to be withheld from the public. Any reference to the eruption in our letters going back home was censored out. At night from far out to sea that glow was like the sun coming up. It was an eerie sight to see a sunrise from a bearing other than from the East. But the idea that the Japanese did not know about that eruption was ridiculous, for any submarine operating within a hundred miles of Hawaii could not miss seeing that heavenly glow. And there were Japanese submarines in the area all the time. The port of Hilo came under bombardment from one of them from time to time, so to try to keep a serious eruption a secret from the Nipponese was a waste of time.

CHEW was lucky in that one warning that came in by radio turned out to be a false alarm instead of the real thing. We got word that a tidal wave was on its way from an earthquake on the Chilean Coast of South America. We were directly in its path and too far from any port in which to take refuge. With a great deal of hullabaloo everything topside that could be taken below was, and everything that could not be taken below was doubly secured and tied down. The water in the Central Pacific can be flat calm and as smooth as an inland lake, but the channels between the islands can be rough due to the conflicting currents and winds. CHEW did not ride rough water very well. It tended to roll and pitch at the best of times and so the warning of a tidal wave brought on memories of a recent Jon Hall "B" movie about a tidal wave that had just about wiped out a whole island somewhere in a South Pacific movie lot. Tension built up as this tsunami roared on toward us.

The bridge lookouts were warned to keep an extra sharp eye out for this oncoming wave and everyone on topside was keyed up in expectation of a dangerous and exciting time ahead. The great build-up and preparation led to a big let-down. The only difference that I could see from the flying bridge was that we passed from a flat calm sea into a slight chop. There was a noticeable line of demarcation, but no wave of any consequence leading it. There was, however, a sigh of relief from the older hands aboard. (In the Fifties Hilo was hit by two tsunamis from South America a year apart that did a great deal of damage to the waterfront area of the city and took a few lives. The direct result of those two waves was the construction of Hilo's beautiful waterfront Liliuokalani Gardens in the damaged area.) I know that after this was all over I was disappointed, and some of the other men voiced the same opinion. The tidal wave was a let down after all the preparation to meet it head on had been made.

Another story, also based on a sliver of fact, has been kept alive by people trying to make a point on the subject of racism in the United States. The Black Congressional Caucus resurrects the Doris Miller story every couple of years in an attempt to have Miller awarded the Congressional Medal of Honor. The facts of the matter are simple. Aboard the battleship WEST VIRGINIA, on the 7th of December, under a severe bombing and torpedo attack, on fire and sinking, Ensign Victor Delano had seen Miller, otherwise unoccupied, at "Times Square," so Delano took Miller to the bridge with the idea of using the strong man to help carry the wounded captain, Mervyn S. Bennion, to a place of relative safety. Times Square was an area where several ladders and passageways came together on the second deck, and was so called because of the heavy foot traffic there.

When Delano and Miller got to the bridge it was too late to move Captain Bennion, as he was beyond help. Delano saw an unmanned 50 cal. machine gun on one wing of the bridge and called Miller to help him man the gun, Miller took the firing position instead of Delano, and let a burst fly through the rigging of the inboard TENNESSEE. Delano thought that would get them into trouble, so the two of them left the bridge and went to the main deck to help fight the fires that were engulfing the ship from the blazing ARIZONA just astern. Delano did not see Miller again that day. [1]

WEST VIRGINIA did not shoot down any planes that day, nor did it claim any.

The story of Miller's heroism was far from my mind for many years. Until 1974 when I was National Treasurer of the Pearl Harbor Survivors Association. I operated the business and membership office of that association out of my own office in McLean, Virginia, a suburb of Washington, D.C. In that capacity I attended many meetings and social affairs in the general Washington area. I met and became friends with a great many people of varying experiences. One of such friend was retired Rear Admiral Robert E. Cronin, a man with whom I shared many similar interests. Cronin lived in Northwest Washington,D.C. Bob had been Engineering Officer of the battleship USS MARYLAND on December 7, 1941.

On July 10, 1974, I received a telephone call from him, and I made a record of that call, as he had been quite upset and agitated over a newspaper article describing a TV program that he said was wildly inaccurate and damaging to the reputations of those "who had been there." at Pearl Harbor.[2] He sent me a copy of the newspaper article in a letter dated that same day. Cronin said that as a national officer of the Survivors Association I "had to do something about this" article and to rebut the slurs against the Survivors. After reading the article, [3] I telephoned the TV producer of the program and offered to appear to give them the facts as set down in the original battle reports from 7 December 1941 by officers on the WEST VIRGINIA. [4] The producer was not at all interested, the story was now too stale for his taste. The TV program was a "public affairs" program on Black History, written and hosted by a con artist whose main claim to fame was his success at conning his way out of the D.C. Prison at Lorton, Virginia.

In the program this host had been fulminating about the poor treatment that blacks had received from the white establishment in the past. He mentioned Joe Louis' tax troubles among other items, but the part that Cronin was objecting to was that "Dorie Miller had shot down twenty planes while everyone else was splittin' out of there and all they did for him was to name a ship after him. [5] That's all they did for this Black American." The gist of Cronin's telephone call that day was that, in order to pick up the recruiting of blacks into the Armed Forces, which was not going well, an order "came out from Washington" to find a black and give him a medal. The only black mentioned in any of the battle reports from that date was Doris Miller, MAtt 2/c. From that mention he was awarded the Navy Cross, the second highest heroism award, after the Congressional Medal of Honor. His citation read "For distinguished devotion to duty, extraordinary courage and disregard for his own personal safety during the attack on the Fleet in Pearl Harbor, Territory of Hawaii, by Japanese forces on December 7, 1941. While at the side of his captain on the bridge, Miller, despite enemy strafing and bombing and in the face of a serious fire, assisted in moving his Captain, who had been mortally wounded, to a place of greater safety, and later manned and operated a machine gun directed at enemy Japanese attacking aircraft until ordered to leave the bridge."

Much has been written about Miller that is absolutely untrue and incorrect. A neighbor of mine in Virginia, a black man, showed me a clipping from "Ebony" magazine, with photographs of the ship and planes, that had Miller aboard ARIZONA and named four Japanese torpedo planes as ones that he had shot down. The facts of the situation are heroic enough, without unnecessary politically motivated embellishment and distortion.

Dorie Miller served his country well, and made the supreme sacrifice. It is too bad that the memory of this good man is besmirched by the efforts of others trying to make a political point, and does no service to the many others who fought and died without recognition in that conflict.

Miller was serving aboard the escort carrier, USS LISCOMBE BAY (CVE 56) when it was sunk off Makin Island by the Japanese submarine I-175 on 24 November 1943, and went down with about 650 of his shipmates.

Footnotes.

1 *Memo of telephone conversation with Victor Delano, Capt., USN, Rtd. 12 July 1974.*

2 *Letter and telephone conversation with Robert E. Cronin, RADM, USN, Rtd. 10 July, 1974*

3 *Washington Star-News June 19, 1974 "Petey does his bit" by Earl Byrd.*

4 *Letter 12/13/41 Combatships to CINPAC (1)*
Letter 12/11/41 Hillenkoetter to CINPAC (4) ***
Statement LtCdr John S. Harper (5)
Statement T. T. Beattie (3)
Statement E. E. Berthold (2)
Statement D. C. Johnson (2) ***
Statement L. J. Knight (2)
Statement C. V. Ricketts (4) ***
Statement H. B. Stark (2)
Statement F. H. White (2) ***
Letter 12/11/41 CO USS WEST VIRGINIA to COM 14
Letter 12/13/41 Combatships to COM 14

Number in parentheses denotes number of pages in report ()
*** *Miller mentioned in this report*

5 *USS MILLER FF-1091*

Chapter XII

From Here to There, and Back Again

The way CHEW's duty was assigned and carried out during the early days of the War is shown by excerpts from the Log for the period 1 to 12 June 1942. In those twelve days CHEW spent one period of 45 hours in Pearl Harbor refueling, having a repair job done, and having the 50cal. anti-aircraft guns exchanged for new 20MM weapons. Of the rest of the time, less three hours and five minutes in Pearl to refuel, eight days were spent on inter-island convoy duty, with two days on Offshore Patrol. It went like this:

1 June 1942. Escorted SS Fisher Ames (freighter), Honolulu to Hilo, released convoy at 0730 2 June and proceeded to Kahului, Maui. Circled outside that harbor until 1950, left Kahului escorting SS District of Columbia (tanker), SS DeSota (freighter), and SS Lake Francis (freighter) to Hilo. Arrived off Hilo the next afternoon at 1600. After convoy entered harbor CHEW entered and anchored for two and a half hours. CHEW left for Pearl Harbor, arrived the following morning, 4 June 1942, entered, fueled ship, took on 300 pounds of bread and 20 gallons of ice cream, and at 1220 got underway again and relieved USS GAMBLE (DM 15) from patrol on the Eastern half of the Defensive Sea Area.

The next day, 5 June 1942, relieved at 1450 by USS WARD (DD 139) and with GAMBLE took a short high-speed escort job to return to the picket line at 0001 6 June. That morning assisted in an Entry Sound Lane operation and returned to picket duty again.

7 June assisted in a Sortie Sound Lane operation from 0730 to 1010, and on the completion of that action was ordered in to Pearl Harbor, to refuel and have the AA guns exchanged (As noted previously). The 50 Cal ammunition was unloaded and replaced by 6,540 rounds of 20MM ammunition the next day.

Got underway at 0828 9 June to the assigned Eastern half of the Defensive Sea Area, where we operated until assigned that afternoon at 1855 to escort the SS Waialeale and YP-237 to Maui. That overnight convoy ended on the morning of the 10th when the ships escorted went in Kahului. The new 20MM guns were test fired on the return to patrol duty, and on that passage picked up the SS Gulfbird at sea and escorted it to Pearl Harbor. At 1800 took station on the picket line, and patrolled until 2010 when we were ordered to Hana, Maui, to pick up another convoy. Picked up the SS Mapele, a Matson

Line big freighter, at 0652 11 June to escort her to Kahului, then to wait outside and circle for ten hours while SS Mapele loaded/unloaded cargo and then escorted her to Hilo. On the morning of the 12th we entered Hilo at 0633, anchored until 1500, when we got underway for Pearl Harbor escorting the SS Waialeale on her return trip. While at anchor in Hilo Harbor, took on from the USS SACRAMENTO (PG 19) 50 pounds of avocados, 100 pounds each of tomatoes, lettuce, and cabbage, and 150 pounds of bread. From that record it would appear that the crew enjoyed some fresh salad for a change.

These twelve days are merely an example of the constant use to which ships were put during the early hectic days of the War, and CHEW especially for her reliability and dependability.

Ross Ainsworth Dierdorff, Jr., 401-46-21, O-1, USNR, Seaman First Class, came aboard CHEW as a transfer from the Section Base, Bishop's Point, Pearl Harbor, T.H., on 24 February 1942. He was a slightly built, awkward, bashful, quiet, young man who kept to himself and did not mix very well with the other young sailors who tended to be brash, noisy, and raucous. Dierdorff had been in the Signal Gang at the Section Base and was immediately assigned to the same duty on the bridge. He did his work quietly and almost unseen. He was transferred 25 September 1942, to Receiving Ship, San Francisco, for further transfer to new construction. During his brief tour of duty on the CHEW he was advanced a grade to Signalman, Third Class, without any fanfare.

During those seven months, the ship was at sea on Offshore Patrol. A large Navy task force left Pearl Harbor headed West. Normal operating procedure for that period of time was for all the destroyers in the task force, and the others available on patrol, to make a "sound lane" parallel to the outgoing or incoming forces course to protect it from submarine attack in those restricted waters. The lane was made by destroyers making a high speed run close to the task force in order to make a strong wake to interfere with the sonar of any attacking submarine, and then on the return leg outside of the roiled waters to go slow while sound ranging (by Sonar) outward to detect any lurking submarines. A column of destroyers on each side of the task force racing out and then reversing in a listening mode, made for a hectic operation.

CHEW was on such an assignment near one particular task group when a blinker message came from the battleship of the group bearing the flag of the group commander. Dierdorff manned the signal light with another signalman writing down the incoming message as Dierdorff called out the letters. As the message was just about completed Mr. Mush-mouth came up on the bridge, took in the scene of Dierdorff manning the blinker light and asked what the message from that mighty warship was all about. When he was told that it was a personal message for Dierdorff he flew into a rage and started to berate the young man "How dare you? What is the meaning of this?" etc and etc. The Exec was engaging in one of his favorite pastimes - chewing out an enlisted man, until the duty signalman held the clipboard with the written message on it up to where the Exec could see it, and said "Read the message, Mister Blank", and when Mister Unmentionable read the message his attitude took an instant 180 degree turn. The message on that board was from the admiral commanding that task force from that battleship, to his son, serving on that screening destroyer, Ross A. Dierdorff, Jr.

That incident gave the ship-board comedians grist to grind. One would play Dierdorff, a second would be Mush Mouth, and the script would run something like this - "Ahhh, Deahdo'ff, deah boy. Have a seegar." With variations, mock hand-kissing, and a great deal of merriment, these scenes played behind the back of the Executive Officer. To have performed one of these charades, and gotten caught at it, would have been the equivalent of putting in a chit for brig time.

At this time I had taken up pipe smoking as something to do, and I didn't like cigarettes. Since the selection of pipe tobacco in the ship's store was limited I had to hike over to the Sub Base to the excellent store in order to buy decent pipe tobacco. One afternoon as I was standing at the counter paying for my pouch, the clerk had a sudden change of expression. This made me take notice of a man wearing khakis standing just behind and to my left side. Yoicks, it was the new Big Boss, Admiral Nimitz himself, waiting for me to complete my purchase. No fanfare, no big deal of someone yelling "TENSHUN", the man just walked into the store to buy a bag of tobacco for his pipe. I grabbed my change with one hand and saluted with the other and gulped out a "Good afternoon" as this quiet, grey-haired man put a bill on the counter, picked up his bag of tobacco, smiled slightly, and turned and walked away out of the store. I don't think more than two or three men of the fifty or so in that place even noticed him. They were too busy gawking at the big, jar-headed, Marine sergeant orderly following behind Nimitz as he left. That incident personified Nimitz. He did his job quietly and efficiently without stirring up a big fuss. Some of the other admirals just a few months previously would have had everyone in the store at attention when they walked in. That is, if they even deigned to go to fill their own tobacco pouch.

In August 1942 CHEW was assigned an escort, code named Mike Seven, for a quick run to Midway, to enter with USS REGULUS (AK 14), take on 1,026 barrels of oil, and leave the same day for Hilo. The five days to Midway were spent with CHEW steaming in the usual zigzag pattern in front of the escorted vessel until we spotted an unidentified warship coming in from the West. From the first we could see that this was a cruiser. Size didn't scare Captain Hummer one bit, or so it seemed. He sent us to General Quarters, trained out the torpedo tubes, and headed for it at Full Speed. Before we came into range it answered our challenge satisfactorily. It was USS BOISE (CL 47) a veteran of Asiatic duty returning to Pearl Harbor. There was an audible sigh of relief when we turned back to our escort. Out there that cruiser could have been flying the Rising Sun instead of Old Glory. If that had been the case this story would be different.

On 28 September 1942 CHEW was assigned under code name "Mike Three" to convoy the SS Waialeale of the Inter-Island Steamship Company to Canton Island to strengthen that island's defense by the addition of a regiment of combat engineers. It was a simple assignment: escort the surprisingly speedy little liner down over the Equator, circle the island while she unloaded the men and their gear, and then back to base again. Canton Island was under constant enemy surveillance and the waters were classified as "submarine infested." Because of the distance involved and the need for quickness this operation was planned closely. There was no time to spare, and every day counted. But, like most military operational plans, something on this one went awry.

On the way South we had to cross the Equator, and traditionally, the ships held "Crossing the Line" ceremonies that were the talk of the Navy. Each story of a certain crossing ceremony had to be out-done by the next teller of a bloodier, or more ingenious, doings, usually with some poor gob being accidentally killed or maimed. Our Fleet Reserves had plenty of these gruesome whoppers to relate, and as we got closer to the Line they got more and more graphic. However, Captain Hummer wanted no part of any tom-foolery on this dangerous assignment, and it took a lot of convincing for him to finally allow one hour at noon for a quick ceremony. The strongest argument in favor, as he told it later, was that as he was a Pollywog, he was being chicken just to avoid being initiated as a Shellback. (I don't know who had the temerity to tell him that. Of all the Chief Petty Officers my idea of who had the nerve is Pat Sheedy. I give none of the officers enough gumption.) We had our ceremony on 3 October at Longitude 171-06 West, and the Skipper took his rotten egg shampoo in good grace. He was allowed to skip crawling through a garbage-filled canvas tube while some Shellbacks on the outside pummeled the poor Pollywog in his transit into Shellbackery. When I saw that set-up, and what was in store, I managed to get at the head of the line and be one of the first ones through that tube and be ahead of the others that would be added to the line of pummelers, kickers, and paddlers.

On departure day from Canton, 5 October, Waialeale fouled her anchor, which caused a delay while we used more of our precious oil in circling. We could not stop or lay to or stop searching by Sonar with the possibility of a Japanese submarine dropping by. Then a lookout spotted a mast over the horizon off to the Northeast. There was a ship coming our way, hull down, where no other ship was supposed to be. Captain Hummer, spoiling for a fight, ordered GQ, Full Speed Ahead, and we headed for the stranger, guns manned, torpedo tubes trained out, with a signalman up on the mast searchlight platform, sending out the challenge on the 36" searchlight. Dit dah, Dit dah, (A A) "Who are you?" was the standard challenge, but this ship, which was now slowly coming up over the horizon, was not answering!

All glasses on the bridge were watching that ship. I was at my battle station manning the three-meter range finder, which was the best set of optics, by far, on the ship. The ranges were being fed into the rudimentary computer and then to the guns. I was also relaying by voice down through a voice tube to the Skipper on the bridge just what I was seeing. The hull came into my view. It was a four-masted ship. The British and the Japanese, used Q ships, ships that were designed to appear helpless and innocent to lure a submarine to the surface and into the range of a large, hidden, gun. Our Navy was experimenting in the use of such vessels. This vessel had the look of a Q ship. Here it was, 'way off the beaten path in Japanese waters, plodding along, not answering our challenge. Then I could see lumber stacked on deck, perfect camouflage for a gun. We were coming into range now. "Load Gun One," from the Skipper, then I could make out, lashed to the top of the lumber, fore and aft, a pair of Army 4 X 4 trucks with a big white star on the door. At about that same instant that I yelled this information down to the Captain, she answered the light signal! We circled her close in, still suspicious, until it was determined that she was an Olson lumber schooner en route from Coos Bay, Oregon, to Australia, unescorted, with a load of lumber. Her one man who was capable of reading and sending by light was slow in getting to his post, and that slowness almost got them under fire. Hummer was not going to fire one across her bow, he would have aimed to hit her with the first salvo. I am pretty sure that he was disappointed.

We returned to our escort, which had finally gotten untangled, and got underway for Palmyra Island to be refueled for the trip back to Pearl. The in and out stop in that protected harbor gave us an over-the-side swimming party to refresh and clean our unbathed bodies. We entered the harbor at 0629 Thursday 8 October, 1942 , and departed after taking on the oil at 1001. Oil was a major problem. The island could only spare us the absolute minimum, 1244 barrels of Bunker "B" oil, to get us back to Pearl Harbor. When we did get back, on Sunday 11 October, Captain Hummer said that we had less than forty miles of oil left in the tanks. He used artistic license to say that we used tomato cans to dip oil out of our bilges to feed the boilers.

Captain Hummer was too ill to attend our ship's reunion in 1989, but he did send a video tape. On the tape he said that he had met Commodore Fullinwider, who had been our Division Commander in 1942, in Washington, DC, about ten years after the war was over, and over lunch he asked Fullinwider why he had sent CHEW, a short-legged ship, on this assignment. (short-legged refers to short cruising radius) Fullinwider's response was that the other two good ships were being converted to high-speed transports, and he sent us because he didn't think we'd make it through the submarine cordon, and he didn't want to risk one of the others. ALLEN had not even been considered for the job.

Saturday, 31 October 1942, starting late in the afternoon, under Code name "Queen Three", we escorted an odd group of ships back to San Francisco, passing Farallon Island Light at 0715 Tuesday 10 November 1942 and passing the Entrance Buoys at 0958, after the convoy had entered the safety of the harbor. We moored first to Pier 28-S, and for several days we underwent Degaussing exercises and compass adjustment and calibration in the Bay. We tied up each evening at Pier 54, which was a gateway to the nightclubs, hotels, bars and everything else that the Barbary Coast was noted for. Bimbo's 365 Club on Market Street always had enough CHEW men in it during performances to make up an entire ship's duty section. This was a most enjoyable port that offered a great deal of R & R, and the men made hay while the sun shone, so to speak. Some of them became acquainted with the Shore Patrol's free taxi service back to the ship, but most of us had a very enjoyable time in the City By the Bay.

On the last day in San Francisco we were shifted to an anchorage out in the Bay near Alcatraz to await the making up of our return convoy. Queen Three did resume on Monday 23 November 1942 as we left in company with USS BARKER (DD 213) as the second escorting ship. On the fourth day out we met the second group of ships assigned to us and took over from the Coast Guard cutter W 109 HERMES that had brought a group of tankers up from Long Beach. This trip lasted until Monday 7 December 1942 when we finally shepherded our group into Pearl Harbor and passed the entrance buoys ourselves at 1456. It was memorable only in that it was a slow trip and the convoy commander, as I recall, flew his flag on the SS Santa Cruz Cement, a bulk cement carrier. The amenities in the owner's cabin on that vessel must have outweighed the lack of flotation ability of a shipload of cement.

WEST VIRGINIA was raised from the mud of Pearl Harbor and entered Dry Dock #1 in June 1942 for a big patch job and enough work to get her fit to go to sea, but not to fight. She required considerable rebuilding that was beyond the capabilities of the Pearl Harbor Navy Yard. WEST VIRGINIA was a good ship with a good crew. The ship was commonly called by her nickname - WEEVIE. On the last day of April 1943 she left for the Bremerton Navy Yard to be refitted, modernized, and returned to the fleet in fighting shape.

In those ten months the Pearl Harbor Yard had replaced her shattered port side armor with steel plating enough to make her seaworthy, but she could not operate any of her guns. Her appearance was lopsided as her top hamper did not match, and she had taken torpedoes after she had settled to the bottom, with damage to her port side above her main deck. Her starboard side retained all its original structure and bulk, while the other side was bare. She could make 18 knots but was defenseless otherwise.

During the salvaging of WEST VIRGINIA it was necessary to remove a total of sixty-six bodies of crewmen killed in the December 7th attack. A grisly tale unfolded that became general knowledge despite official attempts to keep it quiet.

Evidence showed that some of these men had lived for a considerable period of time after the bombing was over. In his report, Admiral Wallin, said that the bodies were widely scattered about the ship and "considerably dismembered." Some bodies were found in the engineering spaces where it seemed that the men had gotten in to an air bubble and survived for some time. However, there were three bodies found in Storeroom A-111 that showed indisputable evidence that these three had survived for a long period of time trapped under

99

water. The men had found blue uniforms and jerseys to keep warm, and had eaten the emergency rations stored there, and had access to fresh water tanks. But the terrible part was that they had marked a calendar with an "X" for each day from December 7 to December 23! 1

CHEW was handed the job of escorting her back to Puget Sound as "Assignment Queen Three." We took off eagerly that Friday to escort her back, zig zagging on Plan #10, more or less in front of WEEVIE, headed around Diamond Head, marking our passing that rock at 1155 Bearing 335 degrees 45' True, 3.7 miles to take course 090T. It was an eerie trip, moving back and forth in front of what was almost a ghost ship, manned by a skeleton crew.

We soon left the blue sky and blue waters of the mid-Pacific for the grey skies and grey waters of the North Pacific. This trip was far too long for our oil capacity, especially with the wide zigzag pattern that was used, so we had to refuel from WEEVIE, an operation that went off without a hitch. The refueling process took less than two hours and the Log shows that CHEW received 26,744 gallons of Bunker "B" Fuel Oil. At the conclusion of the operation, the captain of the battleship, as was the custom after oiling an escorting destroyer, offered to send over a quantity of ice cream for our crew. For some unknown reason, Mr. Nameless, who had assumed the post of commanding officer on the illness of Peter Horn, refused the kind offer, saying that he had a baker aboard thank you, a statement that caused loud groans from our crew. Was he trying to make points?

We were on the third day out from Pearl, Tuesday, 4 May 1943 to be exact, when we had a sound contact at 0950 that proved to be false, but it set the stage for a lookout on WEEVIE to spot a periscope off her port beam at 1230. Good old CHEW dashed to the rescue, going almost immediately to GQ and picking up a sound contact at 1238. At 1245 we dropped and fired a total of 11 depth charges on this contact. We circled the area while WEEVIE steamed away to safety. At 1312 we secured from GQ, with the Log reporting "Results Unknown". Those of the crew on the bridge knew what we had depth charged from the blood that came up to the surface. We bent on some turns to catch WEEVIE and continued our escort onward.

Friday, 7 May, dawned as a beautiful, clear, cold day, with snow-clad mountains ahead on either side of the Straits of Juan de Fuca as we prepared to enter that body of water. As we zig-zagged through some heavy rollers just at the entrance to the Sound, our steering engine, always balky and cranky, decided to jam with the rudder hard over. Whoever was the OD at the time made the mistake of stopping all engines, so that we were stopped broadside to the swells and in the path of the oncoming WEST VIRGINIA. I was at my station on the flying bridge as the ship rolled hard one way, and then back the other way, so far that I stood on the bulwark. I could hear the sound of pots and pans crashing off the hooks in the galley. We had rolled 62 degrees! The order was given at once to ring up Ahead One Third to get out of that trough before we rolled over. We got out of trouble as the engineers got the steering engine unjammed before we made a complete circle and then we entered the smooth waters of Puget Sound.

That series of rolls wrought havoc in the galley, not only the pots coming off the hooks to crash to the deck, but sea water had come in the hatches from the main deck. The fire in the range was washed out, and the big pans in which the cook had been cooking pork sausages, had also fallen to the deck, with the resulting melange of utensils, sausages, and everything else that had come loose, sloshed back and forth from hatch coaming to hatch coaming in an oily, lumpy, mess. Poor old Stormy had that watch, and that mishap was the straw that broke the back of that ex-battleship cook. He sat on the coaming, almost in tears, head in hands, "I quit! This pig-iron SOB isn't fit for humans to live in. I quit!"

This 235 pound cook had spent a hitch as a butcher and had the heavy torso that comes from such a job. There he sat, a mound of blubber, dejected, bemoaning his fate, until the First Lieutenant came up on the scene, sat next to Stormy, put his arm around his shoulder, and assuaged him with kind words. The Chief Bos'ns's Mate turned a gang to in cleaning up the mess and getting the galley back in operation again. The sausages were fed to the fish.

Despite the initial excitement, this day was one of unrivaled beauty sailing through calm blue waters with the mountains of Vancouver Island on one side and the snow-covered Olympic range on the other, dominated by Mount Olympus towering over it all. That morning outside of the Straits, snow on the Canadian mountains came down to the water's edge. As we progressed toward Seattle there were logging operations underway on the sides of the mountains with an occasional log sliding down a chute to hit the water with a high splash. I kept my eyes glued to the rangefinder to take advantage of its superior optics and to take in as much of the scenery as I possibly could.

The beautiful calm was disrupted by a Canadian patrol vessel sending a message that it had a sound contact up ahead. We went again to GQ at 1040 and dashed on ahead to help out. The contact had petered out and we secured from GQ at 1115 and went on with our business. WEEVIE left us and turned in to Bremerton while we continued on to tie up at Pier 41, "Easy" berth, in Seattle, where we were to have liberty. But before we tied up the thrust bearing on the starboard Low Pressure Turbine carried away and we proceeded on to port on one screw. CHEW held off a serious breakdown until she had carried out her assignment. That night in Seattle four of us went in to a gin mill for refreshments. We took a table, sat down, and ordered our Shirley Temples. The place was full of sailors, not too surprising a development in that Navy town. One man at the next table asked the usual "What ship, mates?" When we said "CHEW" he roared, "Put your money away! You guys saved our ship! The drinks are on us!" They were WEEVIE sailors, and we were careful not to tell them that we had depth charged and killed a whale that day at sea, and not a submarine. They were grateful for the protection we had given them on the voyage in from Hawaii. Free drinks are tasty.

Just a short time before we left Pearl to escort WEEVIE back to Bremerton, an ex-longshoreman named "Whitey" had come aboard. Whitey was made into a cook's striker rather quickly. It is beyond rational understanding why a semi-literate dock-walloper was put in the galley, but the Navy went out of it's way to do such unrational things as a matter of course. He was in his early twenties, a nice looking lad with a little white mustache and white wavy hair. Whitey was happy that we were headed for Seattle as he was from that area, and had drawn liberty the first day we were in port. Accordingly he had departed alone, all spic and span in his dress blues and giving off a strong aroma of aftershave. I had drawn the 0400 to 0800 Gangway watch that next morning and it was a chilly one, with a steady, cold drizzle falling, there in the Pacific Northwest. CHEW was moored on a long pier, with a gate and a civilian guard at the head of the pier for security. A 'phone hookup from the guard shack went to the only ship on his pier. Just past daybreak the guard phoned to ask if we had a man aboard named Whitey. When I said that we did, the civilian guard asked if he could let this man on the pier, as he had shown up out of uniform and without any identification. Here came someone running down the pier, barefoot, hatless, wearing a pair of paint-splattered coveralls.

It was Whitey. He said that he had gone ashore the previous night to see one of his girl friends. He had been at her house, some place in the suburbs of Seattle. Sometime during this visit they had gotten around to a serious discussion that was taking place in her bed. They were "au naturel," when suddenly her husband burst in the bedroom door. Depending to whom he was relating this tale, said hubbie was waving a six-shooter, or a tomahawk, or even a claymore. This was obviously no time for parleying, so Whitey went out the window forthwith. Unfortunately for Whitey, the owner of the house had been a lover of roses. Our boy landed in a real bed of roses, but with what he expected to be coming after him out of that window, he could not carefully pick his way. He had to save the rest of his hide in a hurry with the result of his lower portions getting more than somewhat lacerated from his rapid progress out of the thorns. He made his way in the dark, without clothes or money, back to the ship. He walked to a through road and started to hitch hike, but he was not having much success in getting people to stop. (once they had slowed down enough to get a look at him) Finally a man came driving by on his way to work, picked him up, and gave him an old pair of coveralls that were in the back of the car.

After our return to Pearl Whitey was quickly rated as Third Class Cook and transferred to a Marine outfit. We did not miss his cooking, but we cheerily allowed that the lucky Marine bunch had a reason to charge up a beach - anything to get away from Whitey's cooking.

We had just a couple of days in the hospitable port of Seattle, from that Friday afternoon when we tied up to the following Monday, 10 May 1943, when we shoved off for San Francisco. The Black Gang had worked through the night to get that Thrust Bearing repaired and got it done by 2000 on Saturday. There was enough time for the crew to get ashore and put a few dollars in circulation. We also received 23,160 gallons of Grade B Fuel Oil from the dock, and passed the quarantine inspection of one Mr. John C. Pritchet of the Bureau of Entomology and Plant Quarantine. We all certainly felt better after his approval of our ship.

We were ordered to San Francisco to pick up a convoy being made up, and take it to Pearl Harbor. We were needed at work in COM 14, so we were underway at 0800 and passed outbound through the Straits of Juan de Fuca at 1100 at 18 knots steaming independently.

As we were working our way out of Puget Sound that first morning we in the firecontrol gang were testing all the gun ready lights and firing circuits throughout the ship, a routine daily procedure at sea to make sure that the night's salt spray hadn't opened up a circuit. We had tested all the gun circuits and found them OK, and had worked down to testing the firing circuits on the six K-guns that fired depth charges. Eddie Greco was handling the light at the guns that would show a complete circuit when I, up on the bridge, would press the firing key for that particular gun. The procedure was simple. He would open the breech, to make it impossible to fire the charge, attach the test lamp with alligator clips to the primer, and turn on the ready light switch. When the light came on at the firing key, I would press the key. The light would light, he would report over the phones we were wearing, and then go on to the next position.

At the middle gun on the port side there was a group of the Black Gang standing around rehashing their deeds in Seattle the previous night. When Greco, a natural-born comic showed up, the chaffing back and forth started. One of the snipes had been leaning on the depth charge sticking up out of the K-gun and when Greco started to hook up the test lamp he made a crack that he'd better get away as "Those bright Firecontrolmen might just fire that gun." Much laughter. Up on the bridge the ready light came on, so I pressed the button, "KABAWHOOOM." "What was that?" the Skipper yelled as he popped out of his bunk in the bridge ready cabin. As I helplessly watched the hammer-shaped depth charge sail out in a graceful arc to plop down among a fleet of small fishing boats "I just fired a depth charge, Sir." In a matter of minutes Greco and I were standing before him to explain why. It seems that Eddie just omitted opening the breech of the gun during the chit-chat with the Black Gang, and when he turned on the ready light the circuit was complete ready for me to press the firing key. That small fishing fleet scattered like a covey of quail when that depth charge landed in their midst. They didn't know it, of course, but it was set on "Safe" and would not detonate. That live lump of TNT is still lying on the bottom of Puget Sound waiting for some unwary scuba diver to come along.

The surprising thing about this incident was that the skipper took no disciplinary action of any kind. He had been ashore the night before too, and he needed his rest before the ship got out to sea, so he dismissed us rather quickly and crawled back into his bunk and covered his head. No report has surfaced about the firing of one depth charge that day by CHEW.

With a couple of minor steering engine casualties we made an otherwise uneventful passage to San Francisco, passing under the Golden Gate Bridge at 1134 on Wednesday 12 May 1943, and moored starboard side to at Pier 54. We stayed in San Francisco at that Embarcadero pier until Sunday 23 May when we were underway at 0731 to commence our escort duties on our new assignment.

While at Pier 54 those eleven days the ship took on some food items not normally shipped aboard. All food items are logged in with the same notations from the procedure followed. "Inspected as to quantity by Ensign John J. Smith, USNR (or whoever) and as to quality by Richard C. Roe, Chief Pharmacists Mate, USN." Nothing was omitted, every pound of potatoes, every coffee bean, was accounted for in this manner. But the log for those days reflects the changed eating habits of the crew while tied up at a Pier in close proximity to the many good food establishments in San Francisco.

Day and Date	Ice Cream Gallons	Fresh Milk Gallons	Pies	Cinnamon Rolls	Bread
Wed 12	10				
Thu 13	10	10	15	16#	100 loaves
Fri 14		10	15		
Sat 15	05	10	15	14#	100#
Sun 16	05	10	15		
Mon 17	05	10	15	15#	
Tue 18		10	15	14-3/4#	
Wed 19	05	10	15	14-3/4#	
Thu 20	05	10	15	15#	
Fri 21	05	10	15	15#	
Sat 22	05	10		40#	
Totals	55	100	135	144-1/2#	

From that listing one may rightfully suppose that the crew were eating the things that were in short supply under normal circumstances, like the fresh milk, and the pies (no flavors noted), but the pounds of cinnamon rolls require explanation. Such rolls are normally associated with breakfasts, and I read into that total that the crew did not seek out the normal eggs and bacon for breakfast, but that after a hard night along the Barbary Coast, a roll and mug of hot coffee was sufficient to get one started.

Sunday 23 May 1943 CHEW passed the "A" buoy to port at 1156 on course 250 True, escorting transport USS REPUBLIC (AP 33) and the following afternoon rendezvoused with another old transport, USS HENDERSON (AP 1) and USS DOHERTY (DE 14) for a four ship convoy to Hawaii. On the last day before ending this trip, CHEW had two more steering engine problems. These were easily taken care of, and on Monday 31 May 1943 at 1310 we passed the Entrance Buoys in to Pearl Harbor and tied up at Berth Baker 6 outboard of USS BOGGS (DMS 3) and received 2,350 barrels of "B" fuel from a Yard Oiler at the end of the assignment.

CHEW had many escort assignments, some lasting but a few hours, and other longer trips as ordered, with any time not specifically assigned to be spent on the Offshore Patrol going back and forth from Diamond Head to Barber's Point guarding the approach to Pearl Harbor and Honolulu. After a week on that boring patrol any escort assignment was welcomed as a break in that routine.

FOOTNOTE

1. "Pearl Harbor: Why, How, Fleet Salvage and Final Appraisal. Homer   L. Wallin. USGPO

Chapter XIII

Bits and Pieces of Flotsam and Jetsam

It was early in 1942 when CHEW limped into Pearl Harbor with a serious engineering problem and was given immediate attention by the Navy Yard. Things were not going well in the war and everything in that Navy Yard was on an emergency basis. We were tied up at a dock with steam up, just in case we had to get out of port quickly. That night I had drawn the 0400 to 0800 Gangway Watch, with Fredie the Fox as my messenger. We relieved at 0345, with the Petty Officer that I was relieving passing on to me all the pertinent information; who was OD; if the Skipper was aboard (he was); and also that there was a crew of Navy Yard workmen doing something below in the steaming hot fire room. The Yard was as blacked out as a working Yard could be, and before my cup of coffee was cool enough to drink Fox found four Yardbirds flaked out under the torpedo tubes napping.

Hoo boy! This would not do. I kicked them out on deck and asked them whatnell they were supposed to be doing. A spokesman replied that they were working on some pump or other in the forward fire room. With that, I said there was no such pump under those tubes, where they had been napping, and for them to get below and get cracking on the job. To forestall any gripes or murmurs Fox and I gave them our best fish-eyed stares, and adjusted our holsters. Without further ado they went below.

An hour passed and the workmen, or what I thought were the same four, came up through the air-lock hatch out of the fireroom. We herded them back below again. 0730 finally came and a wet and bedraggled gang of workmen came up and beat it down the dock looking over their shoulders muttering something that we couldn't understand. Then their leadman reported that the job was completed and the ship was ready for sea again. Fox and I had breakfast, the crew went to quarters, set special sea details and CHEW departed. After quarters was over Chief Engineer, Lieutenant (jg) Morrison called me aside to say that the foreman of that yard crew was unhappy with him. The Yard had sent over two crews of four men each to work in relays in that hot fireroom on our problem, but that some mean, gung ho sailor with a gun had made both crews work at once instead of spelling each other four at a time. They did finish the job in half the estimated time.

Clovis Wain Phillips, Gunners Mate Second Class, had come to CHEW as part of the recommissioning crew from one of the heavy cruisers, where he had been a champion heavyweight wrestler. He had several nicknames, such as "Popeye" from his large muscular arms, but "Jeep" stuck to him for no known reason. He was a joy to stand watch with as he had an active, dry sense of humor. He was in Honolulu, probably looking for the Public Library, down on lower Hotel Street, when he came upon a sailor getting the whey beaten out of him by a civilian who Jeep recognized as a preliminary event pro boxer. Jeep asked the pro to let the boy alone, but that 125 pound dynamo had his blood up, and wasn't to be kept from whipping up on a sailor. He proceeded to pop Jeep a fast one on his nose, making it bleed down the front of Jeep's pristine white jumper. He tried it again, only Jeep grabbed him this time and clamped him in a tight headlock. Jeep then screwed his knuckles into this Hotshot's ear. He held on until the man went limp. He then let go and the man slid to the sidewalk in a heap, just as the Police arrived.

The original sailor who was the cause of Phillip's concern, saw the police and melted into the crowd. The boxer got up and yelled to the police that this big man had assaulted him, so Jeep was hauled off to spend the night in the pokey. The next morning he went before the Provost Marshal, as Martial Law was in effect in Hawaii at that time. The complaining witness was there complaining shrilly. The Judge was a Navy Commander, who asked Phillips how he got all that blood down his front and when Jeep told the full story, the Judge advised him to counter charge the boxer with assault. Done, case dismissed. The Provost Marshall gave Phillips a slip exonerating him of any charges so that he would not be charged as an AWOL back aboard ship. When asked about this affair, Jeep said, "All I'd did was to hold him a bit."

"Doc" Peterbilt (not his name, but close enough) came aboard as a Chief Pharmacists Mate. Doc was a likable man, with a cheerful demeanor, but he did love alcohol. One of the young officers had a tummy ache and went to the Sick Bay up forward of the Forward Guinea Pullman to get some medication but he couldn't locate the Pharmacist's Mate. The Sick Bay was a little wire-wall enclosed cubby hole with a Dutch door arrangement so that the Doc could stand inside and dispense medicine out through that half door. The top part of the door was open, which meant, usually, that the doc was around close by because that place was never to be left unattended when the door was open. It held a quantity of alcohol, and a bottle of brandy, hence the lock and key. A search throughout the ship was started, still Peterbilt could not be found. Topside, in the crew's quarters, in the engineering spaces, any place - could he have fallen overboard? Then a cooler head looked in the Sick Bay, and there folded up on that tiny deck, fast asleep was one drunken Pharmacists Mate.

Time passed, and on one of the longer trips away from port Doc started to appear as if he had just had a belt or two, and as a matter of fact, he was drunk. All the alcohol had been removed (what was left) from the Sick Bay, there was no booze of any kind on that ship. But there he would be standing, leaning against one of the torpedo tubes, with a big grin on his face, and a cup of black coffee in his hand. This went on for about a week, until we hit port, and Doc was sent to Aiea Hospital to dry out. We received a replacement pharmacists mate to tend to our needs. About a month later "Snap" Whittington, who held forth in the topside machine shop, was doing some cleaning up and straightening out when he came upon a nearly empty gallon jug with some blue liquid in it, marked conspicuously with a large skull and cross bones. A sniff of the contents revealed the source of Peterbilt's hooch. He had set this up well before all of the alcohol in the Sick Bay had been removed. This was his "rainy day" supply. His procedure was to draw a cup of coffee from the galley, and then walk with it through the machine shop, pause briefly at the scrap box where this bottle of poison was kept, and then step out on deck with his cup of fortified coffee. Later we got word that he had been advanced to Warrant Officer at the hospital.

I had made friends with a Yard workman named Dean at the Pearl Harbor Navy Yard. He was a shipfitter, which meant that he worked in every part of a ship. Every department had had contact with Dean. He was a better than average Yard worker, neat and clean, and always willing to do a little more for you. I had done a favor of some sort for him, so inconsequential as to be forgotten almost as soon as it was done. Dean took leave to go back to the "States" to marry his girl friend and was gone about a month. One morning CHEW pulled into Pearl and docked back in the Repair Basin at Baker 6. We were going along in normal port routine, repairing the ravages of the sea and getting ready to go back out again.

I was up on the flying bridge with my tool box opened doing some repair work, when Dean came clambering up the vertical ladder from the bridge and hoisted his big tool box up right after him, and set it down next to mine. We exchanged greetings, how is married life, and so on, and while we talked he opened his box and removed a fifth of Bottled in Bond Tennessee whiskey and handed it to me saying that it was a thank you for that past favor. WOW! That thing was like having a live grenade ticking in your hand. Possession of whiskey on board a United States naval vessel by an enlisted man was a ticket to Portsmouth Naval Prison! I stuck that thing in my tool box and covered it with tools in a trice. If any of the other crew members had seen it there would have been an instant cry of "Gimme a drink" and that bottle of good stuff would have been gone at once. Dean departed, with my thanks, and left me with mixed feelings.

I was on the horns of a serious dilemma. I couldn't share it with any of my shipmates, as the cat would get out of the bag, to all of our regrets. I couldn't leave it in the tool box as there were three of us with keys to that box, and the Radio Gang was always trying to break into it and steal some of my tools. I couldn't carry it below to my locker two decks below, down a vertical ladder to the bridge, past the bridge gang, down past the ship's office, and the wardroom passage, then down one more ladder and forward through the seamen's compartment. I couldn't even stand up and toss it overboard without it being seen and reported "That man threw a bottle over the side" and the damned thing would float anyway. I sat there on the closed lid of the tool box until I came up with the best hiding place on the ship, right there on the flying bridge.

This area was a place out of the passage of most of the crew, and restricted to those who had business there. Some of the officers would sometimes come up there and sun themselves on a cot that they had a mess attendant bring up and set up for them. I know quite a few people that if they read this now will react with awe to my daring. I opened the battery access door in the base of the rangefinder and put that bottle in there wrapped in rags to protect it and muffle any noise it may make as the ship rolled and pitched. I was the only man who ever opened that access door to check on the range finder's battery. That space was never inspected, and most officers did not even know that the rangefinder had cross-hair illumination for night ranging that required a big 6-volt wet battery.

I had a bunk up there on the flying bridge that was the leading firecontrolman's private bunk. Walter Aldridge, a Fleet Reserve First Class, was first to lead the group. With plenty of foresight, he had installed that fold-down bunk up against the forward bulwark when the ship was put back in commission. The Chief Engineer had put his bunk up there too, with the result that an officer and an enlisted man slept at sea head to head in two bunks under the stars. In 1944 one of the new junior officers decided that he wanted my bunk at sea and ordered me to give it up to him forthwith. No way! I went to Lieutenant Joseph Mannion, who was the Exec at that time, and he backed me up. That bunk was on my battle station, and so that pipsqueek had to remain below in the wardroom.

I sipped on that bottle for about six months before I emptied it. On rare occasions I would cadge a couple of ice cubes from the officer's galley and have some on the rocks in a highball glass that one of the officers stewards had "acquired" from the yard's Officers Club and passed on to me. There is nothing as efficient in settling one's nerves as a sip of good whiskey.

Gene Thomas was one of the Reserves who came aboard with us from St. Louis who had one of those "feathermerchant" rates. He was third in line of the deck force group under Chief Bosn's Mate Bill Hudson. Red Fehr was Second Class Boats, and a real ear-banger, then came Gene in that hierarchy as a Cox'n. Gene was a hard worker, and kept his kids in line. We were good friends and were always trying to pull something on the other guy. We played Acey-Ducey (The Navy version of Backgammon) and went out of our way to cheat the other man. That was the game, to try to cheat in some way. We didn't play for money, Gene never had any as he was married and sent most of his pay home to his wife. We tried to put the dice down on the board with a number up that we needed, and then snap our fingers as if we had rolled the dice. This was called "skidding" the dice, and we called each other "Skidmore", among other names. All in good clean fun.

Red Fehr had "inherited" a bunk on the well deck that Newt Dupuy had installed as his private space. We all tried to get a place to sleep up out of the compartments below. Foul air was one reason. Sixty men in one room was another, and then there was the thought that if one slept topside he couldn't be trapped when the ship went down. Red was transferred away and Gene took over his bunk as a matter of seniority. One night Gene came back aboard after dark to find a Yard workman asleep in his bunk, a welder wearing his dirty clothes and boots. Gene threw this big man off the ship bodily down the gangplank, ass over appetite. About a week later in Honolulu I ran in to a soldier from Schofield Barracks that I had gone to high school with. Who was also a neighbor of Genes in St. Louis, Hamilton "Hammie" Carter. Hammie had a cushy billet at Schofield playing on the Post baseball team. Hammie was also one of nature's noblemen, "laid back" before the term became common usage. We spent a happy hour talking over old times and replaying ball games and as we parted we set up a date for Gene Thomas to come in to Honolulu and meet Hammie. Gene did not make that trip as he was so suspicious of me setting him up for something that he accused me of taking a bribe from that welder in order to get him off the base so the welder could waylay him and take revenge for the way Gene had tossed him off the ship.

After the 7th of December 1941 debacle we received a number of men from the sunken battleships to fill out our crew. Some of these people were petty officers and some were non-rated firemen. One Second Class Bosn's Mate had been a "shylock" (loan shark) on one of the sunken battleships and carried his now worthless account book around and moaned over how much money he had lost when his ship went down. He got very little sympathy from any of us, as some of the men who still owed him money never made it off that ship alive. He had spent a hitch in the paint locker of that battleship and knew too little of deck seamanship to be of much use to us, and it wasn't long before he was transferred away. Jock McQuilkin had been on the OKLAHOMA when she rolled over and he was so jumpy that when he was awakened at night to go on watch the man waking him up was careful to wake him gently so that Mac wouldn't jump up and strike his head on the bunk above him. He did get over that nervousness eventually.

We also picked up a First Class Gunner's Mate who had received the Purple Heart from 7 December action on one of the sunken battleships. He had dropped a fire extinguisher on his big toe and mashed it, and was treated at the Navy Yard Dispensary for the injury, and his name was listed as having received medical treatment, so ...... This man picked up the nickname "Shotgun" for one of his deeds. He unlocked a topside locker that held four new short-barreled riot guns that had just been issued to the ship. He intended to clean these guns, but after unlocking the door to this cabinet he stood the four guns on the deck and leaned them against the side of the locker while he re-locked the door. The ship was at sea, and this ex-battleship sailor wasn't used to the action of a tin can at sea. The deck was canted to allow sea water to roll off quickly, and without warning the guns slipped and fell. He caught three of them, but one went over the side.

He looked around, no one had seen this accident, he thought, so he replaced the three guns and hot-footed it down to the Gunnery Officer to report a missing shotgun! Up over his head, Fredie Fox was working on the two 20MM guns on the tub, and saw the whole thing. Nothing was said at first, but within the hour the ship's company was called to quarters and whoever had taken that gun was told to return it. When no one returned the gun, the ship was searched from stem to stern without results, of course. Fox told one person what he had seen - me, and we kept quiet just to see how long it would take for this First Class Petty Officer to speak up and take his medicine. He knew that we knew when we started to call him "Shotgun." He never did 'fess up and the affair blew over and was forgotten.

In 1953 I made a one-day trip from San Francisco to sea on the USS HANCOCK, a big ESSEX Class carrier, for a demonstration of a Terrier missile as a member of the American Ordnance Association. As the ship was coming back through the Golden Gate that afternoon getting ready to debark the passengers the ship's Chief Petty Officers came topside to go on liberty and when I saw one of them and called out "Hey, Shotgun" the man nearly fainted, for that's who it was, now a multi-hash-marked CPO.

From the sunken USS CALIFORNIA we received Gerard "Red" Driscoll, and Harold "Pete" Peterson, a pair of Third Class Firemen who reminded me of a pair of range colts, full of The Old Nick, and always ready for anything. Two handsome six-footers, a red-headed Irishman and a blonde Swede, they managed to get in and out of scrapes continuously. They had been to the Marine Barracks beer garden one afternoon, and on their merry way back to the ship they passed Dry Dock #1. Whether or not it was break time for the yard workmen down in the dock, the workmen were lying in the shade resting. This lack of motion disturbed Red and Pete and so they yelled down for the workmen to get off their duffs and get to work. They used colorful and insulting language to the men, who replied in kind. The pair of sailors looked around for something to throw down on those loafers but there was nothing at hand, so they did what they thought was the next best thing: they relieved themselves of some of the Marine Barracks' beer down on the men. That got results. The Navy Yard Police escorted the pair back to the Marine Barracks and tossed them in the cooler until they sobered up. The ship's Master at Arms came and escorted them back aboard ship to stand at Captain's Mast. I thought the whole affair amusing.

Ten of us, most of the baseball team, were sent to a recreation camp at Nanikuli on the North Shore for a weeks R & R. That was tough duty. We slept in tents under the trees, just off the beach, no reveille, good food, ping pong in an open air pavilion, volley ball on the beach, and swimming in the surf, where the rollers come in unimpeded directly from Japan. At night the beach was patrolled by Marines with dogs to watch for someone being landed from a submarine: spy; saboteur; or whatever. At dusk one evening a Marine came along with a gigantic Great Dane as his helper. The one wearing the tin helmet was the Marine. I had to see this dog so I walked up slowly to the man and asked if I could pet the dog, or if he'd bite. "If he

113

doesn't bite you, I will." That Marine was an old grammar school classmate from St. Louis, Frank Weisler. We spent most of his watch talking over old times in Walnut Park. During his stop-over from his beat a whole raft-full of spies could have landed that night. It is a small world.

There was a sign on that beach warning not to swim there in the evening. No reason given, but I found out why the hard way. I dove out through the breakers late in the afternoon and came up outside the rollers and turned to swim back in with the breakers, only I was going backwards in the undertow! I started to whistle and wave, and as luck would have it there was a life guard still there, but about to go off duty. He swam out with a metal buoy with lines attached to it as grips. The two of us had trouble making it back through the surf to the beach swimming as hard as we could. I lay on my back getting my breath back and when I got up to thank the man, he had caught his breath, and had left without a word. Whoever he was, he saved my life, as that current would have taken me out to sea for good.

I don't remember how or when it happened, but I read someplace that there was a USO acting troupe going to give a performance of "MacBeth" at Schofield Barracks. I carried a large volume of the complete works of Shakespeare that I had bought in Honolulu as reading material, and to see a live performance would be a welcome change from the printed page. (that volume is still in my bookcase) DESDIV 80 had two tickets, and no takers for them, so I was welcome to them if no officer wanted them first. Schofield Barracks was not exactly next door, and transportation up there would be difficult, perhaps that is why no officer wanted the tickets, so they were mine. I needed a suitable companion. That was no problem as Earl Loeb was the first man that I asked and he jumped at the chance. We were both petty officers and were able to be freed from duty that day, so we hitch-hiked up to see the performance. The show was at the base movie house, which was a nice pre-war building with good seats and a big stage. We had left the ship in plenty of time to hitch up there and got there with an hour to spare so we were able to get good seats close in to the stage.

The troupe had a nucleus of professional actors, with the extras filled out from the thousands of men at that huge base. We did not know who the main actors were until we walked up to the movie house, Maurice Evans and Judith Anderson! Wow! We had a top Broadway cast, and were they good! The house was packed and after the performance Evans and Anderson had all the curtain calls that they wanted. Loeb and I were very appreciative of the show and as we

114

stood up for the applause I noticed that we were almost the only sailors there standing out in our whites. Earl Loeb left the ship for new construction in a short time, and it was several months more before the good news of my transfer came. About at the time I left for the Mainland Bob Hope showed up out there on his first of many USO trips. I don't remember much about Bob Hope's show, but I sure do remember MacBeth.

Some of the newly commissioned ensigns that came aboard had highly developed ideas about their exalted station as officers and how the lowly enlisted man should jump at their whims. They had to be shown the light quite often, such as the one who had coveted my flying bridge bunk. One such occasion arose during an at-sea showing of a newsreel movie in the After Engineers Quarters. This was the only place large enough to show a movie to a dozen people during daylight. On this day I had been out of the Black Gang for a couple of years but I still had buddies in that bunch and was not considered an "outsider" by the snipes. One of the Black Gang collared me in the "head" (Navy for toilet) to tell me a problem he was having right at that very minute. He had gone to his bunk only to find an officer was up in his bunk watching the movie. This officer had his shoes on and had marked up the clean sheets in the bunk. When my friend asked him to please get out of his bunk, the officer refused curtly and more or less told the man to get lost. He came to me with his problem.

I went below and confronted this future Horatio Nelson and asked him, not only to get out of that man's bunk, but to take the mattress cover and wash it. My answer was that not even a First Class Petty Officer could tell him what to do, he was a commissioned officer. "Aye aye, sir," I said, knowing better than to argue, and left at once for the Executive Officer, who I found in the Ship's Office, shuffling papers, as Execs are prone to do to pass the time of day. When I told him the story, he thanked me, and ordered the Yeoman on duty to go to the Engineer's Quarters and tell Ensign Big Shot to report to him "On the Double." I returned to the movie and took a seat just in time to see that ensign hustling forward to the Office. In a few minutes one of the Officer's Stewards appeared, asked for the location of my friend's bunk, and proceeded to remove the mattress cover and replace it with a fresh one, and told the man that he would return his mattress cover as soon as he could wash it and dry it. Some of those new officers needed more training than others.

CHEW's duty got to be more and more boring as time passed. She had been working with COMSUBPAC as a school ship training sound crews and submarine crews. In working with the subs one of my jobs was to watch the torpedo wakes to record where the fish would have hit us, if it had been set at the proper depth. They were set at a depth to safely pass under us, and then out behind us would be a retrieving vessel to hoist the spent fish with its hollow yellow dummy warhead aboard for reuse. The war had moved to the Western Pacific and our old ship was doing its bit. One day on liberty Fred the Fox and I were walking around the freight waterfront in Honolulu just rubbernecking, when I spotted a sign "Help Wanted" at the gate to the American Can Company's plant. I nodded toward the sign, and Fred, a man of few words, nodded too, so we went in the Personnel Office and asked if we'd do. CHEW was undergoing a thirty day repair job and we wanted to get away from the boredom and do something different. We could work every third day, our liberty day, if they could work us in.

I thought the Personnel Manager was going to kiss us. Here were two big, strong, young men walking into his life, but there had to be a catch to it. If we could get a permission slip from our Commanding Officer, he would make good use of us. We got the slip, and reported for work with our dungarees under our arm. The foreman that we were sent to could not believe his eyes. Neither could the hundreds of women working in the plant. To say that we stood out would be the understatement of the century. A few maintenance men, this Japanese foreman, and the two of us were the only men in the whole plant. The foreman, who we referred to as "Bugs Bunny" almost at once, was very happy to see us, and shook hands at length and bowed Japanese style at our introduction. He had a facial resemblance to Bugs, and traveled about the plant at a Bugs-style lope, just about the way Bugs himself would have done. Bugs put us to work unloading narrow gage railroad box cars that were full of shiny cans without tops. He'd set up a conveyor in the door of the car, and we were to pick up the cans with a wooden fork-like gadget that would pick up ten or twelve cans at a time and then turn and place the cans on the conveyor that would take them up and over to the cannery next door to be filled with pineapple.

There was no food in this big building, just millions of cans tinkling away on their trip to the cannery. It wasn't really noisy, just a constant tinkling. The job took a certain amount of dexterity to insert the fingers on the tool in to the row of cans, tilt it back enough to keep the cans from falling off, and then deposit them on the moving conveyor. It took a little getting used to, but it was a simple operation. Fred was too tall for the cars and dropped too many cans to suit Bugs, so he gave Fred a job of pushing small wagons of cartons around. Bugs ran the only forklift in the place, and that was the only sit down job to be had. We had only worked about two hours when the noon whistle blew, so we had to stop work too as everything stopped even while the sound of the whistle was still echoing in that cavernous old wooden building and the building emptied out. The women had someplace to eat and had disappeared. We wandered out of the plant in search of something to eat. Across the street was a place with a dirty glass window, with some Chinese lettering over the door. What gave it away as a restaurant was a large Oriental gentleman coming out the door picking his teeth. We went in, and saw it was half full of longshoremen and other dock walloper types, stuffing in bowls of white boiled rice and plates of dark stuff, all using chop sticks and fingers. There was a steady sound of slurping noises, which we took as a favorable sign regarding the quality of the food.

We found a little table and sat down, but there was no menu on it, no silverware either, just a huge bottle of black soy sauce. Obviously there were no waitresses or waiters in this place but finally, in response to our waves, a skinny, wrinkled old Chinese man wearing an apron over a long underwear shirt came over carrying a huge beat-up white pot of tea and two handleless Chinese cups. "Uhh?" was evidently asking what we wanted. When I asked what they served he waved at the wall behind the counter where I could see a lot of faded Chinese characters, each followed by Arabic numbers, like 35c and 15c. Then I could see a twinkle in this fellow's eye, he could see we were baffled and was enjoying himself. In the meantime men were coming in and leaving all the time, so obviously they were doing a good business. We each finally got a plate full of pink pork and vegetables and a great big bowl of steaming, white rice. When I went up to the counter and asked the old man for silverware he had to rummage around in a drawer before he found a couple of forks and big spoons. We ate there every time we worked and never had the same thing twice, except for the bowl of rice. The food was good and plenty of it and it was cheap. I found out how the Chinese eat soup with chopsticks. They pick up and/or spear the lumps with the chop sticks, and then pick up the bowl and drink the liquid. Quick and easy. We fiddled around with the chop sticks but in the need to eat quickly we stuck with the fork and spoon method.

We were paid by check for our work, and the paymaster of the plant immediately cashed the check, so we really received our pay in green backs. It wasn't much, but the job got us out of our routine, and away from the Navy Yard and put some money extra in our pockets. It was fun, too, watching Bugs flit around that plant. The Can

Company had withheld our income tax and a few years later I received a small refund check from the IRS. (It beat a sharp stick in the eye)

Chapter XIV

Athletes and Athletics

Of all the things that the Armed Forces did during WWII, one thing that stands out in my mind as something commendable is the way they handled the induction of major league baseball players into the services. Granted that a lot of movie stars, politicians, and other celebrities were given cushy assignments to make movies, sell War Bonds, whip up the war workers, and the like. The decision to have the ball players play ball was a good one.

In 1944 the military stations on Oahu received many major league ball players. Immediately the stations fielded good teams for the enjoyment and entertainment of the ordinary man in uniform. The Army Air Corps had Joe DiMaggio at Hickam Field, where the officially named Hickam Bombers were known by all the men as "DiMaggio's Team." Johnnie Mize of the St. Louis Cardinals played at Kaneohe Air Station. Barney McCoskey of the Detroit Tigers had a team, and Walt Masterson of the Washington Senators pitched at the Sub Base. It was a good move for morale to have these men do what they did so well. Some of the DiMaggios' games were played at Honolulu Stadium, a place where Joe was supposed to have cleared the stands many times.

In 1944 while in port one time we got word that the DiMaggios were going to play the McCoskeys up at Aiea Rec Center, so I wangled time off, and with Fred the Fox, hiked up to see that game. Aiea had been carved out of the hills up above Pearl Harbor by the Navy as a beer garden to replace the old Tin Roof, which had occupied valuable space in the Navy Yard. Then Aiea was expanded to include a pool, handball courts, football field, and a big baseball field. Along the left field foul line, because of cutting off a slope for the field, there was a natural grandstand with grass planted that made a good place to see a game. Fred and I got there early enough to get a good perch on the grass up behind home plate on the third base side, looking out along the first base line. Excellent seats, and by the time fielding and batting practice was over the place was jammed. Thousands of men in dungarees, fatigues, and even some in whites, had arrived to see this game. The DiMaggios had Merrill May from the Reds at third, Johnnie Berardino and Lucadello from the St. Louis Browns at short and second, Ferris Fain, who would become a star with the Phillies in '46, from the San Francisco Seals at first, with DiMag himself in center. McCoskey played center field for his team, and Mike McCormick from the Cincinnati Reds played left field for one of the teams, which one now escapes me. These were two teams of professional baseball players of note.

The game started with the Air Corps team as visitors batting first. McCoskey's pitcher, a lanky ex-minor leaguer, got the first two out, then up to the plate strode DiMaggio himself, in the flesh. He settled into the box with his familiar spread stance, and coldly eyed the pitcher, who was showing the strain of facing Joltin' Joe by fidgeting, scratching, hitching up his pants, readjusting, then, finally, took his signal. A hush fell over the crowd waiting for that first pitch to Joe. That week, YANK Magazine had come out with a full-page cover photo of DiMaggio in full battle dress, rifle, pack, steel helmet down on his brow, one hand on the rail of the gangplank of a troopship, looking firmly up to the ship with the same gaze that he was now turning on that nervous rookie pitcher. The caption on that magazine cover read "Joe DiMaggio is off to fight the Japs". Just then, in that hush, a leather-lung seated out along the third base side, yelled "Hey, Joe, seen any Japs lately?" The crowd roared and DiMag himself broke up and stepped back out of the box to laugh. Then he bounced out back to the pitcher and the game continued.

Late in the game Joe did hit one up on the roof of a barracks out beyond right center to the delight of his fans, but Barney McCoskey did it three times. I don't recall which team won, which wasn't important, but seeing that game was. It was a memorable occasion for thousands of us. I don't think that anyone envied those men their cushy assignments. I'd much rather see Joe DiMaggio hit the ball than read his obituary from some God-forsaken Pacific islet. Thousands of men like me, maybe millions, left whatever chance they had to play professional baseball behind when they spent a half-dozen years in uniform. One of my North St. Louis schoolmates, Emmitt Mueller, had been the regular third baseman for the Phillies when he was drafted and after four years of playing easy service ball he couldn't make the team again after he was discharged.

At Aiea Rec Center many gallons of beer were served to go with hot dogs and such to off duty sailors. This required a substantial staff of Ship's Service types to man the place, do the work, and keep the peace. The chief petty officer in charge was a portly, red-haired Chief Specialist, who was, at least every time that I saw him, seated at a table holding court and a bottle of beer. This man had a feather-merchant chiefs rating and we all knew that he had come in as a CPO. No one voiced any complaints about him or his rate because he was the current Welterweight Champion of the World, Freddie "Red" Cochrane. Red spent a couple of years in the Navy doing his bit, and lost his Belt in his first post war title defense as he had too much trouble making the weight. He held the title from 1941 to 1946 as he was unable to defend while in the Navy. He was a gregarious man, and liked his duty, and was not one bit swell-headed.

In some way or other I was put in charge of the ship's athletic locker and gear. With that great honor I assumed the duty of scheduling and arranging softball and basketball games when we were in port. With the type of duty that CHEW had in the last couple of years that I was aboard, those shoreside games became very important for morale. I developed many contacts with shoreside athletic officers in order to schedule games on short notice. I was able to scrounge the use of the Division's laundry panel truck for transportation; it had Navy tags and I had a Navy drivers license, which obviated the need to have to go through the Motor Pool in order to get transportation, a process that often took a lot of doing. Most of the games that I scheduled were at nearby bases or with other ships at the Bloch Recreation Center field.

The ship pulled ready duty often at the Bishop's Point Section Base right inside the entrance to Pearl Harbor. There was a ball field right next door in Fort Kam, and the men at the Section Base had set up an inside basketball court in a large warehouse. Those fellows had a sympathetic chief, and they had the court all marked permanently and in a matter of minutes could clear out the warehouse of the pallets and equipment stored there, set up the baskets, turn on the lights, and close the doors, and the Forum was ready for the gladiators. The building even had a mezzanine deck that made a good grandstand. The fleet of mine sweeps tied up there so there was always competition for CHEW's teams of varying quality.

We had in late '43 and in '44 a good basketball team, considering the size of the ship's complement that we had to choose from for players. Ensign Clair Callan gave us the necessary "gold braid" for entrance to some of the bases. Fred Fox was our mainstay, not the highest scorer, but a rock in the middle of our zone defense. Leo Coe had two years at Louisiana State and could score. Callan, Sleepy Wilcox from LA, and I rounded out the first five, and we usually had a couple of substitutes, often another unrelated Callan, Ace, who had been a Junior College quarter-miler in California. We won the greater portion of our games, by far, but we more than met our match in one particular game.

I had made a date to play one of the regimental teams at Hickam Field. When we showed up, all seven of us, and were changing into our home-made uniforms in the gym locker room. In walked a bird colonel, in uniform, and asked me if I "minded" playing against a large squad that he, as officer in charge of all 7th Air Corps athletics, was trying to winnow down to a traveling squad to compete in the world-wide Air Corps championship. OK with us, we came for a game, and we'd take on whatever he threw at us. We went out on the court for a shock. This game was set for the Memorial Gym, what had been the mess hall on 7 December 1941. Hanging on one wall was a giant Gold Star flag with several hundred gold stars on it, for each of the men killed there that morning. There were jam-packed grandstands on each side, all of which impressed us, but what had shocked us, there in our blue shorts and crudely numbered T-shirts as uniforms, was the sight of about fifty giants, all dressed in fancy warm-up duds, taking practice and flying and leaping about.

I had agreed to unlimited substitutions so that the Hickam coach could run in his squad and evaluate his candidates. We huddled and talked this over. It was apparent that we were to be the Christians in the Colosseum that night. I knew one of the Hickam candidates, "Ice" Brinkman, from St. Louis, where we had been teammates in an amateur league in '39. Ice was a big man and had been a star center in high school, but here he was scratching to be a guard! We should have been outclassed, but by the second half the crowd, all from Hickam, was cheering for us. The obvious underdogs were not keeling over and playing dead. We played them hard and close and gave them more than a mere workout. They beat us by only about fifteen points. As we were dressing after our shower many of their players and their coach came in to thank us for the game and to congratulate us for the way we played. One of their lanky centers shook Fred Fox's hand and when we were in the truck headed back to Pearl Harbor Fred said how lucky he had been, he had been beating up on a colonel all night and got away with it. That lanky center was a bomber pilot and had been a varsity college player, but Fred held him in check and showed him a few moves of his own.

When I was at Mare Island in 1945 there was a football team formed at Camp Shoemaker, the "Fleet City Bluejackets" that was composed of many college football stars, most of whom went on to play in the professional leagues when the war ended. The Bluejackets played in a "service" league, and I can recall seeing them play the El Toro Marine Base team at Kezar Stadium in San Francisco. Crazy Legs Hirsch played in that league and the Bluejackets had Buddy Young and Steve Juzwik of Notre Dame among other ex-college stars. These teams played a good brand of football and I, for one, appreciated them more as athletes than if they had been merely Seaman Seconds doing a job at which they knew nothing. They could have learned to be sailors, but why waste their talent?

The Navy made many mistakes in its handling of people. However, having star athletes perform as athletes was a good idea. It made sense for the men at the big camps to have a good team to root for, and to identify with.

"Ships are but boards, sailors but men: there be land-rats and water-rats, land thieves and water thieves."

Shakespeare
The Merchant of Venice. I,iii,22.

Chapter XV

How to get a Free Haircut

CHEW was in Pearl Harbor for repair that involved putting the galley out of commission. We were moored in the Repair Basin outboard of the USS AULICK (DD 569). AULICK had scraped bottom on an unmarked reef some place in the South Pacific and was in Pearl to be dry-docked and have her bottom repaired, and was waiting to be scheduled in one of the dry docks. In place of her galley CHEW had a portable cook wagon set up on the dock where all the cooking was done. The food was served from the galley, however.

We had a ball game that afternoon and as I returned from the game to the ship I crossed over AULICK to the plank that was being used as a brow between the two ships. While I was on the AULICK one of our cooks, Choteau Saffa, was crossing in the opposite direction carrying a large tray of cut celery on his shoulder. As we passed I reached up, took one of the stalks of celery, took a bite off the end and stepped on the plank.

Suddenly a hand reached over my shoulder from behind and snatched the celery out of my mouth unceremoniously. "You stole that celery!" came from an ensign with shiny new gold braid on his hat, and he was clutching my stalk of celery. I reached over and took it right back, and took another chomp off of it, and turned back on to my ship and left him standing there fuming. That fresh celery sure tasted good. I'd hardly gotten below and changed clothes when the Gangway Watch appeared - "Pond, the Captain is holding Mast on you right now on the well deck, and that's no vulgarity." I went along with what I thought was a gag, and followed him up the ladder to the well deck. Sure enough, there was Captain Whose-Name-Will-Not-Be-Found-in-These-Pages, standing there, along with our Mr. Bunny Slippers; the Yeoman with his book; and the ensign from the AULICK, hopping up and down mad. So Captain's Mast was held right then and there with me being charged with "disrespect."

At first I didn't think this was going to amount to much, and presented my case fairly well, I thought, but Captain Mush-Mouth was not having any of this disrespect stuff, and ordered me to apologize to Mister Whateverhisname was - "Or, I will send you to the brig!" in his most threatening manner. He had recently seen Charles Laughton play Captain Bligh in the movie "Mutiny on the Bounty" and was playing the part fairly well. I was a second class right arm petty officer by this time, and I felt that I had been wronged, not the other way 'round. My own commanding officer was taking the side of someone from another ship. Making the scene all the more ridiculous was this pipsqueek wearing a big smile and nodding his head in agreement, and Captain Mush-Mouth's slew-footed side-kick, Lieutenant (jg) Bunny Slippers was also nodding in accord with the other pipsqueek.

I took a deep breath, "Aye Aye, Sir, I'll get my tooth brush." The Chief Master at Arms, our chief bosn's mate, was also present at the Mast, as required. We started for the Marine Barracks and its brig at once. As we left, Lieutenant (jg) Bunny Slippers hissed "I'd have given you thirty days" as a send-off. As it was just about meal time a large group of the men were at the rail as we walked down the pier and their faces showed what they thought of the Skippers sentence, no grins, no wise cracks, all frowns. The walk to the Brig took fifteen or twenty minutes during which the Chief Bosn's Mate kept saying, "Why didn't you apologize?" It could have been that he was missing his dinner. If I had kissed that ensigns foot (or whatever) it would have all been over and done with and he would not have had to go through with all this bother and trouble, but he was sympathetic.

My stay at the United States Marine Brig, Pearl Harbor, T. H., was a whole semester in my continuing education. We walked into a receiving room, where my detention orders were handed over to a desk person who signed a receipt for my body. Before the Chief could say "So Long," and get out the door I had been marched through a barred steel door that was shut behind me with a positive "clang" that meant I was "in." I was ordered to strip, put my clothes into a basket, and stand in front of a Corpsman, who made a cursory examination after the guard who was giving me orders had said "three days." Possibly this meant "quick and easy," for that is what his examination was, quick and easy, and he passed me as being physically able to stand imprisonment. "No blood, cuts, or bruises." Then I was ordered to sit on a stool, still stark naked, while a man in prisoner's grey coveralls took a whack at my hair with a set of hand clippers. "Three days" again to this "barber" who made the job in a matter of seconds. The guard then pointed at a shower with his big billy club and hurried me through an ice water drenching, followed by his throwing a thin towel at me to dry off, all the while urging me to "shake a leg." After I'd used this tar paper towel he threw a pair of those designer coveralls with a big white letter "P" on the back at me, "Git your shoes, no socks", and I was ushered down a concrete hallway to my room.

The passageway had about eight steel barred doors along each side.

The next to last one on the left was open and the corporal gave me a poke with that club into that cell and slammed the door behind me with a very definite clang. The whole place was grey. Painted concrete, steel bars, the walls that weren't concrete were steel, the ceiling was grey, my uniform was grey, except for that big white "P" on the back. The guards were all in Marine OD's, with their chevrons on the sleeve. There I was, still pretty wet from that shower, in a room with three concrete walls, each about seven feet long and ten feet high, with a ceiling of heavy iron bars, open for light and ventilation. On the back wall was a plain steel shelf, no mattress, no pillow: that was the bunk.

The corporal was at the door laying down the rules of conduct for the establishment: No talking with the other prisoners; during working hours you will stand at the door with your nose against the middle bar; you will not sit down until the noon bell rings, then you may sit. At 1300 the bell will ring, and you will stand at the door again until 1800, when you may sit. Trustees will bring you a cup of water and a piece of bread at that time for your daily meal. After the meal your block will be let out to go to the head. He gave a clang on the door with his club for emphasis, and left me alone.

I could see into two cells across the passageway. One had a skinny kid standing at the door facing me. In the other I could see a man lying in the rear of the cell, on a very wet floor, with a rivulet of water coming out the door and running into a drain in the middle of the passageway. The skinny kid, in a whisper, asked "Hi, watcha in fer?" and he cautioned me to whisper as the "screws" would try to sneak up on you and wet you down with a hose, or use their clubs on you. He had a week to go, he said, on a thirty-day sentence for missing his ship. After I had pointed at the other man lying in the cell I got the story that this other man had been in for over a month and was in very bad shape, physically. He refused, or was unable, to stand, and had been hosed down and beaten several times, even that day. Shortly thereafter a bell rang, and with a sigh, the man across the way sat down, and I followed his example. Then a man appeared pushing a cart, and handed each of us a battered tin cup and a slice of dry bread, for our daily meal. Just about two hours before this I had been chomping on a piece of moist, fresh celery.

In a few more minutes a guard unlocked the door, and we stood outside our cells until the guard ordered us to double-time in to the head to answer Nature's call. In the area where the files from each row of cells converged there was organized confusion; guards yelling; and the sounds of several dozen pairs of feet slapping on the slick concrete. One file of runners had a problem when one man fell, causing the others to stumble too, that brought more guards swinging their clubs to spur the men on. Moral to that - don't fall down! Back to the cell again we went, on the double, and the doors slammed shut. None of those doors were ever just closed, they were forcibly slammed, the ringing sound of the metal on metal echoed through the brig. This was sit-down time so I sat where I could see out somewhat. The kid across the way stretched out on the floor, but the other poor guy was still flat on the floor, where he had stayed all the while we were out attending to our business.

After a while a large, burly, Warrant Officer, with a face right out of a Hollywood San Quentin movie, and the wearer of that phiz would never play a hero, walked along looking into each cell. He stopped across the way, whistled at the guard stationed at the end of the row, and then, with another guard to help, the two of them dragged this man out of his cell and down the hallway out of my sight, never to be seen by me again. My buddy across the way whispered, when it was safe to do so, that the Warrant Officer was the Warden of the Brig, and that he was a mean so-and-so. I believed him.

The next day was a long one, especially after a night that had no dark, as the lights stayed on all night. Standing at that door all morning was bad enough, but the afternoon seemed as if it'd never end. The monotony was broken from time to time by one of the guards tippy-toing along the passageway in an attempt to catch one of the prisoners sitting down. One sneaky so-and-so clanged his club on my door when he caught me leaning on my nose on the door. These were United States Marines, and the prisoners were mostly from the United States Navy, with a few Marines mixed in. Some were in the Brig waiting for transportation to a Stateside prison for some serious crime; some were doing thirty-day sentences; but most were short-timers like me. This place was not a prison, it was a holding establishment only, and was not set up for long-term "guests". These guards went out of their way to be sadistic and mean, and that Warden had to be aware of what was going on in his Brig. No wonder sailors don't like Marines.

I had just been returned to my cell on the third day after the morning run to the head when a guard unlocked my door and marched me out through that inspection room. Thrusting my basket of clothes at me, he said to get dressed as "they" were out there to get me. It was the third calendar day of my incarceration, I had been in that Brig for one evening, one full day, and part of one morning. It was good to see Chief Bosn's Mate Hudson, for once. He had to sign out for me, but this time he wasn't wearing a side-arm, so I wasn't a prisoner anymore. He said that he came to get me early in the day as I was needed aboard ship as my absence had left a gap in the right arm petty officer's Watch List. It was about 1030 when we came down a different pier to the ship, as it had been moved while I was "in." There were about a dozen men at the gangway when I walked aboard and saluted the colors, and reported to the OD for duty. My shipmates let out a yell, a warm greeting that made me feel good, but another pleasant surprise awaited me.

Stormy, the cook, had made me a huge sandwich for lunch, and it reposed on a steel serving platter on the chopping block outside the galley: a whole loaf of bread sliced in half lengthwise with two complete bone-in pork chops on the bread, and a mug of fresh, hot, delicious, coffee. There was no sign in or other procedure, I was back aboard and on duty. Years later, after I had been out of the Navy for many years, I got a copy of my service record, and found that I had been charged with, and found guilty of "disobedience of an officer's orders." A charge, that if it had been made during action, could have gotten me hung! Snatching that piece of celery out of my mouth from behind was an order? It seems that The Honorable Captain had named a charge that would look more logical to have sent a petty officer to the brig for.

From that day on Captain Mush-Mouth and I kept a wary eye on each other.

I enjoyed a small measure of revenge of sorts some months later. Captain No-name (thankfully) had been transferred back to the States for another command, USS RALPH TALBOT (DD 390). CHEW had a new skipper, LtCdr. Alan Grant, who was an entirely different type of officer from his immediate predecessor, to the immediate improvement in the morale of the crew. Not too long after his arrival I made First Class Petty Officer. Grant and his Executive Officer, Joe Mannion, *led* the men instead of trying to "catch" someone and "make an example" out of him. Grant and Mannion were excellent examples of what a captain and exec should be.

The ship came into port one morning and the quick scuttlebutt was that the RALPH TALBOT had just arrived from Mare Island and that Mush-Mouth had a serious problem with his new crew. It seemed that his infamous brand of discipline had resulted in quite a few desertions there in California, and the ship had sailed short-handed. To top off his crew problems, they had ran through a bad storm and that three of his senior petty officers had been injured and were now in the

Hospital in Pearl. That afternoon I was up on the flying bridge working when the word came up that Mush-Mouth was back aboard and was in the wardroom at that very minute talking to Captain Grant. There was no loud speaker system on CHEW, but as soon as that man came aboard we all knew it. The air seemed to change with his presence. I'd hardly had time to digest this bit of news when one of the yeomen came up to tell me that the Skipper wanted to see me right away. The yeoman confided to me that he had already called for Sam Curtin, a soft-voiced Georgia boy who was a First Class Electrician's Mate, and another First Class PO from the Black Gang.

When the three of us were assembled in the Office, we were summoned at once to see the Captain in his cabin. To get to the captain's cabin we had to walk through the wardroom, which took up the entire thirty-foot width of the ship, and past the mess table to the starboard side to get to the door to the Captain's cabin. Seated on the far side of the table, facing the three of us as we filed by, was Old Mush-Mouth himself, sipping a cup of coffee. He said nothing to us, just watched as we went by. We said nothing as mere enlisted men did not speak first to commanding officers, and we were not required to salute in a compartment. We were uncovered, of course, being in the wardroom.

We entered the tiny cabin, and stood in a row facing Captain Grant, who was seated at his built-in desk. He came right to the point of his summons to us: "Captain Dash Dash has requested that I transfer you three men to his ship, which is now on its way to the Western Pacific. He promises you action against the Japs." He assured us that this was entirely voluntary on our part as there was a certain amount of paper work involved in getting three Petty Officers from DESDIV 80 in COM 14 to a DESDIV in an entirely separate command but it could be done without too much trouble if we initiated the request for transfer. I was the spokesman as usual for the three of us, and my reply took only a minute. I started off by saying that I would not repeat what others had said about that man's lack of competence, and before I could get warmed up to my subject, the Captain interrupted me with "That's enough. Dismissed." He could undoubtedly visualize what was coming and he wanted to avoid a possible embarrassing situation. We filed back out through the wardroom with one of our group muttering something about "not even with a Marine holding a bayonet to my back" past a red-faced Lieutenant Commander looking deeply into that coffee cup. The three of us went back to whatever it was we had been doing, but I didn't let my breath out until I was sure that our visitor had left. The Gangway Watch told me that when he came up from the Wardroom he was really making tracks and had his cap jammed down over his nose.

If we had a different type of commanding officer, we might have received orders transferring us to RALPH TALBOT, and our refusal might have put us in that Brig on a serious charge. It was also fortunate for us that RALPH TALBOT had to get out of there fast, and that Mush Mouth had to take what he could get from the transients at the Receiving Station to fill out his crew.

It wasn't too many more months later when Captain Grant did get orders to transfer me back to the Naval Gun Factory In Washington, D.C., for an advanced school. I had spent 42 months overseas.

"A ship is always referred to as "she" because it costs so much to keep one in paint and powder."

Chester W. Nimitz,
in a speech to the "Society of
Sponsors of the United States
Navy," February 13, 1940.

Chapter XVI

Back to the States

By July 1944 the duty on CHEW had become a steady diet of training trips for COMSUBPAC, and most of the old crew had been transferred away to new construction or to different ships. All of the Fleet Reserves were long gone, and so were most of the original Reserves. Replacements were new men who were, in the main, raw recruits. This was dull, boring, duty. Right after the Fourth of July, I received orders to leave CHEW to attend the Advanced Fire Control School at the Naval Gun Factory in Washington, D.C. starting in early September. This was the Navy's top school for Firecontrolmen and was a real plum.

But before I was able to get away from CHEW and head for the States something unexpected came up that could have thrown my rating and therefore my orders out the window, or in this case, over the side. That morning I was walking on air getting ready to leave. I went below to the forward Guinea Pullman for lunch and took my regular seat at the mess table. Seated across from me was Charlie, a First Class Gunner's Mate, who had come aboard from one of the new battleships and had not liked his assignment to CHEW. He was a large man, with a constant scowl, and continually compared this duty disparagingly to his previous duty, and in particular to the fact that he had to put up with Reserves. He was a loner without any buddies, but with his surly disposition, that was not surprising. This day he was picking on George Hoffmann with a litany of complaints. George was a mild man and was not responding to his heckler. Heckling was commonplace but it was usually in fun, but not this batch of guff that Charlie was heaping on George, it was mean and nasty in the extreme.

The steady stream of abuse got on my nerves, so I asked him to lay off George and let us eat in peace. That gave him an excuse to make me his new target and he proceeded to get nastier as he warmed to his task. He finally told me not to get smart or he'd take me out on the dock and whip my butt. I ignored this, as I had just a few hours left on the ship, but he got worse and worse, and liked the sound of telling me how he'd take care of me. Finally, with the realization that I was doing something stupid, I said that he'd gone too far, and that I would meet him at the end of the dock and we would find out why the rabbits ate the cabbage. By engaging in a fight, I was risking my trip to the States, and I knew it. Plus, this man was about thirty pounds heavier than me, heavily muscled, and had a bad disposition.

He had been given a wide berth, up to now. I asked the others at the mess table not to go out and crowd around the fight and so draw attention to it. Except for Bud Harnett, an ex-pro football player, who acted as an observer.

I went on ahead of Charlie and picked a place off the dock in the shade of a tree where there was a soft, sandy, area, and maneuvered it so that I stayed on the hard ground while Charlie was in the heavy going. We squared off, and I took Uncle Billy Jackel's advice to heart - when in a street fight use your jab. I made the heartening discovery that this big guy just did not know how to fight. He threw some real round houses that raised a wind, and started some uppercuts, one of which landed on my hip, but nothing else landed. After a few minutes of hitting my fist with his face, he decided that there was no profit in this and dropped his hands and quit. He went back to the wash room to care for his split lip, bloody nose, and lumps. I didn't even raise a sweat and had only used one hand. My sole casualty was a set of skinned knuckles. We had just cleared the area when one of the Division officers showed up in a jeep and hopped out to walk down the pier to the ship and went aboard. Lady Luck smiled on me that day. Hoffmann later told me that Charlie was very quiet from that time on, even past the time when his face had healed.

Captain Grant arranged for me to leave the ship at once and take leave enroute, a typical generous gesture by that man. This gave me half of July, all of August, and a week in September to get from Pearl Harbor to Washington, DC, seven or eight weeks altogether, depending on how long I took traveling. I had not had any leave since going aboard ship and this was his repayment to me for that time. As a First Class Petty Officer I had the option of arranging my own transportation, and I took full advantage of the opportunity . I packed all of my gear, except for a ditty bag of personal needs for the trip, in a large wooden chest, and shipped it on ahead by Railway Express to my parents home in St. Louis. Everything shipped or mailed from Hawaii had to be passed by the Naval Censor, so I packed the chest, locked it with a USN padlock, made out a shipping label, and took the label to the Ensign that had the censor duty that day and asked him to censor the tag, which he did by stamping the Passed By Naval Censor stamp on it. He didn't see that the tag was going on a big chest, so away it went. If I had known it was going to be so easy to get it by the censor, I could have put some real goodies in it. That chest, by the way, got home to St. Louis before I did.

I left the old CHEW with hardly a backward glance, happy to be away from her and the boring duty that had become her lot. During those three and a half years that I had been a part of that ship we had sailed thousands of miles and had escorted hundreds of ships in and out of many ports, without the loss of, or damage to, any of our charges. A conservative estimate of 60 percent of time spent at sea versus time standing still in port (it was more like 75 percent at sea.) at various speeds the ship would have steamed well in excess of three hundred thousand miles, or, ten times around the world. In those years the main battery of four 4" guns had not been fired once at an enemy; the torpedo tubes had been silent also; the two 50 caliber machine guns had been fired only on December 7, 1941, and the four 20MM anti-aircraft guns had never been fired except at target practice. The three inch AA gun had been fired only that one morning. However, the depth charge racks on the stern had been used often, as were the depth charge K guns to lob the depth charges out in a wide pattern. I have no count of depth charges dropped other than partial records from the Roberts Commission Hearings, Volume XXIV, that record 66 charges dropped between December 15 and 28, 1941. (This is not a complete count but just what appeared in the records of the Hearing) My guess is that CHEW dropped well over a hundred charges in the first month of the war alone. An excerpt from that record is "CHEW was attacked by a second submarine while she was attacking one west of the Island." More than once we had seen torpedo wakes meant for us.

Japanese submarines were active in and around the Hawaiian Islands. A Matson freighter, SS MANINI, had been torpedoed and sunk December 17th off Hawaii. Twelve survivors of that sinking were picked up by ALLEN after spending a week at sea and returned to Honolulu with one man of the twelve dead and another insane.

Another sub had shelled Hilo from outside that port's breakwater and done little damage, but it was enough to get an emergency call for CHEW to come to the rescue, but the sub was long gone when we arrived. Another had shelled a refinery near Long Beach, California. Several other merchant vessels,including the SS Barbara Olson had been sunk between Hawaii and the Mainland. My opinion is that we were fortunate that the enemy subs were Japanese and not German U-Boats with aggressive skippers. If that had been the case things would have been different.

CHEW was lucky in that few of the crew died during the long conflict. Two men, Matt Agola killed and Clarence Wise missing and presumed killed in the first hour of the conflict, and Harvey Schlessinger, Clarence Bueltmann, and Cyril Nennig, who went down with other ships after being transferred away to new construction, were the only losses. None died from any other cause, such as accidents, which claim many sailors lives. Life at sea is not always a cruise.

DESDIV 80 was assigned to COM 14 to protect the Pearl Harbor Base from submarines. That was the original purpose and that goal was met. Duty to escort merchant shipping was an extra that was handled expertly and with dispatch. CHEW and the other three destroyers in DESDIV 80 were not technically advanced enough to perform with the high-speed task forces of the Navy and were relegated to duty that it could perform. The occasional plane guard duty with aircraft carriers was very hard on the old girl for her to keep up and change screening positions with a fast carrier. CHEW operated with USS COPAHEE (CVE 12), USS BOGUE (CVE 9), USS BARNES (CVE 20), among others. A memorable carrier operation was with the British HMS ILLUSTRIOUS when that ship was trying out American-built Corsair planes. We had to fish some of the pilots out of the water after landing accidents.

CHEW, and DESDIV 80, was called on to provide anti-submarine protection to the Hawaiian Sea Frontier. It had done its duty, and more.

I made my goodbyes and left for the Receiving Station to pick up transportation to the West Coast. The Receiving Station was a madhouse, jam-packed with people going in every direction at once. No one was apparently in charge when I walked in that afternoon. A good term for it was "organized confusion." A yeoman at the desk merely glanced at my orders, just to see that I really belonged there, told me to pick out an empty cot in one of the many tents out on the baseball diamond and to sit tight until my name appeared on a sailing list on the bulletin board. When I asked how long I could expect to hang around there, his non-committal answer, with a shrug, was "a week or so." These people in their cushy shore-side office jobs did not have much interest in getting me back to what was still the U S of A. This was far from satisfactory to me, as I wanted to take full advantage of making my own transportation arrangements and spend as much time as I could in good old St. Louie putting my feet under my Mother's table.

I went out to the tent city to reconnoiter and found a tent with an empty cot. Three other men were lying there dozing, waiting for chow call. These three were traveling under orders and had been there for more than a week each. They were just marking time, taking a look at the sailing list, and then loafing around until the next list was posted.

They were in no hurry, and didn't seem to mind. I could see me wasting days, even weeks, in that dusty place waiting for a troop transport, tearing my hair out, so I hustled back to the Administration Building to see if I could expedite matters. One wag in the office suggested that I see the chaplain and fill out a chit, and I imagine that my withering look in reply to that sally stopped any further attempts at humor on his part. Captain Grant had marked my orders on the top of the first page, above the printed form, "42 months overseas without leave," and I started to flash that around the office hoping to arouse some interest.

All that anyone seemed to know around there was that a transport was due in "soon" and that if it was turned around for the States it would carry about a thousand passengers. Finally, I hit pay dirt. A sympathetic yeoman said that the escort carrier USS LONG ISLAND was in the Navy Yard getting ready to sail to San Francisco in the morning with a load of planes to be repaired. It had already taken a group of passengers, and was supposedly full, but I might as well try to see if any of the assigned passengers had dropped out. The Receiving Station had fulfilled its obligation to the ship and they had nothing to do with any more passengers for it. I hiked over there at Flank Speed and went aboard. As luck would have it, a First Class Firecontrolman had the Gangway Watch, the OD was below having his dinner, and my name was added to the passenger list in a matter of seconds. I had to be aboard early the next morning as she was to cast off at 0800, July 8, 1944, for Alameda Naval Air Station in sunny California.

I took no chances. Up at daybreak, shaved, I took off for the ship and had breakfast aboard with the ship's company. I spent the five days in transit in the LONG ISLAND's armory/firecontrol shop drinking coffee and swapping lies with the ordnance gang, who had little to do on that ship, and a new set of sea stories was welcomed. That First Class was a good egg, and he warned me that the Master-at-Arms gang on that ship had its' own way of welcoming travelers back to the States. LONG ISLAND had a crap game in the passenger's compartment, and it's bunch of "jimmie legs" had a system wherein they raided the crap game on the last night at sea just before entering port, and then the next morning during the hustle and bustle of getting ready to moor, they would turn in the confiscated money to the Executive Officer to turn it over to Navy Relief. Only this bunch would skim the pot first! None of the passengers would complain, as they were primarily interested in getting off the ship and on their way, and, besides, gambling was illegal, and there was the possibility of being held for some kind of a hearing and delay. Sure enough, on that last night at sea, from up in my top bunk, at about fifteen minutes before "lights out", I watched the MA gang as it swooped down on the crap game and scooped up a large bundle of cash. Entrepreneurs all over the Navy.

LONG ISLAND took five days to get to the Golden Gate, that sight of unrivaled beauty to my eyes, and tied up alongside a dock at the Alameda Naval Air Station. There were fewer than a hundred passengers mustered on the flight deck as she tied up, and there on the dock was a big Navy band playing away in our honor and as a welcome to us! Superb, and most heart-warming.

As the band played we were loaded on an open barge, a Yard Tug was brought alongside, tied on, and we slowly moved out of the Air Station and across the Bay to Treasure Island, which held the Receiving Station for San Francisco. Even though I was traveling on my own, I still had to check in with any station that I passed through, with the only deadline set for Washington, D.C., in September. It was a warm day, and the view from that open barge was outstanding. The City by the Golden Gate never looked better. Traveling alone meant that I was to be processed before the ones traveling as a draft or a group. A young jg read Grant's note on my orders and whistled "Wow, this is your first leave since '40. We can get you out of here the first thing in the morning. Just go over to the Transient Barracks, or have chow first, see me in the morning, I'll stamp your orders, and you'll be off." Nice enough young man, and when I asked "Where's chow?" he pointed out the window at a line of men about six abreast and stretching away out of sight, "That's the chow line." I asked, "How many do you feed here" and when he answered "Ooh, about twenty-five thousand each meal." I pushed my orders back at him without a word. Without a word, he stamped them and wished me well as I lit out, ditty bag in hand, for the cab stand and San Francisco. In thirty minutes I was seated in a booth at 886 Broadway, sipping an Old Overholt, while I read the menu prior to ordering one of the steaks that ex-speakeasy was famous for. [1]

I spent that night with some friends that I had made on one of CHEW's convoy stops. The next day I made a phone call to get a ticket on the first eastbound commercial flight to St. Louis. The ticket clerk assured me that I really didn't need to take the time to go to the Ferry Building first and get one of those "priority numbers" as this was a night flight and I'd get right through. Going to the Ferry Building would have been a bit of a bother, so I took the easy way. The skipping of this step and the lack of that number made for an interesting trip. The flight left at dusk for the first stop at Los

138

Angeles. Just as we were in our approach to land, I was admiring the lights, the stewardess tapped me on the shoulder with the news that I was being "bumped" there, and I'd have to catch a later flight. Some civilian had a number, and wanted my seat. That meant waiting all night for United's next flight, or to try another airline for an empty seat. That wasn't too much of a problem. In a couple of hours I was airborne again, headed for Phoenix, the next stop, on TWA.

The plane was bouncing along to Arizona with me trying to catch a few winks when this second stewardess awakened me with the same sad story, I was being bumped again! I spent all morning in that airport trying to catch a flight without any luck at all. There was a Naval Air group at that airport that had a torpedo plane to be ferried back East and I could ride in the back seat, if I wished. I hitched a ride to the far side of the field to their hangar, only to find that the ferry pilot had chosen to fly a fighter plane, without a back seat, instead. Leaving his disgruntled passenger behind. That afternoon I did get on an American Airlines flight to St. Louis by way of Dallas, with intermediate stops at El Paso, Big Spring (Texas), Fort Worth, Dallas, Oklahoma City, and then finally St. Louis.

The stop at Big Spring was interesting. The plane, a DC-3, sat on the runway after an extremely rough session with a thunderstorm East of El Paso. All the passengers left the plane to stand in the shade of the wing, to get out of that non-airconditioned oven of a fuselage. This time as we were making the approach to Amon Carter Field at Fort Worth I had another visit from a stewardess. I was going to be bumped again at Dallas. That did it! "The Hell I am!" I stomped off that crate right there in Fort Worth and telephoned my Aunt Al to tell her that she had a drop-in visitor. Uncle Bill Pond picked me up in a matter of minutes and I was in his bathtub getting rid of the dust I had accumulated in getting from San Francisco to Fort Worth. In honor of his surprise guest, Uncle Bill took time off from his job as Yardmaster for the Fort Worth railroad yard of the St. Louis and San Francisco Railroad Company. The Frisco did not run to San Francisco, but was an important artery between St. Louis and Texas. Uncle Bill asked me to do the driving and we drove down to Stephenville to see his parents, my grandparents, who lived on a farm outside of that town.

We enjoyed a joyful reunion. During the couple of days I spent with them Granddad insisted on taking me in to town to see some of his cronies who hung out in the hardware store facing the Courthouse on the Square. He introduced me as his grandson, who had been off "fightin' the Japs, tooth and nail." Some of his cronies had done some of that kind of fighting, only their foes had been Comanches. After we returned to Fort Worth I had to visit some girl cousins from Wichita Falls who had come to the big city to work in the war effort and were living in a women's residence club. This was a dreadful chore as that club was full of comely lasses, including some Delta Airline stewardesses, some of whom insisted that we sit for a spell on the veranda and chat on this or that. It seemed that sun-tanned sailors were a rarity in those parts and it was my duty to let them see one first hand.

After a couple of days of this family visit I got over to Carswell AFB and hitched a ride to Olathe Naval Air Station in Kansas. That ride was worth the fare - nothing. The plane was a C-54 in paratroop configuration: two planks running along the sides as seats, and the little plastic windows had small rounds holes in the middle for the troopers to fire out of at the attacking fighter planes. These whistling little holes were also the air conditioning system. No toilet, not even insulation on the aluminum skin, but it did fly. This plane was used as a pick up and delivery truck all over the country out of Olathe. On this particular trip it was bringing some electronic equipment to Olathe, and it was also hauling a few passengers, mostly Navy people going back to Olathe, with a few other hitch hikers like me. It had a crew of three: pilot; co-pilot; and a crew man in dungarees.

The crewman closed the door at Carswell, and while the plane was taxiing to the runway to take-off he spread out some mail bags aft and promptly went to sleep. At least he kept his eyes closed. He had more or less tied down some large boxes of freight in the center of the deck, and when the plane bucked in flight, as it did constantly, you could see air under those boxes. The passengers, sitting facing this menace, had to keep their toes back and stay alert. Airedales don't seem to know anything about knots and tying anything down. I didn't mind so much, but the Miss Prim Wave Lieutenant seated opposite me sure seemed to mind. She had a problem keeping her seersucker skirt tucked modestly while holding on to the seat and keeping her toes clear of the bouncing boxes with that sailor over there grinning at her. She got off at Norman, Oklahoma, ending the impromptu peep show.

Olathe Naval Air Station was not located in a metropolis of any kind. The little town had daily bus service to Kansas City, Kansas and Missouri, but it had left for its trip that day. I was offered an overnight bunk in the barracks, but there was a Navy bus that had an incoming draft to pick up at the Kansas City, Missouri, railroad station, that afternoon, and I could ride in to KC in that bus if I wished. If I wished!

I almost kissed that driver but I doubt if he would have appreciated it. That bus arrived at the station in plenty of time for me to buy a ticket and board the Wabash Flyer. I had dinner in the diner, and slept in a Pullman to St. Louis, finally making it home on July 28, 1944, twenty days after leaving Pearl Harbor. I had traveled on an aircraft carrier; a barge; three different airlines; a Navy freight plane; a bus; and a Pullman; and I had a fun week in Texas. I still had about six weeks to get to Washington, D.C., a nineteen-hour run on the B & O's crack Capitol Limited. Home!

I had barely got used to sleeping in my own bed, eating Mom's cooking, and checking up on what had happened in North St. Louis while I was away, when I received a telegram from the Captain of the Navy Yard in DC notifying me that I had to report in by the middle of August. Some spoil-sport in BuPers had decided that no one, there was a war going on, you know, could have more than thirty days leave, and so Captain Grant's good effort went for naught! My nice long delay en route had been slashed to thirty days. (In 1946 I received a large check from the Navy to pay for my unused leave, so I got the money at a time when I really needed it). The rest of my leave was spent loafing around the house and eating, as most of my friends were gone to the Services too.

The civilians like my parents had to live with the system of coupons for meat, gasoline, and all sorts of things, and I went downtown to the City Hall the first week with my orders to pick up what ration coupons I rated as a citizen for a month in St. Louis. There was an office just set up for such a purpose, and there was a sort of an examining board to make sure that these service men really were deserving of these valuable coupons.

I was wearing civilian clothes with a short-sleeved shirt and loafers. The chief examiner of the three-woman board read my orders without saying a word, all the pages, both sides, showed them to the other two ladies to read with their heads together, while I spread my liberty card and Navy drivers license on the table in front of them. The chief said that she wished that I had worn my white uniform as she "liked whites to show off a tan" and then she stamped my orders with some notation about ration stamps being issued and the date. She started to stuff all sorts of coupons of various colors into the envelope that held my orders. In the meantime all three of them were smiling at me and thanking me for coming downtown for the coupons. They thanked me for being in the Navy. They thanked me again as I left. When my Mother saw all the meat coupons she wondered why those women had miscounted as there was enough points there for a year's meals.

My Dad never did use up the gasoline coupons. I wonder what those ladies would have given me if I had worn my uniform?

It is hard to imagine that my first visit home in three and a half years would turn out to be boring, but it did. Dad worked long hours at the GM plant turning out amphibious trucks. He was tired when he got home, wanting only to wash, eat, read the paper, and go to bed. Having nothing to do gave me the willies. To relieve the boredom we did take in a night baseball game to see the Browns, who won the American League pennant that year, play the Red Sox. The Browns had one-armed Pete Gray in center field, and the team was filled out with an assortment of old-timers and kids, but it was Browns baseball at Sportsman's Park, and Dad and I drank bottles of good old Hyde Park beer during the game. Beer was still served in tall-necked brown bottles in St. Louis.

I was relieved to see my leave end. I was well-rested and eager to get to my assignment at the Naval Gun Factory, and to begin a new chapter in my life.

Footnotes.

1. 886 Broadway was the scene of my wedding dinner three and a half years later.

Chapter XVII

The Naval Gun Factory

I took that civilized method of transportation, the B & O's Capitol Limited, to Washington, D.C., arriving one hot, muggy, evening at Union Station. I took a cab to the Navy Yard and reported to the Annex, over the Anacostia River from the Yard, just before midnight. The man on duty in the Receiving Station office directed me to a small Quonset type building set down in a swale that was used for the sole purpose of housing people who arrived outside of regular office hours. This Annex was a big operation as the Navy had schools there not only for Firecontrolmen, but also for Gun Hydraulics; for Electricians; for Cooks and Bakers; for Divers; and for Musicians. There were a lot of comings and goings around that place at all hours of the day. I was introduced to Washington's August nights right then, muggy, humid, swelteringly hot, and not a trace of a breeze, and a smell from the river, too. As I undressed the quiet in that small, stuffy, poorly ventilated, building was broken by the sounds of slaps and muttered curses. The place was a mosquito heaven. I had stuffed my tropical mosquito net into that big chest when I left CHEW, and it came in handy that night.

I checked in officially the next morning in a big, busy, office where I met my first Waves on duty. I didn't really gape at these females in uniform, but I did look them over closely. Most of the office staff were girls, with just a sprinkling of enlisted men, but most of the officers were men. I found out later that there was a reason why most of the officers had that billet - political clout! The chaplain was Francis B. Sayre, Woodrow Wilson's grandson, and he was not the only scion of a family with pull on duty there. I was given the news, as if I didn't already know it, that my class didn't start for a month, and that I had to hang around there until it started. To keep my hands from being idle, and getting into mischief, I was told to report to a little feathermerchant Third Class for work. He in turn, told me to get into my dungarees, to find a man named Burke, and to help him do whatever he was doing.

I found Burke sitting on the sidewalk at the side entrance to the Administration Building picking blades of grass slowly one by one to trim the edge of the sidewalk! Jim Burke had been doing this job, without question, for two weeks, since he had reported in to attend the same class that I was assigned to. I could not believe my eyes. They had taken away some of my hard-earned leave to put me on a make-work job, and one that didn't make sense to top off this

143

outrage. I was appalled at this blatant waste of manpower. If I had been put to work in one of the shops , or even been sat down in the library to read up on the complicated gear that I was there to learn about, it would have been bad enough, but not this.

Burke had come in from duty on a heavy cruiser in the Atlantic Fleet and had been picking grass with his fingers without a word. I sat down beside him and got the story, and started to pick a few blades as we talked, I quickly had my fill of this nonsense. I got up, went back to the barracks, changed into my whites, picked up my liberty card from an unquestioning Wave in the office, and walked over to Nichols Avenue in Anacostia to the People's Drug Store on the corner. I bought two pairs of cheap grass shears, and sat in the bar on the opposite corner having a few bottles of beer until Burke showed up. From that time on we spent perhaps an hour a day trimming grass, and then after lunch we'd check out to D.C. to see the sights.

Most of my sightseeing time was spent at the old Smithsonian gawking at the oddities on view in "The Nation's Attic." I wonder what ever happened to those grass shears? This business proves the saying: "The Right Way; The Wrong Way; and the Navy Way".

That first month goofing off in Washington was a real vacation for me. Nothing to do but that grounds detail, which was nothing, as our nominal boss, the little Third Class who ran the grounds detail, was afraid of us, and he had more men than he had work for, so he let us alone. We were not yet under the jurisdiction of the school, as our class had not started, and that left us in limbo as transients.

I picked up a bosom buddy, who was my identical twin physically, we were the same size: hat; chest; waist; shoe; but where we differed was in our outlook on life, especially the variety that we found in the U. S. Navy. John C. Mazurkiewicz was also a First Class Firecontrolman who had served in the Asiatic Fleet before going to the light carrier, USS BELLEAU WOOD, on which he had seen action, and from it to the Gun Factory for school. No one was a stranger to Mazurk after the first minute. This ebullient extrovert had a booming bass voice that got louder and louder with each dram of whiskey, but he never got drunk, just more and more sociable. There was little doubt in anyone's mind that he was Russian from his face, square-jawed, Slavic features, with a Cossack mustache to set it all off.

We were assigned to Class 3-2-2-A that met daily five days a week from 1600 to 2400, which left us free all the other hours of the day

144

except for the shift when we pulled Junior Officer of the Day at the Main Office for a one night shift every second week. I heard a rumor that some of the students used their free time to hit the books. This Advanced School was to increase the knowledge of the men from the Fleet who controlled the fire from the guns. Technology was advancing at an astounding rate. I was getting a jump of over fifteen years in knowledge of equipment. Others, the ones from the capital ships, were getting a jump of about ten years. Optics was being replaced by Radar. Gear drives were being replaced by hydraulic drives. We received a course in electrical theory, followed by one in electronic theory, and that followed by practical work on the equipment. The only vacuum tubes that I had seen on CHEW were in the radio shack. Now I was learning about vacuum tubes used in computers instead of the old familiar gear trains. Terms like "grid bias", "selenium rectifier", "amplidyne drive" were on the menu.

The courses were "cram" courses in every sense of the term. Most of the instructors were good and knew their stuff and the pace was rapid. Those students who had problems with math, as an example, got extra help and were required to study during their off hours if they were to keep up with the class. The school operated on the carrot and stick theory that worked out very well. Passing meant going on to a new ship. Fail, or get kicked out, and you went down the river to the Amphibs, the garbage can of the Navy.

After our class let out at midnight, Mazurk and I usually went out to get a bite to eat, quite often to Ted Lewis' place on Capital Hill, or to one of the White Castles for our snack. The District of Columbia had some sort of a silly midnight closing law on Saturday night, and after an experience with some friends Mazurk picked up, we would ride a B & O bar car up to Baltimore, a city with brighter lights, friendlier people, and larger bar glasses. Mazurk ran into an old shipmate who told us of an after hours joint up in Northeast DC, Tex Baker's by name, that was a good place to go after everything else had closed up. We went there once, liked the music and the ambience and the crowd that filled this row house.

It was a hot night the second time we went to Tex's establishment, and we were in whites. The place was not air conditioned, so we went to the back room of the ground-floor walk-out basement and sat around a table quaffing our refreshments and chatting with the other patrons. Then the music, which was live up in the front room of the basement, suddenly stopped, and from where I was sitting I could see blue uniforms headed our way. The joint was being raided! I grabbed Mazurk and we escaped by way of the back window out into a black courtyard, through a gate into the unlit alley at Flank Speed. The only problem in that alley was that it was filled with garbage cans and we fell over them and slid along on the contents of the cans. We hailed three cabs before one would let us in to ride back to the Navy Yard.

Several things happened in Washington that were rare to me. On a night in November great big, wet, snow flakes fell, the first snow I had been in since 1939. On my way to breakfast one morning a B-29 taking off from Bolling AFB flew directly overhead low enough to count the rivets. That impressive monster had not yet gotten to the Pacific when I left.

Phil Hull, one of our classmates, had a sister who was a sergeant at Bolling Air Force Base. She invited Phil to come down to the NCO's Club on Saturday night with some friends, have a few cheap drinks, meet some WAACs, and take a few whirls around the dance floor. The club had a good band. The next Saturday Phil, Mazurk, and I took a cab to Bolling and we had a good time there as we stood out as the only sailors in the crowd. The WAACs were good hostesses and closing time came too early. As we regretfully filed out of the building we found that it had been snowing heavily while we were inside and the wet stuff was falling and piling up in drifts. Luckily, Mazurk and I found a cab right at the gate and left. Phil Hull stayed to visit with his sister, so we left him behind.

We were in good spirits as we ran from the Navy Annex gate to our barracks in the falling snow. All was quiet. As we passed the Administration Building we saw a solitary Marine pacing back and forth on guard duty. No one else was in sight. Mazurk and I were always on the same wave length and this moment was no exception. Mazurk called out in his basso profundo after we had passed the sentry pacing his beat - "Hey Mac, do you have any bullets in that rifle?". The man got to the end of his path nearest to where we were standing and answered "Hell, they didn't even issue me any clips." "WHAP, WHAP," we each let him have it with a big snowball that we had made while his back was turned. Our aim was good, he dropped his rifle in the snow and started to grope for his weapon, all the while blowing on his whistle to summon the corporal of the guard.

We took off around the building and into the barracks. Mazurk was ahead of me as we ran up the stairs, and I saw that we were leaving tell-tale wet tracks on the wooden steps. We stopped at the top and took off our shoes. We skidded on stocking feet into the wing where we bunked, just as we heard the noise of the guard bursting in down below. Our bunks were more than halfway down the row of about

146

fifty double-decked bunks. We just made it into our bunks, still wearing our pea coats, and covered up with the blankets when someone with a flashlight came in the door from the landing and started flashing it around. I couldn't see what was going on but the guard gave up quickly and left. He probably did not relish the thought of waking up a hundred sleeping sailors in their barracks to look for a snowballer.

The next day at school there was a rumor going around that the Marine sentry had been ambushed by an outsider of some kind. I wonder what was so important in the Ad Building to require the protection of an all-night sentry.

Our normal night life schedule meant that we would get back to the barracks any time between 2 and 8 AM, depending on what had went on that night. But, each and every morning at 0630 some dash-dashed bugler would blow Reveille and clear the barracks for the day. This procedure was hard on us, until one day I saw a card on the bulletin board at People's Drug offering a room to rent in a house that was directly in back of the Annex where we had to report in at 1500 each day. We rented that room and moved out of the barracks and away from that bugler to this big, old, rooming house at 1100 W Street, Southeast. (1100 W was replaced by a warehouse in the Fifties).

To get out of a one-mile walk around the six-foot high security fence that surrounded the Annex to get to the gate we made use of a piece of ladder that was left lying behind one of the buildings. We made a stile to hop that fence and cut our walk down to a mere few hundred feet. That was a breach of security of the Base, but no one seemed to touch that piece of ladder but us. It didn't need painting - maybe that's a reason it was untouched.

Our landlady, Dougie, a young mother of two little boy brats, was married to a DC Diamond cab driver who worked odd hours, and to help make ends meet, she rented out two of the upstairs rooms. The family was from the far, far, hills of West Virginia, and were authentic hill billies. She eschewed the wearing of shoes as much as she could and was pleased that she had rented the room this time to a pair of young, single, men as her previous tenants had been a couple who didn't have much to say to her. She enjoyed our conversations, and brought young unmarried female cousins up from "back home" to meet us several times. We steered clear of these lassies after we found out that being unmarried meant that they were teen-agers with one idea - catch a man with a paycheck.

Thanksgiving Day, 1944, was a day to remember. Dougie had invited Mazurk and me to partake of their dinner, which we gladly accepted. Her husband, and Uncle Roy, who slept on a cot down in the basement next to the furnace, were going to go duck hunting on the Eastern Shore of Maryland and bring back a duck or two, or perhaps a goose, but that was going to be the entre'.

Uncle Roy looked the part of a real duck-slayer. His only clothing that I ever saw him wear were hunting pants and lace-to-the-knee boots, topped off with a deer-slayer type hunting cap. He usually had a handle-less tea cup in hand from which he sipped whiskey.

The two men loaded up his cab with enough armament to invade Sicily, and several containers of white lightning, and took off in a pouring rain on their quest. They had planned to return early on Thanksgiving Day in plenty of time for Dougie to bake the fowl.

Mazurk and I had taken someone elses' place on the duty roster so this other pair could go home for Thanksgiving as we had this feast planned locally, and we were on duty all that morning, getting off at noon. We scrambled over that fence all primed for a big meal, only to find that the Nimrods had not yet returned, and while Dougie and a niece were preparing the yams and dressing and other yummies, they had been nipping at Dougie's jug of corn squeezin's.

The two girls were angry at the men for being late. They had most of the food ready, and during the wait had kept at the jug. They were in a drunken, foul, mood, sitting in the parlor grumbling. The girls fell into a sodden sleep just an hour before the hunters drove up, wet, tired, and hung over.

Instead of a pair of ducks, or a goose, the intrepid hunters had bagged some poor farmer's bedraggled rooster. They threw the carcass on the kitchen table. The husband lurched into the downstairs bedroom and fell across the bed fully clothed, muttering "Let's eat." Uncle Roy, however, rose to the occasion and saved the day by cleaning the bird out on the back porch. Mazurk and I were in a quandary. It was mid-afternoon on a miserable, wet day, and a holiday to boot. We were too far away from any restaurant to walk to in order to get a meal. Hell, I'd seen my Mother stuff and bake many a chicken, so without any fuss, I stuffed the carcass, and put it in the oven and baked it. It was well received by those who were still on their feet to eat it, Mazurk, Uncle Roy, the two brats, and me.

There was a railroad switch siding running between the house and the back fence that was not used very often. One Sunday we were off duty partying at Dougie's with a couple of the nieces. The one that I was favoring was indeed a comely lass, tall and well-endowed physically. A troop train lumbered slowly along the track, and stopped. I went out on the porch to look at the train full of GI's hanging out the windows as it moved and stopped and moved and stopped the way troop trains seem to do when on sidings. These men were most likely on their way to a port of embarkation headed for Europe, so to cheer them on their way my lady friend and I, each with a tall glass in one hand, and the other arm around the other person, stood there and waved to them. The roar from that train brought Mazurk and his lady friend out to see what had caused the racket, and they joined in the Bon Voyage act. I don't know why those dog faces seemed to resent two sailors in dress blues with their arms around a girl toasting them, but they made rude gestures and yelled unhappily until their train chugged on out of sight.

On another Sunday afternoon, Mazurk had gone home to Clifton, New Jersey to see his parents. Willie Williams and I had the bright idea that it would be nice to take the street car over to Griffith Stadium and see a professional football game. We were babes in the woods in our knowledge of football in D.C. We arrived at the stadium to find out that it was a sell-out, and the only tickets left were in the hands of scalpers. Willie and I were haggling with one of these characters, when a well-dressed man, who had overheard Willie's high-pitched South Carolina accent, walked up to me, and without any preliminaries handed me two forty-yard line tickets, "Here, boys, enjoy the game" and he left without another word. I've often wondered who that nice guy was who was so generous with a pair of valuable tickets. Many people in those times went out of their way to be nice to men in uniform, and that man did his part, and more.

Sammie Baugh had a good day against Boston, passing, punting, and playing safety.

On a chilly afternoon in late September, 1944, the loudspeaker in the class building blared out to ask for volunteers to march in the upcoming Navy Day parade. Without a taking a breath, the announcement continued, "Class J, Fall in on the ramp." That was our class so we were mustered out in back of the building, formed into two ranks, until Lieutenant Grosvenor arrived to call out "At ease". He told us that we had been selected to represent the school in this first war time Navy Day parade, and that President Roosevelt, as an old Navy man, would be the reviewing officer. And as our CO wanted us to be a good example, he was going to give us some drill out on the parade ground to sharpen our marching skills. For that task he need someone with experience in military drill, and my buddy, Mazurk, with his ready needle, called out "Pond's your man" and Lt. Big Stoop (our pet name for him) called me forward and asked me to recommend another experienced man, so what else could I do but call out "Mazurkiewicz" to even things up with that scamp.

We marched out to the parade ground, me as Left Guide, and Mazurk as Right Guide, and commenced wheeling and marching and countermarching all over the place. The scene was right out of Abbott and Costello. Big Stoop, with an open manual in his hand for constant reference, stood there calling out orders at the top of his squeaky tenor. This drilling went on for a week, an hour at a time, four ranks, wheeling, turning, obliqueing, halt-one-twoing until we were doing a passable imitation of the Coldstream Guards.

Navy Day arrived, a cold, blustery, day with a penetrating wind off the Potomac river. We were ordered to wear our ribbons, no pea coats allowed so to show off the ribbons, and were bussed to the Mall, where we stood for what seemed like hours, shivering and cold. The boots from the Naval Air Station stood behind us, snug in their pea coats. Finally, we swung out behind the full Navy Band and started up Constitution Avenue toward the Lincoln Memorial past thousands of people jammed along the sidewalks cheering. It was good to get moving and to get our blood circulating. My blood had extra impetus to circulate, for as being Left Guide, I was marching in the gutter close to the crowd. Someone in the crowd saw the four rows of beribboned Bluejackets and yelled out "Here comes the Fighting Navy" and then it started.

Women started to kiss me as I passed and when we broke ranks at the end of the parade up at the John Paul Jones monument my left cheek was solid lipstick. There must have been more men on the other side as Mazurk had a lot less of the red stuff smeared on him. Along the way a newsreel cameraman was lying in the gutter to get a different angle shot and I had to step over him.

Two hundred miles North in New York City a young lady saw that newsreel and did not suspect that the high-stepping sailor she saw in the newsreel was soon going to enter her life.

It was nearly dark when we were finally dismissed. At least a couple of lives were saved by the proximity of the Sea Gull Cafe on Pennsylvania Avenue, and its ready supply of The Water of Life. After a couple of doubles of Rye, neat, I started to warm up. Mazurk caught a world-class cold despite taking the same remedies. By the way, FDR was not the reviewing officer, as advertised, of that big parade, it was Admiral William Leahy on the reviewing stand, all bundled up in blankets.

Another cool October morning Frank Amirault, a serious-minded lad of French-Canadian descent from Massachusetts, suggested that we spend the day seeing Congress in action. Why not? We went over to the Capitol. The Senate was in session so we went to get the necessary passes from one of the Massachusetts senators but both were gone. The Junior Senator from Missouri was in his office, however, and Lil' Ol' Harry Truman popped out of his office to sign our passes and to allow as how he was always glad to see "our boys." If I had but known that lightning would strike him the next month I could have chatted some with him to get to know him better. That stroke of good fortune for him was the famous (or infamous) "Check it with Sidney" statement by President Roosevelt.

That statement came when Roosevelt was deciding on a new vice president for his third term. He, and his advisors, were unhappy with then Vice President Henry A. Wallace, and were looking to replace him. One of the advisors suggested Senator Truman, who had gotten good publicity with his investigating committee looking into war profits. Roosevelt was not taking much interest in the suggestions and finally before accepting Senator Truman he tossed off "Check it with Sidney" and let it go at that. Sidney Hillman of the International Ladies Garment Workers union was a power in Democratic Party circles. Hillman had no objections to Truman, so he was selected as FDR's running mate and the rest is history.

Truman's path and mine were to cross again a few years later when as President, he came out to San Francisco to address the UN, and I was on his bodyguard.

Frank and I sat in the Senate Gallery watching our Senate in action. There were, at most, ten men in sight, one sitting at his desk reading the Wall Street Journal, Robert Taft and a couple of others standing in the aisle whispering, only two of them actually carrying on the business of the government: a seated man looking at a standing man making a speech. The speaker, Theodore Bilbo of Mississippi, was standing in front of a large easel with a map of the United States mounted on it, waving a pointer around like Cyrano de Bergerac. In his sonorous Mississippi swamp turkey drawl, he was extolling the virtues of a proposed canal, the Tombigbee Waterway, to eliminate the need for barges from the Gulf of Mexico "to go upstream against the swift Mississippi current." The scene was starting to get to Amirault, who was grumbling, but when Bilbo had difficulty in locating the Mississippi with his pointer it was too much for Frank, and his grumbling got loud enough for a guard to come over to caution us that we "were in the Senate Chambers." That did it, we walked out in a huff. What an exhibition of our government in action. The Tombigbee Waterway did get built after the war and is a prime example of a government boondoggle ladled out of the pork barrel. Billions of taxpayer's dollars spent for a little-used canal.

We left and wandered past the side of the White House on our way when a guard stopped us so that a limousine could come out of that side gate. We stood on the sidewalk next to the driveway within inches of the car as it stopped before entering the traffic, no sirens, no motorcycle escort, just one car. As we stood there a face appeared at the back window on our side. "The President himself" I said and saluted. Frank saluted too, but as the car pulled away he said "That old man wasn't the President, was he?" It had indeed been FDR, and he looked terrible, a sick old man with great dark circles under his eyes. He was dead in about six months. Remembering how he looked that day, when Election Day rolled around, I couldn't vote for that man. It was my opinion that any new president in the White House would change all the heads of the various Services, and so prolong the war and keep me in the Navy for another year at least, but I still couldn't vote for that man Roosevelt.

A bright idea flashed through my mind that I would go to New York City for a week-end and see the sights. For some reason I went alone, leaving on a Saturday morning on the Pennsy to arrive in the afternoon at Pennsylvania Station. Right away, in order to have a place to stay that night, I went in to The Commodore Hotel to register. I had read about The Commodore and it wasn't too good for me, that's what I thought. Behind the Registration desk a dude was taking care of a civilian and when it became my turn to register he turned a cold stare on me as if to say "How did this person get in here?" He asked, coldly, if I had a reservation. I did not, and was quickly informed that without a reservation, I was, well, hardly welcome in his establishment. He sniffed and turned away haughtily, leaving me standing there like a dummy. I spent several hours trying to find a decent hotel in busy war-time New York City without getting to first base, until I got a room, as a last resort, at the YMCA. Hardly a lavish hostelry to come back to after sightseeing, but it was clean, and had to do.

I wandered around, took in a show, and found Times Square to be tawdry and garish and not to my liking at all. So I stopped at a bar to have a night cap on my way back to the Y, disappointed after an unsatisfactory evening. I felt that in New York City, if you stood on a corner with your severed head under your arm, no one would even give you a second glance. Sunday morning I had breakfast in a cafeteria with about a thousand strangers, and strolled to the Empire State Building to spend an hour rubber-necking from the observation platform. It was a cool day and that was an outstanding place from which to look at Manhattan. Back on the street again I looked in some fancy store windows and was just plain bored. I had nothing planned ahead to see or do and the afternoon went slowly.

I had decided to get back on the train to Washington, D.C., and leave New York for some other time, when my stomach told me that I had not had any lunch. If I waited until I could eat on the train I'd be starved, and the Pennsy dining car's meals were not that good anyway. I started to look for a place to have a good meal as my last event in New York City. Shortly I passed in front of a large restaurant with a big window facing the sidewalk. Inside I could see that it had white table cloths and few customers, as it was still early for the dinner crowd. I went in, to find no one at the front door to meet customers but very shortly a young man in shirt sleeves came out of the double swinging door in the back to show me to a table and hand me a menu.

Before I had looked at the menu a mature man in a tux came out of the back and took up a station at the door as if he was just starting his shift. I happened to be looking at him when he turned to look at me, and a startled double-take look came over his face. He smiled and came over to my table quickly, stuck out his hand, welcomed me, and thanked me for coming. We shook hands and he left for a group of black clad elderly waiters standing just outside that double door in a group. I watched as he said something to them, out of which I heard "Max's boy" and most of them smiled at me and waved. I saw that this was a high class place, nicely furnished, and if not Kosher, catered to a Jewish clientele. From 1933 to 1939 I had been employed by Albert Jacob Silver as a photographer, so I was not unfamiliar with that type of establishment, and I knew that the food would be good. Al Silver had been a professional boxer, had saved his money, and bought the photo business. I was sixteen when he hired me. Al and his wife, Tillie, childless, were like a second set of parents to me.

A waiter showed up, smiling a greeting of welcome, and served me a bowl of soup, and suggested that the beef was exceptionally good that day. As he left he passed another one of the waiters, who he stopped and pointed to me, and I heard "Max's boy" again. I had excellent service, my coffee cup was always full, the delicious rolls were wrapped in a napkin, and the butter plate was replenished. When I finished and left, after paying the bill, several of the waiters, and the major domo, came to the window to wave goodbye as I strolled away.

Whoever "Max" was, he obviously was well thought of in that place and these men had confused me with his son. I've often chided myself for not asking about Max, but it was too much fun while it lasted getting all of that attention from a crew of elderly Jewish waiters, who are renowned for being surly. It is a good thing for me that Max was liked. What if it had been otherwise?

I returned to the Gun Factory not at all disappointed with my new York trip after all. Max made it fun.

New Years Day was approaching fast, and Mazurk had a plan for the weekend for us that worked out just fine. His plan was for us to go to New Jersey for a celebration with some of his cousins, of both sexes. We would arrive by train in the afternoon of New Years Eve at his parents in plenty of time to get dressed, shaved and showered. His cousin Boris, a war worker, would pick us up in his car, and pick up the ladies and go on to a supper club for a party. In the arrangements Mazurk had given me a choice of girl cousins, blonde, brunette, or red head. I had no idea of what my blind date looked like, nor did she know anything about me other than I was a friend of John's. Boris drove fast in a cold, foggy, dark night, stopping only for a moment to pick up Mazurk's and my dates, as his wife was sitting in the front seat.

Two women in bulky fur coats piled in and away we went, introductions were made on the fly as Boris went around corners on two wheels some place in industrial New Jersey, until we finally slid to a halt in front of a place boasting a marquee out in front. In we went, and when the girls stopped at the cloak room to take off those big fur coats and hats, three tall, beautiful young women in evening gowns appeared.

Boris' wife, a brunette, was the eldest at about thirty, the other two,

Mazurk's date, a blonde, and mine, a striking red head, were about twenty-five, at the peak of Slavic beauty. We made an impressive entry into a big, dimly lit room, escorted with a flourish by the major domo, who greeted Boris by name, and ushered us to a dance floor side table near, but not too near, to the band, which was playing dance music but with a definite Russian overtone.

The night was a great success. We ate, drank, danced and had a wonderful time. There were very few men in uniform in the crowd so John and I were constantly being greeted and cheered at every turn on the dance floor. At midnight the band leader struck up The Star Spangled Banner, after asking me to sing it. No problem at all, I was mellow, among friends, having a ball, and after I hit the high note at the end we shook hands with all of the band.

We stayed until they turned out the lights and we took the girls home just as dawn was breaking for 1945. It is sad, but I never saw "Tasha" or Boris again after that wonderful night.

The Navy Department, in its infinite wisdom, decided to give an intelligence test to all the students at the Advanced Fire Control School In Washington,D.C. It seemed that the Personnel Officer had received the forms and the instructions to proceed so several hundred of us were assembled in the mess hall one morning shortly before the first of the year to take this test. This was a closely monitored affair, with the tested scattered far apart to eliminate cheating, and with alert proctors pacing the aisles. The rules were given out by a Wave Lieutenant in a nasal voice, a low grade meant immediate transfer to the Amphibs, but nothing was said about good grades. From the tone of this damsel's voice she expected most of us to be gone in a day. The test was handed out, about a dozen two-sided sheets of multiple choice and some "reasoning" type questions, all bound in booklet form, with a cover page for your name, rate, serial number, date of the test to be filled in. The tests had to be kept face down until she said "Go" as time was important in this test too.

"GO." This was, I thought, a simple test, with a little bit of reasoning required, but mostly straight- forward questions with no tricks. After about 45 minutes I finished and took my test up front to Lieutenant (jg) Miranda or Mazenda, or whatever, who was known as "The Boid Man" as he ran the identification classes that used silhouettes to train the people who had never seen an airplane before. Mister Miranda had an almost unintelligible Noo Joisey accent, hence the moniker. "Wajjadoo, give up?" "No, all done." "Come awn, go over it again." "I did." "OK" he said, marking the time on the cover,

"It's yer funeral." I went to the Gyp Joint for a cup of coffee and was soon joined by Mazurk, Willie Williams, Frank Amirault, and some others. We decided that it was a stupid test, another waste of our time, and promptly forgot about it.

COMSUBPAC was having losses, and I felt that I could do something about that. I went to see that Wave Lieutenant Personnel Officer to see if I couldn't be transferred back to the Pacific to see if I could help out. My request was taken, considered, and acted upon in a day. The quick reaction time was amazing. I was given a two-week leave, in which I took the good old Capitol Limited back to St. Louis again, and returned to Washington about the 20th of January, 1945.

My orders were to go to Brooklyn, New York, to the Arma Corporation to take a sixteen week course in the Upkeep and Repair of the Mark III and Mark IV Torpedo Data Computers, and its related equipment.

This was in answer to my request for assignment to COMSUBPAC and back to sea duty? Someone in that office must have decided that I had a screw loose upstairs, I thought, so I asked to see the Personnel Officer again. Done, she was reading my personnel folder as she waved me to a seat. She said that she had requirements for people to take care of the new computers (the new what's?) that were going in the submarines, and after my test results, and my record in the school, I had to be one of them. I asked about my test results and she replied that I had ranked in the top half of the top one percent of the entire Navy, therefore, you are going to Brooklyn tomorrow, dismissed. "Oh yes, good luck."

I wonder how I would have made out at that school if I'd tried harder and not had such a good time off the base. That would have been the place to start the ball rolling to get a commission. Most of the desk-bound commandos at that place were impressed by anyone who'd been to sea on a tin can. Another opportunity missed.

I did not know that the good times were going to get better, a whole lot better, in Brooklyn, but they did.

Chapter XVIII

Brooklyn, the one in New York

I was instructed at the front desk to come back and pick up "the" orders the next morning as they would not be ready until then. The word "the" did not register with me as especially significant. The next morning I was handed a large, fat, envelope addressed to the Officer in Charge, School Detail, Arma Corp., 254 36th Street, Brooklyn, New York, and to report there as soon as we had checked in through the New York Receiving Ship, Pier 82. I was in charge of a draft of men all of whose orders were in that envelope, eight men, including me. There were ten men going to Arma, but two were chief petty officers, married, and they had been given separate traveling orders.

We were hauled by a bus to the Union Station and dumped off. They handed me tickets to catch any old Pennsylvania train running to New York. The Pennsy had trains running about every hour for New York, but I held off from the first one as it was a local and the one after that was an express, making only a few stops, that would get there ahead of the local. I suggested to the others that we wait in the bar and get better acquainted. These men had not been picked as submariners to pick up knowledge about submarine gear, but from their records at the school. What we had here was a bunch of serious, hard-working, intelligent types, only a couple having any amount of sea duty.

It was readily apparent why I had been put in charge of herding the bunch to New York. I was senior to the two CPOs in time and in age. One, Louie Clements, had been on USS HELM at Pearl Harbor. Louie's nickname was "Chicken" from his youthful appearance. The other chief, Bill Reynolds, was a dude, the type that if he was abandoning ship would make sure that he had his comb in his pocket. These two had just served under better execs than had been my lot. Red Strom was the other First Class PO. Herb Miller and Bud Boyle were Second Class POs, and four Third Class, Bill Kapfer, Johnnie Johnson, Hiram Seppi, and Bob Pastor, filled out the ten. These men were the cream of the intelligent types in the school, no goof offs, shirkers, liberty hounds, or boobs in the bunch. These were serious, studious men. I was lucky to be with such a group, but, with my skeptical, irreverent, attitude, I probably did not belong with it.

The time spent in that bar at the Union Station waiting for our train was a real attitude adjustment hour, well spent. We got better acquainted on the train ride up to the Big City, where we had to check in through the infamous Pier 82 Receiving Station. Our pay records were to be kept there as we were under that jurisdiction. We had to go through the required sex check for venereal disease. We boarded a bus, driven by an idiot with a death wish, over the bridge to Brooklyn. We debarked at a drab, four-story, warehouse building on the waterfront out at Bush Terminal. The only thing that made this building different from the others were the national Colors flying from a staff at the door. The driver double-parked, gave us barely enough time to get out, and roared away. Our bags had been checked at Penn Station so we were traveling light.

Arma Corporation was a company that specialized in equipment for the Navy. It had been a minor operation until the development of the Torpedo Data Computer by its engineers working with Navy engineers and scientists. Arma had grown at a tremendous rate as the Navy's need for its products expanded, not only in larger manufacturing space, but also in the different products that it made for the Navy. Torpedo Data Computers were the star items, but it also made navigational gyro compasses, 6" gun drives, Stable Elements for gun control, Dead Reckoning tables, and Gyro Angle setters, as major products. Arma was the sole supplier for the computers and gyro angle setters. Security surrounding these secret products was crucial, with the computers being the item requiring the tightest secrecy. There were six to seven thousand people working at Arma's Bush Terminal facilities, in several buildings, in shifts around the clock.

We were in the early days of the computer age. The Torpedo Data Computer was to be our subject for the next sixteen weeks. After this period of time we would be experts on a computer, just the word alone raised all sorts of questions - what was it, what did it do, and so on. The TDC, as it was known, was an electro-mechanical device that solved the complex trigonometry problem of keeping an enemy target in position, and then solving, instantaneously and continuously, the problem of the angle to set the gyros in the torpedoes to insure a hit on that target. The Mark III was currently in use in the latest submarines in the Fleet, and the Mark IV was developed while we were in class, soon to be installed in all the newest boats. There were mostly minor differences between the III and the IV, except for one major item. This improvement was right on the cutting edge of technology of the times. The one big difference between the III and the IV was in the inputs to the computer. Mark III had inputs from Periscope; Target Bearing Transmitter; and Sonar, while the new wrinkle in the Mark IV was the additional input from Radar. This was being retrofitted to all Fleet submarines. The addition of this new data required that the two-section Mark III have an additional section inserted between its two sections, making it into a three-section instrument. The sections had to be able to be passed through the hatch into the conning tower of a submarine.

We took a freight elevator, the only one, to the top floor. Our class room had been put up in a concrete warehouse. Amenities had been added, such as battleship linoleum on the floor. (required waxing) There was a dressing/locker room entered from the hallway, as we had to wear our dress blues on the street, and dungarees in the plant. This assignment was considered to be one of the "cushiest" of all Navy enlisted assignments. We were on Per Diem, which meant that we had to furnish our own food and lodging for some astronomical sum like $7 per day, in advance, in addition to our regular pay. The best part of the cushyness of this assignment was the thousands of girls, women, females, that worked there. So many that the place was known as "The Arma Matrimonial Agency" and it most certainly was that.

We received a very short welcoming address by the Officer-In-Charge, Paul Comer, Warrant Electrician. His staff consisted of one First Class Firecontrolman as instructor, a Third Class Yeoman as paper shuffler, and a Chief Firecontrolman as Master at Arms (to keep the peace? No, to keep the floor waxed). The MA knew nothing about submarine gear as he had served on the light cruiser USS HELENA and had been beaten up pretty badly in some of the many engagements he had gone through aboard HELENA. Tony Ferrari, the MA, was a native of the Bronx. He spoke pure Bronx, and looked like a tough John Garfield. However, Tony was a pussy cat and one of the nicest persons that I have ever met. A warm, friendly man who had a pugilistic alteration done to his nose, and spoke out of the side of his mouth, Tony was OK. We met again twenty or thirty years later shortly before his death, and we had a joyful reunion.

Comer was a practical man. It was in the late afternoon of 22 January 1945, and we all needed a place to stay that night, so he made the welcoming speech short and sweet - see you tomorrow right here at 0800. We took off for a more likely part of Brooklyn to find lodgings. The married men had their wives already started on the search. The single men were on their own. One of the Third Class PO's had sat next to me during Comer's little speech, and we just gravitated together and decided to find a room. That's how Bill Kapfer and I got started as friends. He was twenty years old, had two years of Gonzaga U. up in Spokane under his belt before he enlisted.

Bill and I bought a copy of the Brooklyn "Eagle" and started going through the want ads looking for an apartment to rent, without much luck. We didn't have a map of the city, and were not at all familiar with Brooklyn. Comer had advised us to look around the Long Island Railroad Station where Atlantic Avenue and Flatbush Avenue intersect, and that's where we were looking. We found a basement apartment close by that was just like the one in the movie "My Sister Eileen." It was fine, until that night when we retired in our twin beds, and some awful subterranean rumble shook us awake. Our bedroom was right over the subway! We stayed there until our one-week paid-in-advance rent was up and then left for a place out on Long Island in St. Albans.

That first basement apartment was just a short walk to the subway station, very easy to take in to the plant in the morning. The walk included a short cut through a vacant lot that had a row of big advertising signboards running through it at an angle. Murder, Inc. was supposed to toss bodies behind that row of signs as its favorite dumping off spot. That piece of information was imparted to us by two city detectives who knocked on our door our first evening. These two gumshoes were not just welcoming us to the neighborhood, they were checking our orders looking for deserters. There was a cash reward for catching a deserter.

One my classmates back at the Gun Factory, Bob Linker, wrote and invited me to his wedding, which was to be held right there in Long Island. He also invited John Mazurkiewicz to come up from DC, which resulted in a reunion at Bob's wedding reception. Bill, Mazurk, and I had a ball at that affair. Linker's Dad threw a real soiree. Bob's older brother Art had been shot down over Germany and was a prisoner of war at one of the infamous Stalag Lufts. Art's fiancee, Mary Lang was there, enjoying the party. Some time during the festivities, when she found out that Bill and I were stationed in Brooklyn, she invited us to come to her parent's house in St. Albans "some time" for a Sunday dinner. Her act of kindness was the start of a beautiful friendship that endures even to this day.

Mary's Dad had fought in the Austrian army against the Italians in the Alps in WWI. Julius Lang was originally from Innsbruck and was a quiet man who enjoyed a chuckle. The Langs lived in an enclave of Austrians there on Long Island . Mrs. Lang could cook, and enjoyed the way that Bill and I tore into her Austrian cuisine. Bill and I made it a point to see the Langs quite often on Sunday. Bill and the Langs were Catholics, and would go off to Mass, leaving me at home with Julius and the Sunday newspaper. Mary used to bring a friend of hers, Mitzi Zehner, over to help her teach the two sailors how to waltz and polka with the music from her records. (After VE Day Art Linker was released and returned to marry Mary.)

In between sumptuous Austrian dinners, we had Saturday night parties at Bud Boyles apartment near 42nd Street in Manhattan. An actor friend of Bud's had a fantastic apartment, and let Bud have it for the time he was in New York. The place would be empty while the actor toured Europe with a USO troupe. These parties had to be on Saturday night because one needed the entire Sunday to recuperate from them. The location of that apartment made for some interesting party attendees as it was in the theater district of Manhattan and the first floor bar was a pool of party goers of the fair sex.

Across the hall from our fourth floor class room was Arma's Test Department, run by a nervous, worrying type, George Frank. George had a bevy of women working for him and he was worried that the proximity to a group of sailors would lead to catastrophe for his staff. There were two class groups in the plant of ten sailors each, making a total of twenty sailors in the whole place. The classes were staggered in their entrance in the 16-week course, so that all twenty did not leave at the same time. The curriculum was split between half day in the class room for ten men with the other ten being scattered around the buildings learning how certain sub-assemblies were made, until the last eight weeks when the men spent all day in the shops.

Arma was a genuine war plant, making weapons, but everything stopped for morning and afternoon coffee breaks, and the whistles starting and ending the employees shifts. There were coffee wagons rolled out at break times with urns of hot, brown liquid, at times called "coffee," rolls, doughnuts, and bagels. At lunch and dinner times the carts had other foods. The Crotty Catering Company operated these wagons, and so one of the names was "Crotty Wagon." Some wag in the Expediting Office tagged them "Upchuck Wagons", but the food really wasn't that bad. These wagon stops were a meeting place for the sailor/students and the employees. Whenever one of the sailors would stop by one of the girl's work benches to say "Hello", or whatever, the men employees would whistle the tune "Hearts and Flowers" to protect the girls from those sailors, (Ho Ho Ho) but chit-chat at the coffee carts did not cause any musical comment.

Conversations sprung up between the female employees and the sailors, despite George Franks scowls and sad face. We got to know sweet Mary Dolan, Sweater Girl Dolores Jensen, serious Frances Kane, vivacious Kitty Flynn, curvaceous Louise Gibson, diminutive Margie Madden, and Miss Edith Lazar, over cups of coffee. When the sailors took over the noon-time shuffleboard games, the girls watched and rooted. One afternoon Kitty Flynn asked Bill Kapfer if he'd like to go bowling with some of the girls, and he could bring along his roommate, if he wished. This was a set-up by Kitty and Mary to get Edith Lazar to meet Bill.

Raven-haired Edith was a "junior engineer" as she had been an 19-year old graduate of Brooklyn College, and despite her obvious educational qualifications she was a sweet, naive, child and Bill was a "catch." Or, at least, Mary and Kitty thought so. The bowling that night was highlighted by a strange sailor on the next alley letting his ball slip and fly backwards into the seats. Otherwise Edith had a problem telling which was Bill and which was Jess - at first. After that night of bowling and pizza that same group often met over coffee and sinkers. Bill liked Edith, but not as much as I did. Edith liked Bill too, but I think she liked me better. Maybe that's why she kicked me in the shins as a response to one of my bon mots, and drew blood. I did take Edith out once, to a movie with a stage show. Woodie Herman and his band, The Thundering Herd, were on stage. The movie came after we had steaks at Dan Whalen's Chop House. Edith had never been inside a place like Whalen's, and she liked it.

Staffing the Arma plant had been a problem from the start as it required many skilled artisans to make its products. As an example, in order to get the many Instrument Makers, an extremely rare trade, that were needed, it was necessary for Arma to train its own by setting up an apprentice system. That program had brought in all sorts of people that Arma made into Instrument Makers from its base of Journeymen Instrument Makers. There were ex-divinity students, handicapped men, and watchmakers. Anyone with manual dexterity, good eyesight, and some skills, were molded into those necessary slots. Two of the Journeymen had been German U-Boat skippers in World War I and still spoke with extreme German accents. My favorite Instrument Maker was an 80-year old Scot, John Downie, whose voice brought visions of the Highlands. I spent two enjoyable weeks at his elbow learning how to put a cam assembly together. A widower, Arma had brought him out of retirement. His legs were badly crippled by arthritis, but that fine man took pride in his work and was a good teacher. "It has to be prrroper, Lad, prrroper" was the way he put it.

I am sure that in the thousands of people working there some were there just for the money, but it certainly was not obvious because the morale and effort was tops. Most of the employees had someone in their family away in one of the services. Many of the women were married to service men and that fact had a positive effect on the way they worked. A large Army-Navy "E" flag flew at the main entrance next to the National Colors. It was awarded for "efficiency in meeting contract goals." Arma's products were dependable.

Six days a week we spent in school at Arma. Up early to catch a Long Island Railroad train from St. Albans in to Brooklyn, there to catch the subway at the Atlantic Avenue Station and out to 36th Street. Breakfast at Fred's Place, a restaurant sited between the subway stop and Arma's front door, then pass by the guards at the door and punch in by 0800. This entire trip, including the walk to the train station, and breakfast took just about an hour. The transportation system impressed me in its speed and efficiency. I had ridden St. Louis' trolley cars, and then busses, to get to my first job downtown, but they were hardly in the same class with the New York system.

Every night Bill and I ate at a different restaurant. We had wide variety of choices, with our favorite being Dan Whelan's Chop House right in Flatbush. It had a big, well-stocked raw bar, and we could wash down our clams on the half shell and steaks with porter. We lived pretty well on a high-cholesterol diet. Steaks were rationed but we had made friends (we were good tippers) with a seasoned waiter at Whalen's and he was always able to "find" a couple for us.

Week-ends usually had a party some place on Saturday night, followed by a restful Sunday, unless we had scrounged an invitation for dinner. That usually meant the Lang's home in St. Albans but I did have a couple of dinners at other homes at times. One I remember was after a tennis game with Jane Hagen, one of Arma's finest, who took me home to meet her family. Her Grandfather was interested in talking baseball with me, which Jane barely tolerated.

Considering the way Kapfer and I ate, and the amount of alcohol that I consumed, I should have put on some weight, but I remained at the same weight that I carried when I left CHEW. I remember buying a case of Old Overholt (Bottled in Bond rye whiskey) at Abraham and Strauss' in Brooklyn and carrying the case openly, unwrapped, on the subway to a party. When the party was over that case, and some other bottles were in the trash bin. I was keeping an eye on, and being an example to, young Bill Kapfer and I never got drunk, just mellow. I think I even sang sometimes. Maybe, very mellow.

Bud Boyle got married while we were in Brooklyn, and the whole class attended the wedding. The party took place someplace "way out" on Long Island, and the trip on the late train back to Brooklyn was a hilarious one, especially when the conductor tried to quiet us down. We weren't a mean crowd, just feeling good, and the few other passengers didn't seem to mind. One of the highlights of that ride was watching the sarcastic, snippy, discourse between the red-haired wife of one of the CPOs and the Aussie wife of the other one. They did not get along, and to us single men, the meowing was funny.

Bill Kapfer tossed a quarter into a beggar's tin cup at one of the subway stations, and was surprised when the man swore at him for taking one of the pencils! Bill was learning about the Big City. We both learned something quickly about manners in the subway system. In our first few trips below ground we would be polite as the cars stopped and let women board ahead of us. This ended quickly. We were almost inundated by the crush of humanity charging on the cars. It was every man for himself at first, but then, being reformers at heart, we would pick out an especially uncouth man, give the signal, and we'd give him a high and low block. It got to be fun, if there was fun to be had in that human stream. The subway in the evening was always jammed. One night we squeezed on to see an open space near a door and pushed our way into that breathing space. Seated there was a man with a very pungent hind quarter of beef on his lap. The riders near him were pushing back hard to keep clear of him, hence the open space.

Brooklyn, and New York City, were interesting places in war time. This was The Big City, no doubt about it. I attended a ballet at Carnegie Hall with the Langs; Radio City Music Hall; and many different night clubs, including an extremely rowdy one in Brooklyn, so rowdy that I made twenty-year old Bill Kapfer stay back in the apartment. The comic acts were not for his ears. The subways were always interesting to a people watcher like me as there were a large variety of homo sapiens on view.

Arma was an interesting place. The school was good, and I learned a great deal about a manufacturing plant outside of the school curriculum that came in handy in civilian life later. The time in Brooklyn was almost, not quite, one big party for me. More than what I learned in The Big City, was who I met there. I left footloose and fancy free to all outward appearances, but I had met someone who stayed in the back of my mind for future reference, when and if things settled down.

Chapter XIX

V E Day, 1945, in Brooklyn

May 7, 1945, was just another work day at Arma Corporation. The plant workers were doing what they were supposed to be doing, the sailor/students were scattered about in the various Bush Terminal buildings picking up bits and pieces of knowledge about the TDC. Just prior to noon a rumor started going around that the Germans had surrendered. The rumor was shouted from bench to bench, and all work stopped. We Navy people were in our working dungarees and one by one we migrated to our locker room to discuss this rumor, and change into our dress blues, when the Yeoman burst into the room with the news that he had 'phoned Pier 82 and that the rumor was true - the Germans had quit! Edith Lazar verified this by 'phoning the New York Times.

Pandemonium reigned on the shop floors, whooping and hollering, tears, kisses, embraces, until the word came over the PA loudspeakers that all work was suspended for the day, and to go home! That advice was superfluous as there was a flood of bodies already going out the door. Mary Dolan and Edith Lazar went to church to give thanks.

Several of the Arma service people that we worked with in the plant invited us to go around the corner with them to a bar and have a drink, and we were swept along with a crowd. I had been in that particular bar once or twice before fending off an attack of dehydration, and it was definitely not my style. It was a dark, gloomy, ill-lit, hangout for retired Merchant Mariners. It had a tiled scupper, with drains, running along the floor in front of the bar for easy morning clean up, with a hose. All it needed to complete the picture was a one-eyed, peg-legged man sitting at a corner table with a parrot on his shoulder.

In my mind, other than the dirty glasses and general dingy atmosphere of this waterfront dive, its outstanding characteristic was the resident tom cat. This large, battle-scarred, feline could usually be found sleeping up on the back bar, but he could be persuaded to go into his act by a customer buying one of the five cent hard-boiled eggs. The bartender would place the egg on the front edge of the bar, then Tom would spring across to the bar, roll the egg off the edge where it would crash down to the tile below and break. Then he would jump down and eat the egg.

On this day there was no room for any cat acts, the place was wall-to-wall people, a solid pack of human flesh, pushing, shoving, slapping backs, shaking hands, everyone in an ebullient, uproariously, good mood. There were perhaps a dozen white hats in the crowd, the rest were Arma people toasting the end of the war in Europe. I never heard the cash register ring that day as the drinks were being passed out overhead from hand to hand. The bartender had shanghaied a couple of his steady customers as assistants and they were pouring drinks as fast as they could. The sound was deafening, laughter, screams, a continuous uproar.

Our bunch had a couple of quick jolts, and re-grouped outside, to plan the evening. We settled on having a private party at someone's apartment. Which we did, although whose place and where we had it has faded into a fog. By having our private little party, we missed out on what went on that night in Times Square.

The newspapers had one or two million people congregating in Times Square for a celebration that was fairly temperate in execution. Nothing to compare with what would happen in San Francisco when the Japs quit! We missed that outburst of good feeling in Times Square to celebrate the end of the war in Europe. The next morning when we reported in for duty, no one spoke above a whisper for fear of shattering a delicate skull. I spent the day hid out by sleeping on a shelf in a remote storeroom.

On the East Coast the war in Europe had been paramount in the public mind. The Pacific War was 'way out there thousands of miles from Brooklyn and New York City. The Japanese Kamikaze attacks were wreaking havoc with the American fleet at this time, but war-time secrecy kept the awful truth of that operation off the front pages so only a few people knew what was really happening in the far Pacific. Hitler was the prime villain and now he was knocked out of the war. It was time for a celebration, and celebrate they did.

Chapter XX

Back to The Navy on the West Coast

Finally, our last school day at Arma arrived. In a brief ceremony Warrant Office Comer handed out Certificates of Satisfactory Performance and bade us farewell. He did mumble something under his breath about his pleasure in seeing the last of me.

Once again, we had to be checked through Pier 82, and that meant going through that madhouse again, only this time we had more paperwork as outgoing than we had as incoming personnel. Our assignment as a group of ten was to be sent to Mare Island Naval Shipyard in Vallejo, California, to put the USS NEREUS (AS 17), a submarine repair ship, in commission. She was scheduled to be commissioned later that year and had not yet been launched.

We clustered at a counter in front of a bored Wave yeoman (yeo-person?) who started to assign us en masse to a group that was waiting there for a troop train to be made up. "Hold it right there." I didn't like the way she was handling our orders. The way she was lining things up meant that we would hang around that squirrel cage until they filled up some cattle cars in a troop train. I was acting as the spokesperson for the group, again, and when I saw that I was not getting anywhere with her I demanded to see her boss, who turned out to be a genuine "full" ensign. ("Full" when applied to an ensign is a derisive term for a brand new officer.) The ensign listened to my request for giving us what the original orders called for, the authorized mileage figure, plus per diem, for the trip, with delay en route, and all of us to be on separate orders. I think what clinched the argument was that Bob Pastor's wife was eight months pregnant and couldn't stand being bounced around on a train all the way to California. The Pastors could take a slow trip in his car, which would be safer for Irene. We got some good support from an old chief who heard the commotion and came up to put his two-bits worth in and ended up helping me in my arguments.

The crew in the office started cranking out chits and orders, and finally, the Paymaster gave each of us our pay and travel allowances in cash. On May 12, 1945, we left Pier 82 to go our separate ways and to meet again at Mare Island. Of course, we had to be checked out by a Corpsman to see what venereal diseases we had picked up in our sojourn in New York City. This inspection was done late in the day by a Corpsman who was on his cot on the opposite side of a screen wire wall from us. We stood in front of him in turn and did the partial disrobing required. We were in a hurry, he was bored or sleepy, and really didn't care. That joke of an inspection didn't take long, and we were off to Grand Central Station to catch our train out of town.

Bill Kapfer and I got tickets on the New York Central's Spirit of St. Louis. We made a two-week layover at my parents' in St. Louis, where he made another lady friend, and helped make deep inroads into her larder. Bill and I did our duty by the home folks by squireing some of the younger female types around to some of the night spots in St. Louis. Tough duty, but some one had to do it.

We took four days more to get to Crockett, California, the train stop for Mare Island, on the Union Pacific's "Challenger". The trip seemed to take forever as the steam train chugged along being side tracked several times each day to let a troop train pass. We sat in our Pullman car playing pinochle with two Navy wives traveling to California. We watched those troop trains pass in both directions, full. It occurred to me that there was a couple of complete armies in those trains.

Mare Island is one of the world's largest naval shipyards. It had built the battleship CALIFORNIA there on the Napa River on the upper arm of San Francisco Bay, San Pablo Bay. It had many large shops; a foundry and machine shop able to handle capital ship propellers; with lathes long enough to machine a battleship's drive shaft. It even had it's own paint factory. David Farragut of "Damn the Torpedoes" fame in The War Between The States had once been the Captain of the Yard. Now it had a large vessel up on the ways, with a launching date set for October, NEREUS, our future home. There were between a thousand and fifteen hundred men in sailor suits stationed on the Yard, but very few of them were sailors, they just wore the suits. They were in a Ship's Repair Unit, the unit to which we were assigned pending commissioning of NEREUS.

Because of our rates, schooling, and future assignment, the ten of us were to report daily to the Navy Yard's Fire Control Shop, which was on the mezzanine floor of the main machine shop. The mezzanine was on one side of the building with access from a balcony that overlooked the jumbo machines on the shop floor. An interesting sight from up there was to see the machine turning a twelve-foot diameter carrier screw to balance it. The bald-headed civilian Civil Service Leadman in the Fire Control shop did not have much use for ten men with technical knowledge far superior to his on the instruments that his shop was supposed to keep in repair, and he went out of his way not to make us feel welcome. That attitude of his gave me a lot of spare time as he had no authority over me and I hardly ever so much as sat down in his shop. I think he appreciated that.

We were billeted in a barracks with others from the SRU, most of whom were men who had seen their draft number coming up, and as they had skills as machinists they were brought into the Navy as petty officers without having had any sea duty. They were "feathermerchants," and were also excellent gripers about how tough things were for them - how they had been making so much an hour as a machinist in Cleveland, or Chicago, or some place, running a turret lathe, and now here they were, doing the same work, only now they were being paid at a measly Second Class Petty Officers rate. Their sad tales of woe did not touch my heart, and as a "right arm" petty officer I was assigned the Master at Arms job, and I made my feelings about gripers obvious from the start. They had it pretty easy at that. Most of them were married and went home every night to see their wives, no one was shooting at them, and there was no military discipline bearing down on them.

Many of these "feathermerchants" also had automobiles for commuting, and as they were under strict gasoline rationing rules, they modified the cars to run on kerosene, distillate, and a combination of fuels. These men were innovative, and some of those Chevy fours and Model A Fords were outstanding examples of good old American ingenuity. Some of the modifications to those cars were fantastic.

Bill Kapfer and I had friends in San Francisco, forty miles to the South, and after a few late-night returns back on the Greyhound bus on old Highway 40,and a few trips as hitch-hikers, we bought a 1932 Dodge sedan and fixed it up, later unloading it on one of the feathermerchants. After selling the Dodge I bought a Model A Ford sedan from one of the yard workers, and I thought that when NEREUS sailed off into the Pacific I'd just push the jalopy off a cliff, but that was not to be.

While life at Mare Island was not exactly idyllic, for me it was mighty close to it. I had to muster with the men at 0800 daily and I had overnight liberty with the only rule to be back in time for muster. I had the liberty cards for the entire barracks in my possession, too. Assignment to the SRU meant that there was an officer in charge, but the NEREUS crew had so little contact with the SRU and any of its officers that I cannot recall the setup at all. NEREUS had an office with some staffing getting ready for the commissioning detail, but all of our paperwork, records, pay, etc., was handled by the SRU office.

After muster it was off to the Fire Control shop to see what was up, and then to take off for something important, like working on my car, or driving over to Vallejo to get a steak and eggs breakfast. Often on these trips I had the company of a First Class Gunner's Mate, not of our fire control group, also waiting for NEREUS, who wanted to stop at his favorite lower Georgia Street hangout. It was a bar and restaurant, but his interest was in the back room where he could place a bet on a horse running anyplace in the Western Hemisphere. I never placed a bet, but that place did make up my mind that steak and eggs for breakfast was the way to go.

The old Ford needed a pair of tires so I scrounged a pair of heavy duty tires mounted on pickup truck wheels from the Motor Pool. They were larger in diameter than the stock tires so it gave the old Tin Lizzie a rakish tilt. It looked as if it was moving even when standing still, which wasn't very often. That big Navy Yard was a prime scrounging area, and as a Blackie-trained man, I picked up a lot of goodies for the cars. I had Navy insurance on the car, Mare Island license plates, and a Navy driver's license, so my car ran all over the Navy Yard.

Having an automobile meant that one needed gasoline ration coupons in order to buy gas. There was a Ration Board office right there in the Navy Yard, and as a man assigned to a ship I didn't "Rate" one gallon of gasoline. However, a sympathetic woman in the office showed me how to work in a visit to my married sister down in Los Gatos on an allowable twice a month trip, and with that I was allowed plenty of ration coupons. I didn't have a sister, married or otherwise, but I did have a sympathetic friend in that office. Having those coupons meant that Bill Kapfer and I could visit friends at a horse ranch near Los Gatos every other week-end.

Ex-shipmate George Hoffmann was now stationed at the Submarine Supply Depot on the Island. He had been advanced to Warrant Payclerk and was assigned to that busy office. With his office came the use of a Navy pickup truck, and one evening he came by the barracks in it and wanted to have a serious talk with me. We drove to the South end of the Island out to the Ammunition Dump, where the only interruption was from an occasional Marine sentry and the flight of a pheasant.

George related that the CO of the Sub Supply Depot was a

commander who, rumor had it, had been given this berth to put him in a place where he couldn't do any damage. Another rumor about him was that he was married to a Hollywood starlet, and he helped the rumor along by leaving each Friday at noon in his Cadillac convertible for Los Angeles, and returning around noon on Monday. He did not pay much attention to business.

The officer who did pay attention to business, above and beyond the call of duty, and ran the place, was a Reserve Lieutenant who had been an automobile salesman in Vallejo. Because of his college degree, he came in the Navy with a commission as a supply officer. This man was one busy person, always on the go, in the office early and late. George was his right hand man. George was a serious man, a worrier, and this night, in his talk with me, he had reason to worry.

Lieutenant X had given him a stack of purchase orders to sign and send out, all identical, to the same machine shop somewhere in the East Bay, all for the same item, for the same amount of money, just under $400 each. The rule at that time for outside purchases was that any order for $400 or more, had to go out for competitive bidding. This was not the first time that this had happened, but George, rightly so, smelled a rat, and wanted to discuss this with someone he knew and trusted. The way this worked out it would seem that *he* was the person playing footsie with this machine shop. So old Sea Lawyer Pond advised him to sign "by direction, G. E. Hoffmann," and stand by.

Not too long after the war had ended and George had returned to St. Louis and I was working in California, I heard a radio news broadcast that had an announcement that the FBI had arrested Lieutenant X and had confined him to his quarters on Mare Island. (Oh, how cruel!) Almost at the same time I received a letter from George telling me that he had come home one night from his work to find an FBI agent waiting for him in his Mother's parlor. This agent had flashed his credentials at his Mother and nearly scared that poor woman to death. The FBI had the reputation in those days as the courageous tough guys who had shot it out with Dillinger and Pretty Boy Floyd and here was one of them right here in her parlor waiting for her son.

George went "downtown" where they took his deposition regarding the actions at the Submarine Supply Office in Mare Island in 1944 and 1945. The case against Lieutenant X was so good that he pleaded guilty and George was not required to testify. What had tipped over the apple cart was an order for a large quantity of ball bearings to be delivered to an address in Vallejo. Some functionary in Washington,

171

DC, had wondered why, at war's end, the Navy would order a large quantity of ball bearings with an odd number. A quick check revealed that these were automotive bearings, and an inquiry was started that resulted in an FBI agent from the San Francisco Field Office going to check on that address in Vallejo to see why the Navy had sent ball bearings there. The address was that of a Studebaker/Packard agency owned by Lieutenant X, who had bought the agency cheap during the war.

But more than just ball bearings had been delivered there on Navy purchase orders. Our Lieutenant had acquired expensive machine tools too, but none of those "big ticket" purchase orders had rung any bells in Washington, DC. I surmise that the reason Lieutenant "X" hung around in the Navy so long after the war was to take that time to cover his tracks, (or to keep on stealing) and he slipped up on those ball bearings.

During that summer I played baseball as a "ringer" with one of the Navy Yard shop teams. The shop team needed a hitter, and I filled in nicely, playing the games after work and before dark in a "twilight" league in Benicia at a nice fenced park. I liked that park, the pitchers were not that good on the opposition teams, the fences were close in, and I hit a few balls into the eucalyptus trees behind the fence. But the league folded quickly with the end of the war in August and that ended my baseball career.

Whenever we could, Bill Kapfer and I would pile into whichever car it was that we or I had at the time, and head for the ranch near Los Gatos. It was a nice drive, the people were friendly, and we always had a horse to ride. The ranch was really a rest camp for the staff of the owner's manufacturing and sales agency in San Francisco, and we made lasting friendships. The owner also kept his string of race horses there with a staff to take care of them. It was a large operation and the addition of two sailors as guests during the ongoing war was considered as the thing to do. "Help our boys" sort of thing.

I made some brownie points with the ranch staff by tossing the 18-year old son of one of the partner's into the horse trough after he bothered me with some triviality or other. The owner's eldest daughter, a 21-year old blonde beauty, who rode like a Centaur, was there quite often to sit around the fire in the evenings. A few years later my civilian boss told me how stupid I had been in not making a "play" for her, as her father was so wealthy and needed a strong son-in-law to take into his businesses, as his only son was a real rich man's son playboy. What my boss didn't know, and I appraised him in very few words, that I couldn't stand that heiress and all the money in the world couldn't get me interested in her. In comparison with that black-topped beauty that I was writing to back in Brooklyn she was a wash-out in every way. Disposition, character, intelligence, conversational ability, she was lacking in every characteristic, except, perhaps, paternal bank account, which meant very little to me at the time.

The moving finger writes; and having writ,

Moves on: nor all your Piety or Wit

Shall lure it back to cancel half a line,

Nor all your tears wash out a line of it.

The Rubiayat of Omar Khayyam.
From the translation by
Edward Fitzgerald, 1809 - 1883.

Chapter XXI

V J Day in San Francisco

One of the men in the class ahead of me at Arma Corporation, was James Clyde "Pat" Humphrey, also a First Class Firecontrolman, and a raconteur of the first grade. Pat was a crew member of the submarine USS GURNARD (SS 254), that was at Mare Island finishing up on a major overhaul getting ready to leave for the Pacific on a war patrol when I arrived at Mare Island. Pat's wife was expecting a child in a couple of months so Pat and I were going to try to work a swap with him going to the NEREUS and me the GURNARD. This was subject to approval of the submarines executive officer. However, this swap idea was killed by the NEREUS Personnel Officer who decreed that I'd never go to sea again on a warship as the Navy had invested too much on my education to risk losing it.

I had some big deal cooking one August day, but first President Truman was going to address the entire military establishment and his speech was going to be broadcast over the Mare Island PA system, so whatever I had planned was postponed until after the speech. Mr. Truman came on to say that the war was over, that the Japanese had surrendered. I had been listening up in the Fire Control Shop. Pandemonium broke out as it had at Arma that day. Suddenly all the machinery in the shop stopped and there was a dead silence for perhaps a minute, broken quickly by shouts and cheering, punctuated by odd crashes. The odd crashes were from the Navy Yard workers throwing their full tool boxes off the mezzanine down to the floor below! They were going berserk.

Bill Kapfer and I got into our whites, jumped into the old Ford, and headed across the causeway for Vallejo and Highway 40 to San Francisco to celebrate. At the gate the Marines were not checking liberty cards or badges out, they just waved all the cars on non-stop. The war was over! I needed gasoline and I pulled into a station in town and when I pulled out my gas ration coupons the attendant just waved them away and filled 'er up for the first time. We took off for The City, and our friends house in the West Portal section.

We had a party, neighbors came over, champagne flowed, we danced to the radio music, and just had fun. Bill and I were the only service men there, of about a dozen merrymakers, and we all were celebrating the end of the War. About 10 PM the man of the house, who was an office manager for one of the companies that had an office building on Lower Market Street, received a 'phone call from Security at his building telling him that there was "trouble" on Market Street and he needed instructions. At that time there was an announcement on the radio for all service people to return to their base "at once". This announcement was repeated again and again, but Bill and I were having too much fun to take it seriously, and we were 'way out of the way in a private home, so we ignored the announcements.

Another call came to our host from his building saying that there was rioting going on all over downtown, that the police were powerless, and that the situation was serious. We took the situation seriously enough that on our return drive to Mare Island the next morning we left a bit early. Instead of taking our regular and shortest route, through San Francisco and over the Bay Bridge, we instead went back over the Golden Gate Bridge and up Highway 101 past Hamilton Field and over the Black Point Cut-off. We entered the Ship Yard by the North Gate and got to the barracks just ahead of the 0800 muster call.

The OD was unhappy and wanted to know where we had been, why hadn't we returned as they had called out the Mare Island Marine Detachment and sent it off to San Francisco to restore order and they mustered all the sailors to use as back-ups, but the Navy had not been used. He accepted my excuse that I had been in a private home and did not hear any announcements.

The San Francisco CHRONICLE put out an extra issue on Wednesday, August 15, 1945, with banner headlines trumpeting the war's end. In that issue was an announcement that "Anchors Aweigh" had opened at the Fox Theater starring Gene Kelly and Kathryn Grayson, with Frank Sinatra. A sports page article told of the St. Louis Browns defeating the Washington Senators in an American League baseball game.

However, in the next days issue the Chronicle, in an article 'way back on page 11, mentioned in a humorous vein that some girl was going to have a real hangover after dancing nude in the fountain that was part of the Native Sons monument at Mason and Market streets. It also mentioned that five were dead, 624 injured, 115 drunk arrests and "inestimable damage" had been done. The reporter had not done any leg work before writing that article.

Finally, in Friday, August 17th's issue the Chronicle did come up with a front page article on the seriousness of the goings on. Now it reported eleven dead, "thousand injured" and that after the first night's riot had been quelled, more gangs appeared to loot and burn for two more days. It called the affair "Peace Riots" and tried to keep the reporting low key.

San Francisco Mayor Roger Lapham called a "barn door" meeting, with the press barred to talk things over. Attending for the Army were three Major Generals; Rear Admiral C. H. Wright for the Navy; the Police Commissioners; the Chief of Police; the Deputy Chief; a pair of Police Captains; The DA; and even Louis Lundborg from the Bank of America representing the Chamber of Commerce to get everyone in on the act. After the two-hour meeting was over the Army officers were said to have smug expressions on their faces as there were few khaki uniforms among the rioters. No word on how Admiral Wright felt, or what he said. There were no "exit interviews." The press was barred, so it stayed away. Mayor Lapham had successfully held publicity down on the rioting. There was little press curiosity shown.

In a Chronicle editorial it was said that "the Navy Top Brass must assume responsibility for their inadequate preparation for a Victory Celebration."

The real cause of the problem was a decision by a fairly low-level officer at the Amphibious Training Center down at San Bruno at the old Tanforan Race Track, to allow unrestricted liberty to the men who were held there to man the amphib ships. These men were the dregs of the Navy and were kept under lock and key until their ship was ready to leave port, and then they were escorted by armed guards to their ship. This mob descended upon San Francisco, short of money and ready to rebel against anything and everything. It swept down Market Street looting, breaking windows, assaulting passing automobiles and street cars, and spilled over into the Tenderloin area to continue the orgy of destruction.

Sixty-six businesses along lower Market Street reported 107 plate glass windows broken out. Public Utilites reported over 300 windows broken out of the street cars. Mail boxes were overturned and the contents burned, and almost every street sign of all types were missing. An oddity of the reports was that the Police had no rapes listed, despite many such events witnessed.

That night of rioting, followed by two more days of trouble, left a scar on the collective memory of San Francisco. Any ceremonies to commemorate the anniversary of the ending of the war were low-key from that day on. In its issue one year later, Wednesday, August 14, 1946, "City Takes Stock One Year After" the Chronicle remembered a "three-day hoodlum carnival" in which (now) twelve died. The day was not a holiday in San Francisco.

This was a sad ending to the long, tough, war in the Pacific and made the Navy look bad in the eyes of the very people that it had been fighting for. The Navy had always kept the Amphib Base conditions under the rug, and when it did slip out - it was ugly.

Chapter XXII

Keeping out of Mischief

The quick end to the war caught the Navy unprepared, although in a different way than it had been fifty-six months earlier. Command set up a point system for enlisted men to determine eligibility for discharge, counting months of service, months overseas, and several other things, such as dependents, marital status. Under this system I had points to spare. Then, because of the many complaints about that first system, it was reevaluated and revised. I still had enough points to get out about three times. Then the men eligible for discharge were made into a "Separatee" division at Mare Island, and of the thousands of men there, only eighty of us were eligible for discharge. September passed with the "Separatees" hanging around, playing softball, with no process being set up to separate us from the service. We were in some sort of limbo and I, for one, was on pins and needles in my eagerness to get out and away from the Navy and get into that lush civilian life, and be my own boss.

During this hiatus we had some odd jobs come along. One morning at quarters the Executive Officer, a Supply Corp regular Navy officer, who was one of the people keeping the Base operating, called me aside with the news that he had an assignment for me. He told me to hop into his jeep to receive my instructions and to size up the job. We chugged out the North Gate, turned West on the Black Point Cut-off Road for about a half-mile to a motel on the North side of that road. Here he turned in, unlocked a heavy chain that was stretched across the entrance road, and drove on back quite a distance from the highway to some buildings. I had driven by this motel many times and had paid no attention to it. The looks were not inviting and I did not have any business at a motel that close to my base. There was always a big "No Vacancy" sign out at the highway entrance. There had never been more than one or two cars visible in it, no matter what time of the day I went by the place.

The Exec parked the jeep in a wide area paved with loose stones, between two identical, flat-roofed one-story buildings with rows of windows and doors. It looked like a motel, but upon closer inspection it came out that these windows and doors were dummies. The whole place was a dummy! There were four large rooms at the four corners forming a square around the rock parking space with dummy walls connecting the rooms. The flat roofs on these corner rooms were on rollers, and by means of ropes and pulleys the each roof could be pulled back over the dummy walls, opening up for one 90MM Army anti-aircraft gun! The four corner gun emplacement/rooms had walls made from heavy redwood timbers holding up earth-filled walls about two feet thick. The place looked like a motel, but it was an anti-aircraft battery placed there to protect the North side of the huge Mare Island Naval Shipyard from aerial attack.

Behind this complex, and not visible from the road, was a barracks and mess hall building where the Army gunners had stayed when on duty, and from its appearance, the soldiers had just left with all their mess gear and had returned.

The location of this gun station was about 25 air miles from the Golden Gate and 36 miles East of Point Reyes out on the coast so it was well-placed to protect the shipyard.

The officer gave me a quick walking tour around the four gun stations and the mess hall/barracks and then it was back to the jeep and back to Mare Island. My orders were succinct - "return this place to being a hay field. It was a hay field when the government got it, and it will be a hayfield when it leaves it." I was told further to take as many men as I needed, and draw what tools we would need. There would be a bulldozer on call, burn the burnables, don't set the hay field on fire, what can't be burned, take to the dump.

The next two weeks were interesting. I drew two big stake trucks, one a brand-spanking new International that I used as my personal limousine and to haul my wrecking crew back and forth; the other was a regular 4 X 8 to haul away the unburnable trash, like the hardly used cast iron oil cook stove that the Army had left behind.

I hand picked a dozen men for this fun job. On the first trip I laid out a plan of attack for them, and turned them loose. The first thing they did was to throw those rocks from the courtyard through all of those windows, to let off steam as a release of anger against whatever. Breaking glass seems to have therapeutic value. Then they attacked the doors with crow bars. We soon had a big bonfire going in the courtyard to guard against setting the surrounding hayfield on fire. Each noon when we broke for lunch, my truck went to the mess hall, with number two stopping off by way of the dump. A similar routine at quitting time. It took from 0800 to 1700 daily for two weeks and the "motel" was gone, replaced by a big bare space. Even the rocks had gone to the dump and I turned the chain and padlock in to the Exec. No one had been hurt. No snake bites, just a fun job. I really hated to let go of that shiny, new International truck. It was fun to drive, sitting 'way up there, and it had a big truck business-like roar and cars scurried out of it's way quickly.

Jimmie Graffigna was on Guam when the war ended, and he wrote to ask me to wait for him so that we could go home to St. Louis together. We were sure that I'd have to wait for him as he was so far away, and I was right there in California so, generously, I said that I would. October 1st came, he was in from Guam, discharged, and waiting for me at our friend's home in San Francisco. On that day the eighty prospective civilians were assembled to leave for Camp Shoemaker, near Pleasanton, for processing for our discharges.

The transportation arranged for us was a fleet of beat up old stake trucks, not even busses, with a young Third Class Yeoman in charge of the detail. I still owned the doughty Model A Ford, and after one look at those trucks, I declined the dubious honor of riding like cattle standing in an open truck, and told that kid that I was taking my own car. He demurred, his orders were to take these men to Shoemaker in those trucks and dump them off. After a very short discussion, which ended right after I cracked my knuckles, he handed over my papers, with the statement that if that car broke down it'd be my problem, not his. If anything happened I would miss out on getting discharged, and he washed his hands of the whole affair.

Two other First Class POs in group who had watched this little scene also took their papers from this little Big Wheel and asked me if they could ride with me. Of course. Then the three of us took off following the trucks for the forty mile drive through the fantastically beautiful San Ramon Valley past Walnut Creek and Danville to Camp Shoemaker. Along the way the last one of the trucks started to boil over and we in the Ford got them some water so they could continue. If we hadn't been following there is no telling how long it would have been delayed. At the gate at Camp Shoemaker there was a young sailor as guard checking papers. "You can't drive that car in here." That prompted me to get out and go in and convince the OD that I could drive into that Navy installation with that car as I had Navy insurance, a Navy driver's license, and a Mare Island permit for the car, which was good for any installation in the 12th Naval District. I was getting close to being a civilian again and I wasn't about to take any guff from any kids in blue, officer or enlisted.

In less than five minutes we were tooling up a dirt road against a stiff breeze to brand new barracks on top of a hill. Gunner's Mate Bill Brock, Torpedoman Tom Lavazolli, and I took a quick look at the place, and decided that we'd use the car for our lockers as it could be locked, and the inside of these barracks was bare of everything but bunks, not even a hook for ones clothes. There was a shower room and a head on each deck, no screens on the wide open windows, nothing but wind and dust and wasps, and there were plenty of each. There was a bored kid seaman in undress blues, with a belt and a billy club, sitting in the shade out in front. This was the Master at Arms for the barracks, who was supposed to provide security for the barracks There was a lot of "supposed to" around there..

The next morning, after chow, we reported to a room in the gate building for a scheduled lecture. The lecture was to be on some subject to help us get ready for civil life, only the text had not arrived yet from Washington, so we were told to sit around until noon, and instead of the lecture, read some antique Life magazines that had been piled on a table. At 1300 after lunch we were supposed to report back again for another lecture on a similar important subject. That lecture was still enroute from Washington, too.

We sat around, bored, until one of the youngsters on the Base's staff (they were all youngsters who did not come close to having enough points for discharge, so they were put on duty to help pay off the veterans) came in with the great news that some horseshoes had just arrived and we could go outside in the one hundred plus heat and make a court and pitch horseshoes! You gotta be kiddin', Brock, Liz and I went back up to the barracks to take an afternoon nap, only to run into a big to-do. During the day, when everyone was down below "attending" one of those very important lectures, someone had gone through all of the bags of the Separatees and had removed everything of value. The lockable Ford did well by us.

So for a couple of long, long days, bored silly, we lay around in our bunks in the stifling heat, and then if we did fall asleep, we'd wake up after dark, cold and sneezing, for as soon as the sun went down the wind would come up and the temperature would plummet. Camp Shoemaker was close to Altamont Pass, the present location of some windmill power experiments, as that is one of the windiest spots in the entire U S of A. (Outside of, perhaps, Washington, D. C.)

After several more days of frustration and continual griping to the officers in the Camp office, the three of us were handed without ceremony three large envelopes with a large eagle printed on the outside, and lettered "HONORABLE DISCHARGE". One of my big disappointments was missing those lectures, that never came in from Washington. I am sure that we would have been better able to face civilian life if we had undergone them. We just had to make do without.

October 6, 1945, was the date, one for which we had been working toward for years. Brock, Liz, and I squeezed into the front seat of the old Ford, the back seat piled up with our sea bags. We roared out that gate headed for San Francisco, discharge money in our pockets, and joy in our hearts. Tom and I dropped off Bill at the Greyhound station on Mission Street in San Francisco for him to catch a bus for his home in Reno, and then the two of us stopped off at Oliver's in South San Francisco for our first steak as civilians. Then I dropped off Tom Liz at his mothers in the Mission District and then on to pick up Jimmie Graffigna and go home to St. Louis. (In 1954 I bought a house in South San Francisco, and moved our family in to our new home in Rancho Buri Buri. Buri Buri roughly translates into 'God, it's cold!'. That night for dinner we walked to the corner delicatessen to pick up some sandwiches to find Tom Lavezolli was the butcher)

Jimmie and I hung out in San Francisco for about a week. In that time we bought civilian clothes, (pants with pockets), sport shirts, jackets, things that we hadn't worn in five years. We stayed over to attend a wedding anniversary party given by our hosts, otherwise we would have left for St. Louis a lot sooner. But this was to be the first post-war party, and an affair worth waiting for, so we stayed on. The reception was held at the Century Club in San Francisco, a nice soiree with a piano player and a singer in one corner, and waitresses passing among the partyers with trays of hors d'oeuvres and silver pitchers of Martinis and Manhattans, depending on whether you liked olives or cherries. A nice party. When the formal part of the celebration broke up the family and a few friends, Jim and me included, re-convened at our hosts home for cold turkey and champagne. Our host had an "in" with the monks at the Alma Monastery down below Los Gatos and had bought a case of the monks' champagne. He had let me buy half of the case, and my six bottles were already packed in the back seat of the Ford ready for our departure for home the first thing in the morning. Our hosts plan was that his six bottles would be plenty for this little family get-to-gether after the big party downtown.

The party was in full swing when our host asked me if he could have one of my bottles as his six were all empty. That was fine with me as I was feeling quite mellow at the time, and five bottles would be plenty for me at home. This champagne, by the way, was fit for the Gods. Unbelievably delicious, a worthy product of a beautiful part of the Coast Range. When Jim and I left the next morning I threw the empty case from the back seat into the trash. My case had melted in the warmth of that party.

I felt pretty good the next morning, after a big breakfast, and we set out. Jim passed on breakfast, and again at lunch, as he wasn't hungry. He sat there, held his head, and didn't even groan until after we had passed Stockton. Our original driving plan was to take a week going home by way of back roads, and really take it easy. I had tuned the old Lizzie, added a jeep can on each running board for oil and water. As a last minute idea before leaving Mare Island, where most of the readying for the trip had taken place, I had scrounged a five gallon gasoline can which I had filled, and tied it between the front fender and the hood. We were well provisioned for the long trek.

Instead of going East over Donner Summit we took a route South of that one over Carson Pass up past Jackson to Lake Tahoe. We had a half tank of gas as we left Jackson, and there were several towns ahead on the map, so we started up the grade. The road had turned into a narrow gravel road and we kept chugging along, but first one, and then another, of those towns on the map turned out to be summer camps that were boarded up for the winter, and no gasoline was to be had. We made it up over the 8,800 foot summit and headed down but up there, at just about dark, we ran out of gas in the tank and stopped to pour from our can into the tank. We got out of the warm car to find out that at that altitude at that time of year it got cold when the sun went down.

That night we stayed in a very deluxe tourist cabin in Myers, California, with a roaring fire in the fireplace. That gasoline stop up on Carson Pass in the cold had brought Jim back in to the land of the living again. His head was now clear and he was back to battery. We kept on chugging along at 35 MPH, as that was as fast as I wanted to rev the old engine, through central Nevada, stopping at Ruth/Ely at a tourist hotel that had a coed bathroom. We had intended to take Route 50 across the Rockies East of Ruth/Ely but that night at dinner in the town's one restaurant, a state trooper advised us against that road as it was passable only by a four-wheel drive vehicle, so we opted for crossing the Bonneville Salt Flats through Utah.

This trip was made before the growth of the motel industry, and accommodations, even along a main road like Highway 40 were catch as catch can. At almost every stop for a meal we got into conversation with other folks. We were just about the first real veteran sailors that had come through and the people had all sorts of questions for us to answer. It made for a more enjoyable and interesting trip.

The sun was still up when we left Vernal, Utah, and bore on ahead through dinosaur country, intending to drive for another hour or so, then find a place and turn in. We drove, and we drove some more, no places to stay until we finally saw a "tourist cabin" sign at Elk Springs, Colorado. It was cold and dark, but after pounding away on the door of the cabin marked "office" we roused an old sourdough who allowed that he had a cabin that he'd rent to us. He came out of his cabin wearing a big sheepskin coat and a fur cap, and carrying a bucket of water. He showed us to a one-room cabin, lighted by a single bulb dangling down in the center of the room. At least it had electricity, but no plumbing or running water. There was a double, wrought iron, bed on one side and a small pot-bellied stove on the other side. The stove had been prepared for a customer, for all that he did was to strike a wooden match on the stove and light the pine knots in it, which started up with a sputtering roar, putting out a welcome glow of heat, and an unwelcome puff of smoke.

The landlord put the water bucket and a pair of skimpy towels on a primitive wash stand. As he turned to leave, after pocketing our dollar rent, Jim asked about drinking water. He pulled a tumbler out of his coat pocket and put it next to the bucket with a flourish. He asked if "that A Model had anti-freeze in it" and as it did not, and never had in its life, at his suggestion, I went outside and drained the radiator.

The next morning we got up early, it was cold in that shack. We saw that the water that I had drained from the car was now a sheet of ice, and hanging from the office portico, unseen by us in the dark when we checked in, were the carcasses of two deer. They didn't need artificial refrigeration, it was natural. That bucket of water in the cabin filled the empty radiator nicely. There was no one anyplace around that we could find for information about breakfast. We did find that the closest restaurant was at Steamboat Springs, almost a hundred miles farther on. That was a tough drive without even a cup of coffee after that cold night. We pulled into Steamboat Springs right behind a Greyhound bus that had stopped in front of an eating place right there on Highway 40. Its passengers took up all the seats and were standing three deep in front of the counter waiting for service. That was bad news for us, we would have starved to death waiting there for food, so we stepped outside and stopped the first passerby and asked about a place to eat. There was one a block down on the side street and we stepped off briskly for it. My California car did not have a heater and we were dressed in Navy foul weather gear and our feet made a crunching sound as we walked on the inch-thick snow packed on the sidewalks. Outside the restaurant door was a large thermometer showing an even Zero.

This local beanery was geared for customers who had just come in off the range from punching dogies in their zero weather. It was crowded, warm, noisy, and full of the smells of frying bacon and hot coffee. It was not a formal place. As a waitress sped past us, loaded down with platters, she yelled at us to "find a seat," which we did without waiting for a second call, at a long table of men stuffing food into their faces. As soon as we got seated she was back with two steaming mugs of hot, black, coffee, and took our order. This was a fixed price eatery: eggs, bacon and ham, One Buck; with steak, two bits extra.

The meal was served family style, with a platter of hot cakes and a bowl of hash browns in the middle of the table for one to help himself. Also in the middle of the table were bowls of butter and sugar, and pitchers of cream and syrup. No one seemed to be loitering over the morning paper with a cup of coffee in that place. The customers just came in, sat down, ate, and paid as they went out the door, toothpick akimbo. The food was just huge quantities of good, plain, wholesome grub. Very welcome indeed after that hundred miles on an empty stomach.

The rest of the trip went smoothly. The car did its duty. Going over Berthoud Pass, higher than eleven thousand feet without getting hot. There were other cars pulled over with boiling problems, but we got in behind a snow plow and walked right over the pass at a steady gait. Our only car problem was that it used almost as much oil as it did gasoline. We had to stop at a Sears store in Manhattan, Kansas, and buy a two gallon can of oil to get us home. In the first week that I was home I sold the car to a soldier from Jefferson Barracks, and he tore out the rear end before he got it back to the barracks. It took us three thousand miles without a hitch, and he killed it in just a few miles.

My career as a sailor was over. The first eight months in St. Louis as a Reserve amounted to nothing, and were a waste of my time. I spent 43 months on that old rust bucket, CHEW, and finished off with 16 more months "Stateside" that were better than good, easy living, no supervision, with fun and games galore. I had made some life-long friendships, learned a lot more than just steam engineering on obsolete machinery and how to solve the fire control problem in launching a torpedo, I had picked up an advanced degree in how people work. The dollar value of the lessons learned at the two Navy schools was spelled out to me in detail when I was working later at the San Francisco Naval Shipyard, by the Navy captain in charge of the mothball fleet there in 1947. I was leading a gang of Navy Yard workmen removing the anti-aircraft computers from seven cruisers in mothballs. [1] The computers were to go back to the factory in Brooklyn (not Arma Corporation, but Ford Instrument Company) to be modified to be able to handle jet airplanes. This captain came in the Plotting Room where I was elbows deep into the first computer and interrogated me on my experience on such equipment. What made me think that I was qualified to tear open a computer. After my recital of advanced schools attended he blew up and chewed on me for leaving the Navy after it had spent "thousands of dollars" on my education.

I grew up on the old CHEW. In my travels I met many interesting people, most interesting to me was an outstanding and unique young lady. I had said goodbye to her without making any commitments when I took off for California as the war was still going on and my future was still very much up in the air. Fortunately when it ended and things had settled down she and I took up where we had left off. She eclipsed all of the many other girls along the way.

After almost a year in St. Louis I had returned to California to seek fame and fortune. The time was ripe to write letters to someone who responded in kind. This correspondence persuaded her to come to California to seek fame and fortune. She did, and one night sitting in my car parked on the waterfront of the San Francisco Marina, listening to the fog horns from Lime Point and Alcatraz while watching the fog on the Bay, we decided that two could live as cheaply as one. We were married December 5, 1947 by Fr. Thomas Heyburn at St. Vincent de Paul's Church, corner of Steiner and Green Streets, San Francisco. We have had five children: Susan Mary, 1949 to 1988; Mark George, 1950; Laura Elizabeth, 1953; Jesse III, 1956; and Katherine Anne, 1957. A large, close-knit, family.

I can look back with few regrets, although there are many things that I would do differently, if I had a second chance. Some of my friends followed the old maxim "When life hands you a lemon - make lemonade" by staying in the Navy and retiring with commissions, but I got out as quickly as I could. I was one of the first thousand men "paid off" at Camp Shoemaker. I had served my country and done my duty, and occasionally a bit more, and even played some basketball, and never got close to any trench warfare. With my ingrained stubbornness and cross-grained disposition, if I had opted to make a career in the Navy, instead of retiring as an admiral, or a captain, or a commander, I could have very well ended up breaking rocks at the Portsmouth Naval Prison for throttling some officer with my bare hands. Square pegs, as a rule, do not last long in the Navy.

FOOTNOTES.

1. Heavy Cruisers: BREMERTON CA130; LOS ANGELES CA135. Light Cruisers: AMSTERDAM CL101; MIAMI CL89; OKLAHOMA CITY CL91; VICKSBURG CL86; VINCENNES CL64.

Epilogue

Nearly a half-century has passed since the happenings in the last chapter occurred and many of the characters in this memoir have passed on to their reward. In this period of time things have changed drastically in the world. I have met, and shook hands with, a man who was a dive bomber pilot in the Japanese attack force, Senji Abe. In my capacity as an historian I have corresponded with a Japanese Navy officer. The people who were deadly enemies are now friends.

What has happened to the characters in this book in these years?

I have tried unsuccessfully several times to find John Mazurkiewicz. Two of his ships reunion committees have no record of him. I did find a Russian woman from New Jersey whose father remembers the name, but we have no addresses - yet. We last met in 1947 when he was a CPO in USS HIGBEE (DD806) and I was a civilian Navy employee in San Francisco.

This is a small world. I met a man recently in rural Virginia who had attended the school at the Naval Gun Factory with me in 1944.

People from CHEW take up the first part of this book. However, some memorable characters show up in the later chapters and should not be overlooked.

Ten years ago Admiral Hummer "ordered" me to get up a CHEW reunion, and that I did forthwith. The first reunion of the Crew of the CHEW was held in October 1983 at the Sheraton-National Hotel in Arlington, Virginia, with seventeen men attending. Most brought along their wife. That affair was the start of a series of annual reunions. I set up the first one. Harry Collins has ran several in St. Louis. "Ensign" Jack Tuttle honchoed two good ones: San Diego in 1989; Reno in 1990. Even in St. Louis, where the original Thirty Seventh Division came from, the total number of men who come out remains just about the same.

For the first reunion I found a man who had been one of the original crew from the CHEW's commissioning in 1918. He was living at an Old Sailor's Home in New Jersey. Between the time I found him, and the reunion, he died. I had arranged to pay his way to Arlington for the affair but Father Time intervened.

The "Star" of several of the CHEW affairs has been Horace "Pat" Sheedy, who enlisted in the Navy in 1914. He is a charmer to be with, witty and full of vim.

All five of the CHEW officers who went on to flag rank have died: Edward Beck; Harry Hummer; Peter Horn; Paul Cosgrove; and Charles MacNish, the only Reserve of the five. The losses to the Grim Reaper are to be expected.

Asbestosis in one form or another has taken several men before their times: Jack Grossman and Jimmie Graffigna a long time ago.

Five of the men from the first reunion have died: Paul Cosgrove; Omke Doeden; C. W. Phillips; Phil Hanley; and Jack Tuttle.

My roommate in Brooklyn, and sidekick, Bill Kapfer died just this year. Earl Loeb has been dead for many years and I have sent photos of him to a son who hardly knew his father.

In 1947 Fredie T. Fox had written to me in California from his home in the Missouri Ozarks telling me that he was leaving for California and would see me soon. He never arrived and my efforts to find him since that time have not been successful.

When I sat at a table and looked around at our last reunion and the mature people assembled there, I thought of that rabble on the station platform tearing around like wild Indians. Then I thought of the crew assembled at quarters after December 7th, 1941. I compared the three groups. These mature people, men and women, are the very solid foundations of our country. There are none to be ashamed of. That is a group of substantial citizens worthy to be called a "Great Crew."

The dividing line between officers and men has disappeared and we mix like shipmates should at our reunions. There is a feeling of friendship that brings widows back to the meetings year after year.

I am lucky to have walked a while with these people.

Appendix

Most Monday morning quarterbacks have 20/20 hindsight, and my eyesight after more than fifty years is certainly a lot clearer than it was during the time the game was being played.

Almost everyone now agrees that the Japanese gained a tremendous tactical success with the attack on Pearl Harbor, even if they failed to follow through properly and take full advantage of their position to destroy the exposed fuel supplies and the power plants. We also agree that the strike was a strategic error of the first magnitude. Nothing united the American people as did that "sneak attack" delivered during highly visible and publicized negotiations, and then on a Sunday morning, too.

But let us suppose that they **HAD NOT** struck Pearl Harbor and our Fleet, but instead had continued on the course they were following, and taken the Philippines, the Dutch islands, China, and so on piecemeal. Our pathetic Asiatic Fleet, HOUSTON, MARBLEHEAD, and the rickety old four-stack destroyers would not have slowed the advance hardly at all. Even after the strike on Pearl Harbor our Asiatic Squadron went down rather quickly. The Japanese could have taken all of Asia on their own schedule.

I can hear the debate, if that is the word, for what might have gone on in our Congress. "We can't send our boys to fight for the Spice Islands," "They're all Asiatics over there anyway, let's let them alone." The isolationists would have been loud and strident, and their efforts would have held back our attempts to get involved in Asia. In our hesitation the Japanese would have consolidated their gains, and added to and improved their military capabilities.

Let us further suppose that after a year Husband Kimmel did get orders to carry out the Orange Plan and send his fleet out to clear the Japanese from the Philippines. I admired Admiral Kimmel in his times of trouble, and I was aghast at the shabby treatment he received in life, and even after his death, from his Navy. At his funeral at the Naval Academy, an event that I and several other Survivors of Pearl Harbor attended as honorary pallbearers, the services in his honor and memory were not allowed to be held in the Chapel, but were instead shuffled off to be held downstairs in the crypt. An insult after death to an honorable man.

However, Kimmel was an aggressive battleship man, and his fleet, with its long supply line, would have been exposed to Yamamoto's new concept of the aircraft carrier as being the primary weapon of attack. Remember, the lessons of Pearl Harbor would not have been learned, as it had not happened in this hypothetical situation, and Kimmel's ships would have had a tough time of it. In my mind, the outcome would have been in doubt.

In the meantime, the United States, without the Pearl Harbor attack, would not be at war, and what would be happening to Britain? England had stalemated the Luftwaffe's air attacks, but without the American supplies and the American B-17s how would she be weathering the storm? The bombing attacks that hurt Germany so badly would not be mounted in nearly the magnitude of what the American Army Air Corps did later, after several years of the Arsenal of Democracy running full-tilt at our back. If the United States had not entered the war for another year or a year and a half, would England have survived?

It is possible, with this scenario, that the United States would have protested and deplored the Japanese actions until our cookie pushing diplomats were blue in the face, with no effect at all on Japan. Finally the isolationists would have ruled the day here at home, until the Axis partners became strong enough to try to rule the Western Hemisphere too.

After fifty years many theories have been aired. The revisionists have come up with all sorts of cock-and-bull stories about how Roosevelt knew the time and date of the attack, and kept it to himself in order to bring the United States into the war. How Churchill knew and kept the secret too for the same reason. Roosevelt, the perfect example of the spoiled rich-brat-mama's boy, who cheated on his wife openly, and kept a concubine on the White House staff, and died at his long-time mistress' place in Georgia, could not have kept such a secret. His style was more along the line of sending a small craft out to entice the Japanese to strike it, such as the order of 1 December 1941 from Admiral Stark to Admiral Hart that involved the ISABEL and the LANIKAI. Even FDR would not have allowed a thousand men to die to further his aims. [1]

From all angles have come tales that the Japanese attack was an open book; the Navy radioman in San Francisco who claimed to have monitored the Japanese Fleet while it was en route to Hawaii; an Australian who had broken a "code" and was ignored by the British Secret Service; a Netherlands diplomat with all the details months earlier. The list goes on, but, in my opinion, one of the better analyses of the whole affair was made by Roberta Wohlstetter in her

"Pearl Harbor, Warning and Decision", Stanford University Press, 1962. Yes, with fifty-year hindsight, an attack could have been foreseen, but not by anyone at the time.

Prominent in any discussion of "What if" is the use of the atomic weapons against Japan that shortened the war measurably. The United States had worked up plans for a two-part operation against the Japanese home islands, Operation Downfall, the first part, Operation Olympic, and the second part, Operation Coronet. This two-part operation would have been the end of Japan, and also would have been the end of several million American attackers. This book, on the short career of one sailor, is not the forum in which to discuss this subject, other than in passing. Suffice it to say, the atomic bombs that killed about two hundred thousand Japanese when they were dropped on Hiroshima and Nagasaki, saved more than ten times that number by eliminating the need for Operation Downfall.

FOOTNOTES

1 *"The Fleet the Gods Forgot", W. G. Winslow. Naval Institute Press 1982.*

"Air Raid: Pearl Harbor," The Strange Assignment of the USS LANIKAI, RADM K. Tolley. Naval Institute Press 1981.

"It therefore comes to pass that everyone is fond of relating his own exploits and displaying the strength both of his body and his mind, and that men are on this account a nuisance one to the other.

Spinoza 1632- 1677.

JESSE E. POND, JR. was born in St. Louis, Missouri, January 15, 1917. He was educated in the city's Public School System, graduating from high school in 1933, and received a BS degree, with honors, from Menlo College, Atherton, California, in 1953, through the GI Bill. He has had a business career for over fifty years, interrupted by active duty in the Naval Service from December 1940 to October 1945, serving mostly on an overage destroyer in the Pacific.

He has lectured to secondary school students on the Pearl Harbor attack as director and officer of the Survivors Association and as a founding member of the Pearl Harbor History Associates, Incorporated. He is author and editor of two widely distributed pamphlets published by the latter organization: "What Happened at Pearl Harbor December 7, 1941" (1987) and "Remembering Pearl Harbor" (1990).

THE PEARL HARBOR HISTORY ASSOCIATES INCORPORATED

The Pearl Harbor History Associates, Incorporated, is a non-profit corporation chartered on July 2, 1985, by the Commonwealth of Virginia, for the purposes of "education, research, and promulgation of historical data." The Internal Revenue Service granted advance approval to PHHA to operate under the classification of Section 509 (a)(2) of the Internal Revenue Code on September 24, 1985, and on April 25, 1988, gave permanent approval under Section 501 (c)(3).

The organizers, mostly military survivors of the attack on Pearl Harbor on December 7, 1941, and ex-officers of the Survivors Association, envisioned a need for an organization to concentrate on the historical view of "The Date That Will Live In Infamy."

The Association has received many credits for delivering data to aid in publishing and broadcasting stories and articles for the Fiftieth Anniversary commemoration.

It has published and distributed nationally, "Remembering Pearl Harbor," a fact brochure, and a chart of ship locations in Pearl Harbor at 0755 December 7, 1941. It also maintains a Speakers Bureau to present historical data in the form of lectures and slide shows. Arrangements may be made for this service by writing or by telephoning Area Code 703/987-8515.

Donations to the PHHA may be listed as a deduction in a Federal income tax return. Federal ID #54-1313057.

195

ORDER FORM

To: The Pearl Harbor History Associates, Inc.
      Post Office Box 205
      Sperryville, VA 22740-0205

Please mail _____ copies of "The Square Peg" at once to:

Name_____

Address_____

City, State, Zip Code_____

_____Copies @ 19.95   Total for books   _____

Virginia residents add 4.5% sales tax on books

Shipping charge:
   $2.00 for first book; .75 each add'l.   _____

                  Total   _____

Please make Check or Money Order
   payable to "The Square Peg."

Thank you for your order.